CUSTER'S 7th CAVALRY

Photo by E. L. Reedstrom

The Custer statue was erected in Monroe, Michigan.

CUSTER'S 7th CAVALRY

From Fort Riley to the Little Big Horn

E. LISLE REEDSTROM

Sterling Publishing Co., Inc. New York

TO MY WIFE,
SHIRLEY
who has seen little of a husband —
TO MY CHILDREN,
who have seen little of a father —
ALLOWING THIS BOOK
TO BE WRITTEN

Library of Congress Cataloging-in-Publication Data

Reedstrom, Ernest Lisle.
Custer's 7th Cavalry : from Fort Riley to the Little Big Horn / E. Lisle Reedstrom.
p. cm.
An abridged version of the author's Bugles, banners, and war bonnets.
Includes bibliographical references and index.
ISBN 0-8069-8762-6
1. Little Big Horn, Battle of the, 1876. 2. United States. Army. Cavalry, 7th. 3. Indians of North America—Wars—1866–1895. 4. Custer, George Armstrong, 1839–1876. I. Reedstrom, Ernest Lisle. Bugles, banners, and war bonnets. II. Title.
E83.876.R38 1992
973.8′2—dc20 92-26524
CIP

10 9 8 7 6 5 4

Published 1992 by Sterling Publishing Company, Inc.
387 Park Avenue South, New York, N.Y. 10016
This edition is excerpted from *Bugles, Banners and War Bonnets* originally published by Caxton Publishers

Distributed in Canada by Sterling Publishing
% Canadian Manda Group, P.O. Box 920, Station U
Toronto, Ontario, Canada M8Z 5P9
Distributed in Great Britain and Europe by Cassell PLC
Villiers House, 41/47 Strand, London WC2N 5JE, England
Distributed in Australia by Capricorn Link Ltd.
P.O. Box 665, Lane Cove, NSW 2066
Manufactured in the United States of America

Sterling ISBN 0-8069-8762-6

CONTENTS

LIST OF ILLUSTRATIONS

PREFACE

The cavalry of General Custer's day is no more. Like coal oil lamps, horse cavalry has been relegated to the past. With it went a certain glamour not evident in the army of today. There was a liveliness to a cavalry camp not evident in a motor pool, and an odor that was unforgettable. The pounding of hoofs, clank of sabers and rubbing of leather has gone. Roaring motors, screeching brakes, and an air polluted by a haze of burned petrol have taken its place.

On the Western plains of Custer's day the horse provided a companionship for the lonely trooper a Jeep couldn't provide. It was his fastest means of escape when retreat became a necessity.

The trooper and his horse were constant companions, each dependent upon the other. The mount was the cavalryman's first concern on arising each morning and his first and last concern when retiring at night. His life might be forfeited because of the improper care of his horse. There were instances where the attachment between a trooper and his horse grew so strong that when the latter was transferred to another regiment the trooper abandoned his own friends by requesting a transfer to accompany his horse.

A portion of this volume is devoted to the cavalryman and his horse. Equally interesting is that portion devoted to the cavalryman's adversary during the settlement of the West, the American Indian.

There is a tendency to view the military men and their engagements of Custer's day on the basis of present day standards. To properly and objectively evaluate the subject it is imperative that the reader or student of Western history be supplied with reliable background material of the people, the places, the problems and the accoutrements of that period.

Lisle Reedstrom has spent many years as an artist and illustrator of the Old West. Meticulous in his art and methodical in his research he has accumulated an amazing amount of background material not commonly known, all for the purpose of providing authenticity in his productions.

I recall his desire to obtain accurate and firsthand information of cavalry drills and charges. He was not content with the usual written descriptions. The retirement of the horses from the military service had erased all opportunity for him to view such drills. Learning of a reactivated cavalry unit in Indiana there was no rest for him until he could join them during their maneuvers. It was just a matter of time before he had sketched from life what he had been unable to obtain in any other way.

Since the formation of The Little Big Horn Associates in 1967, he has generously supplied its publications with the products of his pen. Now, just as generously, he supplies all of us with the products of his research.

LAWRENCE A. FROST
MONROE, MICHIGAN

Courtesy U.S. Signal Corps photo (Brady Collection)

After being wounded in Virginia during the War, a clean-shaven Custer returned to Monroe in 1863 to court Elizabeth Bacon.

ACKNOWLEDGMENTS

I wish to acknowledge my gratitude for the never-failing help and encouragement from the many people who rallied to a distant call and helped compile the necessary ammunition to complete this book.

I respectfully mention the following names who graciously submitted a vast amount of photography from their private collections: Dr. Lawrence Frost, Dr. Elizabeth A. Lawrence, Randy Steffen, Gordon Corbett, Jr., Herb Peck, Jr., Arnold Marcus Chernoff, Thomas M. Heski, Grant Dinsmore, Fred Hackett, Robert J. McDonald, George A. Rummel, Jr., Gary Reusze, First Sergeant Robert M. Craig and Sergeant J. J. Narus from the Second U.S. Reactivated Cavalry.

From the various archives and museums around the country, my sincere thanks to the many people at West Point Museum, New York; The Library of Congress, Washington, D.C.; National Archives and Records Service, including the Old Military Branch Division, Washington, D.C.; Smithsonian Institution, Washington, D.C.; U.S. Army Quartermaster Museum, Fort Lee, Virginia; Custer Battlefield National Monument, Crow Agency, Montana; Chicago Historical Society, Chicago, Illinois; Union Pacific Railroad Company, Omaha, Nebraska; Nebraska State Historical Society, Lincoln, Nebraska; Kansas State Historical Society, Topeka, Kansas; State Historical Society of North Dakota, Bismarck, North Dakota; Arizona Historical Society, Tucson, Arizona; U.S. Cavalry Memorial Association, Inc., Midway City, California.

For additional help in supplying books and reference data, I am appreciative to William A. Graff, book dealer in Iowa City, Iowa; George A. Willhauck, Norm Flayderman & Company, Inc., The Westerners, Chicago Corral; and the Lake County Reference Library, Merrillville, Indiana, where the librarians worked endless hours compiling data and requisitioning books from out-of-state libraries.

I am especially indebted to the troopers of the Second U.S. Reactivated Cavalry, particularly Mitchell Swieca, who have all worked many hours in the field with me during weekends, helping to re-create conditions from original cavalry manuals, risking dangerous maneuvers to carry out some task. They are truly cavalrymen.

For documents loaned and permission to reproduce them, I am grateful to Paul Hoag for autographs and books; William A. Bond; Dr. Elizabeth A. Lawrence; and The Library of Congress, Washington, D.C.

Special thanks for photographs taken of Basil White Eagle in costume; J. J. Narus; Robert M. Craig; Victor Studios for their wonderful service in film developing; and many more, whose names were not submitted to me for acknowledgements.

My appreciation to Conrad Kleinman and Petley Studios of Phoenix, Arizona, for assisting in photography. To Mike Koury, Old Army Press; and the Little Big Horn Associates, who graciously gave permission to reprint a number of my pen-and-ink drawings, especial acknowledgment is made.

Above all, to the individuals whose unselfish aid in typing, proofreading and editing made it possible to complete this book, I am indebted—Gib Crontz, Theada Davis, Kay Pleasha, and Joan Tutsie, who served as secretarial assistant. To Don Russell, who edited the book, my thanks and deepest gratitude.

Courtesy U.S. Signal Corps photo (Brady Collection)

A Brady photo, taken in 1864, of General Custer and his bride.

BUNKIES

"I say, Billy, give us a smoke."
'Twas a rough, stalwart, generous fellow who spoke,
With heavy mustache, a sort of devil-may-care;
One of those sort of men who'd go anywhere—
Who'd share half his pay with a bunky or chum,
The first in a fight, the last on a bum.
"Go ahead, Jack"—handing the pipe—"I'm through."
There was a very great contrast in the build of the two.
Bill, quiet in manners, unused to rough ways;
In fact, one of the many who've seen better days,
With very fair hair, eyes decidedly blue—
Yes, a very marked contrast there was in the two.

A sort of attachment had sprung up 'tween the men,
I can't say exactly why it was, how or when.
To proceed with my yarn:
"Bill, have yer made down the bed!
'Cos I'm awfully tired, and very near dead."
(Impulsively striking the bunk with his fist).
"Bill, what a d—— fool I was to enlist."
"Well, it's no use your growling, it makes matters worse,"
Jack only replied with a forcible curse;
"You ain't fixed, Bill, as I am; I do more 'n my share;
You've got a soft thing, and of course you don't care.
I enlisted to soger, and I'm willing to fight—
Not to whack Government mules and stay out half the night.

I've soger'd for years, fit during the war,
But I never did see sich fatiguing before.
One day I'm on guard, the next cuttin' ice,
Then on kitchen police, which ain't over nice;
A fourth, layin' brick (I ain't used to the thing),
A fifth day on guard, with just three nights in;
Sometimes I'm detailed to drive a company team,
Which if yer aint keerful, or the mules rather green,
You're apt to upset, and the Lord only knows,
If yer don't get a tumble, ye're nearly half froze.
Then yer unhitch the mules, feed, and water 'em too,
And it's hard to say which eats the most of the two.
Yer dinner is cold, the soup's all played out,
And at fatigue call you've again to turn out.

"Then, Billy, yer see they've cut the stamps down
That's allowed for the clothin'; a new plan they've found.
It may be all very well, tho' it doesn't look nice
To cut down the stamps and keep up the price.
If a greeny enlists and draws a full rig of clothes,
It'll take near three months to pay it off, I suppose;
Then agin the old hands'll make quite a stake,
And you bet a good many'll soon make a break.
Because, don't yer see, it's the last chance they've got,
And those who don't go'll spend it for rot.
Sogerin's all very well; I'd bet my last picayune
We know more of fatigue than we do of platoon.
Now what d' yer . . ."

"No loud talking up there," roars out Sergeant Schnapps.
(The bugle is sounding the last note of "taps.")

February 14, 1871. F.H.[1]

1. Army Navy Journal, March 4, 1871, page 463. The Army Navy Journal will sometimes hereafter be cited as A.N.J.

FOREWORD

This saga starts on July 28, 1866—the beginning of the U.S. Seventh Cavalry. Assigned to Fort Riley, Kansas, it was one of four new regiments authorized by Congress. The way it began is an often neglected part of the regimental story. There is even some humor—with the description of a dogfight in the back of an ambulance, where Mrs. Elizabeth Custer and two other women sat, while Lieutenant Colonel George A. Custer was reporting in at headquarters.

Major John W. Davidson and some officers from his U.S. Second Cavalry formed the new Seventh. As officers and men arrived, they were assigned to their units. Custer assumed command, although as a lieutenant colonel, he was only the field commander. The ranking officer of the regiment, Colonel Andrew Johnson Smith, was kept in other assignments by Major General Philip H. Sheridan.

Lisle Reedstrom's research is thorough. His citations mainly come from primary sources. Also, the book is profusely illustrated with photographs, sketches, and maps.

Early on, Reedstrom prepares the reader for the events to come by presenting a detailed description of the officers and the ordinary soldiers and the life they led. He discusses the type of men they were, their equipment, the conditions under which they lived, and their training.

The life of the officer's wife is described as well. Living on the frontier was hard, especially for women. They were seldom able to obtain decent housing, furniture, or food. And there was always the fear for the safety of their men, while the troops were out searching for Indians. Often there were long separations while the troops were in the field.

In the summer of 1867, Custer and the Seventh were sent into the wild country, where the hostiles from the Arapaho, Cheyenne, and Dakota tribes were operating. The purpose of this campaign was to protect the settlers and the people crossing the Plains from the Indians. Custer was authorized to use force if the Indians started to fight.

It was an education for perhaps the best army in the world, the one that had just defeated the Confederates. The soldiers chased the Indians for hundreds of miles all over the Plains, but they were never able to bring them to battle.

At the tail end of this campaign, Custer committed several foolish acts, which resulted in his court-martial and suspension from duty for a year.

The U.S. Government made a peace treaty with the Cheyenne, Comanche, and Kiowa tribes at Medicine Lodge, Oklahoma Territory, in 1867. Known as the Medicine Lodge Treaty, it included a provision for the tribes to live below the Arkansas River in a sanctuary where they would be safe from the U.S. Army. The Cheyenne village of Chief Black Kettle, camped on the Washita River in Oklahoma Territory, was certainly well within the sanctuary.

However, not all of Chief Black Kettle's people were with him; many smaller bands were scattered around the country. Starting in August 1868, more than two hundred Cheyenne warriors raided north, hitting the white settlements in western Kansas and eastern Colorado, where over one hundred settlers were killed.

In reaction to these atrocities, Sheridan

decided to punish the Indians with a winter campaign. He released Custer from his suspension from duty and placed him in command of the Seventh Cavalry again. He also authorized Governor Samuel J. Crawford, of Kansas, to raise a regiment of cavalry (the Nineteenth Kansas). The governor resigned from office to lead this regiment. In November Custer moved the Seventh to the newly established Camp Supply, in Oklahoma Territory, to meet Crawford and the Nineteenth.

Reedstrom conveys all of this, setting the scene for Custer's first real fight with the Indians—the Battle of the Washita. There is considerable controversy about whether the U.S. Government was justified in authorizing this campaign. However, Reedstrom builds a careful, thoughtful, and detailed case, showing that Sheridan was correct in his reasoning.

Although the Nineteenth had not yet arrived, Sheridan decided it was time to make a move and sent Custer south in a blinding snowstorm. The Army found and followed the trail of about two hundred warriors, who had been raiding north of the Arkansas River, straight to the village of Black Kettle. In the battle that ensued, the chief was killed along with about a hundred warriors. Custer captured fifty women and children. The cost to the army: about twenty-five killed. I found Reedstrom's description of this event quite accurate.

The next several chapters cover the activities of Custer and the Seventh after the Battle of the Washita up to the Battle of the Little Big Horn. Included are the rescue of some women captives held by the Cheyennes in the Texas Panhandle, the protection of the railroad builders in the Yellowstone country, and the exploration of the Black Hills in Dakota Territory.

In 1875 most of the Plains Indians were living on reservations. However, in the Northern Plains there were a large number of free Indians in both the Cheyenne and Dakota tribes who had never agreed to give up their native life and settle down on a reservation.

The vast Plains were being settled by frontiersmen and there were conflicts between hostile Indians and settlers. The same was true with regard to the people who crossed the Plains on railroads, stagecoaches, and wagon trains. The government decided it was time to place all the Indians on reservations—by force if necessary. The hostile tribes were warned to report to a reservation by the end of 1875 or face the consequences. The free Indians paid no attention to these threats.

Early in 1876, the U.S. Army was ordered to act. Sheridan sent three armies into the field. From the south one was commanded by Brigadier General George Crook, from the west another was under Colonel John Gibbon, and from the east the troops were under Brigadier General Alfred H. Terry. The plan was to find and destroy the Indian villages and horse herds. These tactics had worked effectively during the Buffalo Wars fought with the southern Plains Indians in 1874.

Custer was again in trouble and had been relieved from his command by President Ulysses S. Grant. Again, Sheridan obtained his restoration to duty, but only as commander of the Seventh Cavalry, which was part of Terry's command.

Reedstrom meticulously tells about these background actions leading to the Battle of the Little Big Horn. He is even-handed and fair to both sides of the story.

Terry sent Custer and the Seventh Cavalry to find the Indians. Custer divided his regiment, sending Captain Frederick W. Benteen and his battalion on a scout to the left with orders to rejoin the regiment if he was not engaged. Then he sent Major Marcus Reno and his battalion to charge the Indian village from the front. Finally, Custer took the remaining five companies under his personal command and swung to the right as part of an envelopment.

Benteen found no Indians and started

back. Reno found sufficient Indians to cause him to stop his charge, fight briefly, and then make a disastrous retreat back across the river onto some bluffs, where he established a defensive position. In a short time, he was joined by Benteen and his battalion and the pack train.

Meanwhile, Custer approached the center of the village but did not enter. Rather, he fought at a couple of different positions, and at the last one he and all the men in his five companies were killed. Reno held his hilltop position and was rescued by Terry a couple of days later.

Reedstrom is thorough in recounting the story, and his maps and illustrations are helpful in understanding the actions. The interpretation of specific events has been controversial since the time they occurred, yet I find Reedstrom's version detailed and logical.

JAY SMITH, EDITOR
Little Big Horn Associates
Research Review

Courtesy U.S. Signal Corps photo (Brady Collection)

General Custer was a loyal Republican, while his father Emanuel H. Custer was opposed to him in politics.

CUSTER'S 7th CAVALRY

C H A P T E R O N E

FORT RILEY AND THE 7TH CAVALRY

On July 28th, 1866, under an act of Congress, four new regiments of cavalry were organized. The 7th through the 10th were to be stationed at various posts to restore order on the troubled frontiers. One of the regiments, the 7th U.S. Cavalry, was assigned to Fort Riley, Kansas; its future duty was to protect the building of the Kansas Pacific Railroad against already menacing warlike Indian tribes. During August and September, 1866, Fort Riley was already a concentration of recruits, frontiersmen, fugitives, adventurers from the east, former Union soldiers along with a few rebels in disguise. The men were a rough-looking lot, many of them Irishmen newly-immigrated from the "old country," all seeking a meal ticket and their fortune in the western expansion. Others, while awaiting only to be issued clothing, arms and a horse, would desert at the first available opportunity.

Courtesy Bob McDonald

A classic example of a cavalryman, armed with saber and revolver, and wearing the regulation shell jacket and universal forage cap.

Soon the post became a crowded and dusty parade ground of confused men and horses . . . shuffling about unorganized and restless. By September 10th, Major John W. Davidson of the 2nd Cavalry, an old army regular, carried his orders out to the letter by forming the several hundred recruits into companies. At the end of September, twelve companies had been organized with a total strength of 882 men commanded by officers of the 2nd Cavalry.

All through November and December, 1866, a casual flow of officers assigned to the 7th Cavalry was organized into a headquarters staff. All had served in the Civil War and could produce papers showing their services and combat records. As the officers reported, they were assigned quarters in one of the stone buildings on post. Officers take their quarters according to rank, and it was not an uncommon happening that another officer, already established in quarters, would have to vacate his quarters and give up his place to another who outranked him. The ranking officer is entirely in his right, according to the army code, and generally he does not hesitate to use this authority, although he may be a single man and the man displaced be a family man. Among veteran officers this is so well understood and accepted that no hard feelings or resentment occurred.[1]

---

1. Tenting on the Plains, by Elizabeth B. Custer (New York: C. L. Webster & Co., 1887), pages 372-373.

Most of the officers who served in the volunteer service during the war knew nothing of a full dress uniform, having spent the duration of the war in field tents. And so some ridiculous errors in uniform dress and deportment were made while reporting to headquarters on their arrival. Some sought to alleviate their embarrassment and mortification over these harmless mistakes by laying pitfalls for the greenhorns that were constantly arriving. To quote an example from "Tenting on the Plains" . . . "He wore cavalry boots, the first singularity I noticed, for they had such expanse of top I could not help seeing them. They are of course out of order with a dress coat. The red sash, which was then *en regle* for all officers, was spread from up under his arms to as far below the waist line as its elastic silk could be stretched. The sword belt, with sabre attached, surrounded this; and, folded over the wide red front, were his large hands, encased in white cotton gloves. He never moved them; nor did he move an eyelash, so far as I could discover, though it seems he was full of internal tremors, for the officers had told him on no account to remove his regulation hat. At this he demurred, and told them I would surely think he was no gentleman; but they assured him I placed military etiquette far above any ordinary rule for manners in the presence of ladies, while the truth was I was rather indifferent as to military rules of dress."[2] No excuses were ever made by these pranksters, and none were expected. However, in later years, every time the episode was recalled by 7th Cavalry officers, laughter exploded with tear-filled eyes.

Courtesy Bob McDonald

Cavalry officers — late 1860's.

Courtesy Grant Dinsmore

Packed and ready for field duty a trooper poses for a photograph to send home.

On the evening of November 3rd, 1866, Lieutenant-Colonel George Armstrong Custer arrived at Fort Riley in a somewhat embarrassing commotion. While Custer was reporting his arrival to Major Alfred Gibbs, a dog fight broke out in the ambulance,[3] where Elizabeth Custer, her

2. Tenting on the Plains, by Elizabeth B. Custer (New York: C. L. Webster & Co., 1887), pages 376-377.

3. An ambulance carried the women, dogs and luggage from Junction City to Ft. Riley, some 10 miles distance. Custer rode on horseback.

Custer, brevet major general[4] and permanent captain, was appointed lieutenant colonel of the 7th Cavalry, and second-in-command to Colonel and Brevet Major General Andrew Johnson Smith, a veteran of the Mexican and Civil wars. Custer's appointment as lieutenant colonel was actually a sudden leap in promotion from captain in the regular army, though a step-down

4. Brevet commissions were permanent honorary recognition of distinguished service and an officer could serve, and be paid, in his brevet rank under prescribed circumstances.

Courtesy Author's Collection

Photo taken in Detroit, Michigan the Fall of 1866. Custer seated center, Libbie on the right. Man and young girl in background, standing, unidentified. Woman seated at left is believed to have been an actress starring at one of the leading theaters in Detroit. Photo taken shortly before journey to Fort Riley, Kansas.

schoolmate, Diana, and Eliza, the family cook, were waiting to be quartered. Hostilities between the two Custer dogs, Turk and Byron, brewed during the short trip from Junction City, and now within close quarters they leaped at one another snapping their muscular jaws in rage. When Custer returned, he found Elizabeth and Diana each at a corner of the ambulance, their tiny white fingers clutching the collars of both dogs and trembling with horror. A few stern words from Custer settled the immediate matter.

Courtesy U.S. Signal Corps photo (Brady Collection)

The Custer's "Autie," brother Tom and Elizabeth. The War had finally ended, and the three would return to Monroe.

from the rank of major general of volunteers he had held the previous year. His pay of $8,000 as major general had been reduced to $2,000 with additional allowances and living quarters. Other regular officers found themselves similarly cut back in rank and pay when the volunteers they led as generals, colonels, and majors were mustered out during the process of disbanding the Union Army. Custer was always addressed as "general," as it was army custom to recognize the brevet rank.

To a man full of life and exuberant health, the thought of hunting wildlife on the plains was most enjoyable. Strange birds and wild beasts that roamed the wide and endless sweep of prairie were sufficient to keep a person of his danger-loving temperament continually active. The many herds of deer and antelope, along with the temperamental buffalo, would furnish ample sport for his rifle. Squirrels and jack rabbits, ducks and prairie chickens, were so generous in supply that hardly a day passed that Custer and his greyhounds would return from a hunt empty-handed. But another hunt, that of the hostile Indian would not be so easy.

Custer enjoyed having friends and relatives about him. He helped them to get positions in the new regiment including his younger brother, Lt. Thomas Ward Custer,

Courtesy Union Pacific Railroad *Photo by C. R. Savage*

Union Pacific work train in 1870 near Green River, Wyoming.

Courtesy Union Pacific Railroad
The "Seminole," woodburning locomotive built in April 1867 for the UP eastern district (Kansas). Overall length 50 ft., weight 115,000 lbs., fuel capacity two cords, tender capacity 2000 gallons water, tractive power 11,000 lbs. The cab of the old "Seminole" was of varnished walnut and the engineer's seat was made of ash, the pilot was made of wood. Rogers Loco. & Machine Co., Paterson N.J.

holder of two Medals of Honor for meritorius service during the Civil War.[5] The "Custer circle" formed a clique within the new regiment inviting favorites to dinners and evenings of high-stake poker games. Custer may have been a born gambler in real life; he was, however, the poorest poker player within the circle. Many times his I.O.U. notes went unpaid, and Elizabeth reminded him to practice economy with the reduced income from his army pay. While champagne and light wines were toasting future victories for the 7th Cavalry, Custer accompanied each toast with water or lemonade. Two years after leaving West Point, Custer voluntarily gave up drinking. The reason was he could not be a moderate drinker.[6]

Schooling the young recruits was difficult. Some did not understand English, but they seemed to get by . . . by following the movements of their comrades. First was the "schooling of the dismounted soldier." Then the manual of the sabre, sabre exercise, manual of the pistol, manual of the carbine, and next, the principles of target practice. As the schooling of the soldier continued, endless duties and work details that plagued military life continued to irritate the men.

As one soldier wrote from Fort Harker, some 90 miles southwest of Fort Riley: "There has been no drills here the past

5. Thomas Ward Custer joined his brother at Fort Riley with a first lieutenant's commission, November 16th, assigned to Troop "A", but detailed acting regimental quartermaster. Tom Custer was one of two persons in the army ever to have been awarded twice the Medal of Honor for meritorious service during the Civil War. Tom Custer distinguished himself at Namozine Church, April 2nd, and at Sailor's Creek, Va., April 6th, 1865, by capturing a Confederate battle flag at each position. It was at Sailor's Creek that Tom leaped his horse over the enemy's breastworks and fearlessly dashed up to the rebel colors. When he reached the color-bearer he was immediately fired upon. A musket ball smashed into his right cheek and passed out behind the ear. However, Tom succeeded in capturing the rebel flag and dashed back to his lines, blood streaking his face. General Custer, noticing his brother's severe wound, ordered him to the rear to have it dressed. Tom refused, his young blood up, prepared to spur his horse forward for another charge. General Custer, grabbing the reins of the horse, ordered his brother under arrest and to return to the rear.

6. E. B. Custer; microfilm — Reel 4; Custer Battlefield Museum.

Courtesy Union Pacific Railroad

Construction crew and soldiers fighting off Indian attack (painting). Constant danger of Indian attack kept construction crews on their toes during UP's building. Army detachments helped protect the workers but the railroadmen themselves had to be equally handy with spike maul or rifle.

winter, the soldiers being all occupied in building quarters. Isn't it a mistake on the part of the government to require enlisted men to work as common laborers with no opportunity to perfect themselves in drill? An officer cannot have proper discipline in his command under such circumstances. The men, too, labor somehow under silent protest; desertions are more than frequent . . .," and in ending the soldier makes this point, "... making dirt shovelers of soldiers may make them a source of profit in time of peace, but it is equally sure to make them worthless in time of war."[7]

Many a young man has been attracted by the pomp and circumstance of soldiering, tempted by the cheering music of military bands, the brilliance of a new uniform, and the prospect of a future promotion . . . wilfully signing on the dotted line, selling his soul unknowingly. Anxiously waiting to be sent to his new company to begin his soldiering, he is somewhat shaken to find that he has been sent off to some unknown post amidst the frightful solitude of rocks and sagebrush in the summer, or the Siberian-like snows of the winter. From the moment of his arrival at the post, he is taught to cease imagining himself as a soldier. In his military future he is to suffer all the hardships of a soldier's life to the maximum point of endurance, without any of its privileges. He is issued a musket with hardly any basic training on how to use it; he is posted on guard duty without being instructed his duties, and is forced to work when not on guard duty . . . to work, drudge, shovel with spade or fork, as soon as uniform and belt are off.

Frontier posts were so poorly garrisoned that the number of men at most stations were not equal to the work necessary to be done. After hours of strenuous labor, men depended on the smallest of rations provided by the government, and flour, salt meat, and hardtack were often of the poorest quality. Vegetables and sugar seldom showed up in the soldiers' diet, only now and then did potatoes and cabbage make their appearance. The usual rations of eight ounces of bread, three-quarter pound fat pork or salt beef, or one-quarter pound fresh beef, were daily issues expected while in garrison. Occasionally, one pint of soup made of hominy accompanied a serving, otherwise a pint of hot steaming army coffee washed down the meal.[8] Laughing, singing, and cheerful conversations were seldom heard among men so wanting; and as the heavy hand of time dragged on so did the sad monotony of frontier army life. The majority of the enlisted men, as well as a few officers, considered themselves failures in their object of enlisting, and thoughts of deserting or getting drunk at the first opportunity became critical.

7. Army Navy Journal — Feb. 16, 1867, page 414.

8. Army Navy Journal — Sept. 1, 1866.

Courtesy Union Pacific Railroad

Poster — map

It was not uncommon to witness at a camp or garrison, some six or eight men walking what is known as "the ring," each carrying a log of wood on his shoulder for being dirty. If the offense were more serious, two logs were carried, one on each shoulder. Carrying a saddle for most of the day was a common punishment if the soldier was not present at an inspection at first call. These punishments often lasted 24 hours. For more serious misconduct, the prisoner was arraigned before a court martial, and if found guilty, was sentenced to confinement, and in many cases, with loss of a portion of his pay. Commanding officers called attention to the ever-rising tide of courts-martial. Too many trivial charges were filed, and many should have been brought before a Field Officer's or Garrison Court, and disposed of, instead of being referred to General Courts Martial, convened with great inconvenience and expense. Officers preferring charges seldom examined the case thoroughly before resorting to courts-martial.

Discharging a soldier for desertion was no punishment at all. To the individual it meant a little humiliation and embarrassment, being drummed out of camp before his comrades, but with his dishonorable discharge he was finally free and rid of the army for good. Forfeiture of all pay and allowances then due, except the just dues of the laundress and sutler, were the only things that seemed to concern him. Having his head shaven, and his left hip branded with a two-inch letter "D", only hurt his pride. Punishments given by the courts did not seem to have the slightest effect in preventing desertions. The number of deserters was so high that it was almost impossible to make the soldiers look upon desertion as a serious crime.

Isolation to a soldier in a military fort on the plains was similar to that of a sailor on a ship at sea. Discipline was rigidly enforced

Courtesy Union Pacific Railroad *Painting by J. Gogolin*

One of series of six paintings done by J. Gogolin, famous German artist in 1931 depicting events from life of Adolph Roenigk, member of a section crew working on the UPRR. This painting illustrates a band of Cheyenne Indians led by Tall Bull tearing up railroad tracks near Fossil Creek (now Russell) Kansas, about 1 p.m., May 28, 1869, following the attack upon the section crew.

by the supreme authority, the post commander. All forms of military etiquette were observed. The flag was hoisted at sunrise with the accompaniment of a long roll from the drum and was lowered at sunset with the added reverberations of the evening gun. The frontier soldier found much of his time occupied by many duties. Essentially, a good soldier was to be well drilled. The extent to which frontier garrisons were drilled depended largely on whether troops were veterans with past experience or recruits requiring further drilling. Special duties such as mending roofs, repairing fences, and building additions kept many recruits away from company and regimental drills. There were cases where soldiers served their entire enlistment without once drilling in regimental formation or even in battalion formation.

Another important function on post was guard duty. Government property had to be protected day and night. Guards and pickets prevented Indians from entering the post or lurking near enough to shoot at its defenders, steal horses, or set fire to haystacks or storehouses. It was a very comfortable feeling to hear the hours called late at night, by those on guard duty with the announcement, "All's well." On hearing this the first sentinel repeated the message, and so on around the camp. When the last sentinel repeated the message, the sergeant of the guard called aloud, "Two o'clock and all's well all around." This was repeated at each hour during the night. In case of danger, an alarm to awaken the post was given by a continued beating of the drum — the long roll — without break, until the entire post was fully aroused.

To the soldiers whose lot it was to go on guard duty, hours were spent in cleaning

Courtesy Union Pacific Railroad *Painting by J. Gogolin*

This painting illustrated a band of Cheyenne Indians led by Tall Bull making a buffalo surround near Fossil Creek about 4 p.m., May 28, 1869 after they had attacked the section crew. Later the same band began tearing up the railroad tracks and was instrumental in wrecking a train.

uniforms, polishing boots and brass buttons, and rubbing rifles down, before the time set for "guard mount."

From each guard detail the neatest and most soldierly-appearing trooper was chosen to be orderly to the commanding officer. He reported to post headquarters, where his main duty consisted of carrying messages and making himself useful. It was a high honor, but also he walked no post and slept in his bunk all night. "Bucking for orderly" resulted in rigid inspection of the man, his uniform, arms, and equipment. It was at guard mounting, dress reviews and inspections that the soldier presented his most soldier-like appearance.

Details sent out for escort duty often broke the monotony of "post boredom." It might be escorting the paymaster's wagon, scheduled for a visit every two months, or the monthly military train that supplied the post with mail or rations. Possibly an escort would be required for the inspector-general or the commanding general of the department or district. Soldiers at posts along well-traveled trails, often found escorting was a daily chore . . . and the only work for the cavalry. During Indian troubles, stages, mail wagons, generals, government trains, and paymasters, along with immigrant wagon trains bound for California, and freighters all required escorts; however, the size of the detachment depended upon the character and importance of the object escorted. Army details varied from three to four men to escort a mail carrier, to several companies as escort for a large supply train.[9]

Troops were often called upon to form scouting parties to locate the Indian and

9. My Life on the Plains, by G. A. Custer, pages 62, 68, 74, 78.

keep him in check. Generally, the marauding Indians were scattered in small bands far from their villages. It was a general policy to keep scouting parties out in summer to hold the hostiles in check, and give the impression the army was always ready for them. The soldiers were hardened by the experience of scouting in the field, and practically trained by experiences in maneuvers. For the soldier, it broke the monotony of garrison life with a change of scenery, and of diet. Shooting buffalo, antelope, or other game was encouraged. These expeditions were also welcomed by the men remaining at the post, as fresh meat was brought in to supplement their rations. The anticipation of being chosen to accompany the next scouting party was always the topic of the day. Many stories, somewhat blown out of proportion, of hair-raising experiences, were topics of garrison gossip.

Within a few months, a number of troops of the 7th Cavalry Regiment were organized and sent to more remote posts. Troops B and C were stationed at Fort Lyon, Colorado Territory; Troop E was sent to Fort Hays, Kansas; Troops F and G were assigned to Fort Harker, Kansas; Troop I was stationed at Fort Wallace, Kansas; Troop K at Fort Dodge, Kansas, and Troop L went to Fort Morgan, Colorado Territory. Only Troops A, D, H and M remained with the regimental headquarters at Fort Riley.[10]

10. Of Garryowen in Glory — by Lt. Col. M. C. Chandler.

Courtesy Union Pacific Railroad *Painting by J. Gogolin*

This painting illustrates an attack on a hand car near Fossil Creek (now Russell) Kansas by Tall Bull's Cheyennes, about 10 a.m. May 28, 1869. Several men were killed and Mr. Roenigk was shot completely through the lung.

The deafening "ping" from steel hammers played the first grand chorus across the plains, as railroad crews of gaugers, spikers, and bolters, stretched the steel ribbons of rail westward. The Kansas Pacific had been completed as far as Junction City, and most of the grading had been done as far west as Fort Harker. The end of the Civil War produced an adequate labor force for the first time, particularly as financial depression in the East led many discharged soldiers to seek work on the railroads. The Indians were anything but pleased with the progress of the "iron horse," largely because of its push through their hunting grounds. Serious depredations developed. Engineers, surveyors, graders and bridge builders, plotting a course of construction toward the Rocky Mountains, always considerabley in advance of work gangs, faced the peril of being ambushed and killed. Armed with the best weapons the railroad could supply meant little or nothing against the swift attack from a band of hostiles. Even as the 7th Cavalry remained the watchful dog, the threat of these attacks always lingered and the building of the railroad appeared many times a small scale Indian war.

The overland stage lines to Denver and Santa Fe were protected by two lines of posts, one on the Smoky Hill River, the other on the Arkansas River. These posts, seven in number, were all of a temporary character, rudely constructed, usually of cottonwood logs and rough lumber. At some of them, particularly at Fort Dodge, many officers and men lived in dugouts, with dirt roofs and no floors. Temporary bunks with pole or board slats and a straw tick, empty boxes, cross sections of cottonwood logs, and barrels with the sides out and stuffed with hay, made up the furniture in the barrack room; tallow dips supplied illumination.

The uniformed cavalryman of the 1866-1867 period was bedecked in a maze

Courtesy Union Pacific Railroad

Gaugers and spikers were constantly harassed by Indians. Weapons, supplied by the railroad, were close at hand in case of another attack.

Courtesy Herb Peck, Jr.

Trooper of the late 1860's, with full equipment.

Courtesy The Kansas State Historical Society
Fort Riley Hospital 1867.

Courtesy The Kansas State Historical Society
Custer House, Fort Riley. A modern photo.

Courtesy The Kansas State Historical Society
Fort Riley, 1867.

of entangled leather straps, supporting-cartridge pouches, pistol and carbine. At his left trailed a three-pound, seven-ounce light cavalry sabre[11] totaling 42.35 inches in length and as useful as a club against hit-and-run tactics of the plains Indian. On his right, fastened to a wide leather shoulder belt[12] hung his most effective weapon, the Spencer, a seven-shot repeating carbine, caliber 56/50, model 1865. An average-trained marksman could fire the seven rounds in 12 to 18 seconds. It could throw a ball more than a mile and with a little accuracy, penetrate a foot of solid pine at 150 feet. Indeed, the Spencer was classified a potent short-range carbine. Loading was speeded up when Spencer incorporated the Blakeslee Quickloader. These leather boxes came with ten tin tubes,[13] each tube holding seven .52 caliber rim-fire cartridges. The arm was loaded through a trap in the butt plate, loaded singly one tube after another. This meant that the soldier had a fire power of 70 shots. The overall weapon was 38 inches in length, with a 22 inch barrel, and weighed approximately seven and a half pounds.

Snugly seated in a black holster with a large semi-circular flap, was the soldier's .44 caliber Remington or Colt percussion revolver. This heavy and unbalanced six-shooter could drop a man at 70 paces.[14] The trooper generally wore his holstered revolver on the right side and attached to the sword belt, with the butt of the weapon forward. Historians venture to guess that this

11. Ordnance Manual 1861, pg. 224.

12. This shoulder belt was a carryover from the Civil War and measured two and three-eighths inches in width.

13. In my article in Guns magazine, "Military Accoutrements, part 1, up to the Civil War," Oct., 1971, page 68, I mention seven tin tubes each holding seven cartridges. Scarcely anything has been written on the Blakeslee, so I referred to Bannerman's 1949 catalog, page 223, which advertises a seven-tube carbine cartridge box. Gun Digest, 1962, shows a photo of the Blakeslee as a ten-tube cartridge box, page 8. Collectors Guns, 1963, page 76, mentions that these boxes came in varying sizes, with the largest holding up to 13 tubes. At the West Point Museum, a box in their collection was found to have six tubes, for the 56/56 cartridge.

14. Cavalry Journal, Vol. 16, page 184, "The extreme useful range should be over 75 yards."

position of the revolver made it easier for the trooper to mount his horse. This is pure assumption. The primary weapon of the cavalryman was the sabre. The revolver was introduced much later.[15] Even during the Civil War it was labeled as an auxiliary weapon. Regulations specified that the holster must be worn on the right side, from which the left hand could draw it if necessary.[16]

The dark blue shell jacket with its two and one-half inch choke-collar, waist-length, were Civil War leftovers. Neither jacket nor blue woollen trousers seemed to fit any man without several visits to the company tailor. There appears to be no rule specifying whether trouser legs were to be worn tucked into the tops of boots or left hanging loosely about the boot when strolling about the post. An exception was made, of course, during an inspection or dress parade.

The floppy crowned "kepi"[17] or forage cap was habitual for casual headwear. From a current French pattern it gave a rather sloppy appearance. The crown was either

15. From a letter written by George B. McClellan, Capt. 1st Cavy., to the Honorable Jefferson Davis, Sec. of War, Oct. 3rd, 1856, Phila. "For my own regiment, armed with the revolvers, there need be no holster, (referring to the saddle holster) for the men should follow the Russian system and always carry the pistol on the waist belt." Cited from Cavalry Journal, Vol. 34, pg. 432.

16. The only possible place to hang the holster was on the right side. On the left is where the sabre hung with all its sabre belts sewn in place. Hypothetically, the right hand was meant for wielding the sabre and the left hand utilized the revolver. This, of course, would only be done at either close combat or dismounted close combat.

17. This cap was a poor imitation of the original French kepi, from a French word deriving from German origin to describe a military hat.

Courtesy The Kansas State Historical Society

Fort Riley, 1867.

Courtesy Union Pacific Railroad

Sod houses peppered the Kansas Plains, most of them empty, the owners scared away by Indians or murdered in their bunks. It wasn't long before a new tennant, fresh from the East, would take up quarters, looking for a new life in the great Western expansion. Ox drawn covered wagon pulling up to empty sod house.

pushed back or sloped forward to suit the wearer, as there was no reinforcement to keep the hat in uniform shape. The kepi gave the soldier little protection from sun or rain. One use was recalled by an old cavalryman; filled with oats or corn, it served as feeding bag for his horse. For dress, the flat-topped, wide-brimmed "Hardee hat"[18] with brass embellishments counterbalanced with an occasional plume was seen in ranks. To distinguish cavalry from infantry, the wide brim was pinned up to the right side for cavalry, and to the left side for infantry.

The average weight of the cavalry soldier was approximately 140 pounds. With saddle, weapons, and accoutrements, the horse carried a little more than 240 pounds. Sword, carbine, and tin utensils caused a continual din as horse and trooper crept along the trail at a rate of from three to four miles an hour. The trooper enlisted for five years and received $16 a month[19] in inflated greenbacks. This lasted him a short time, as gambling, whiskey, and the high-priced sutler exhausted his pockets quickly. There was nothing sensational or picturesque about these Indian-fighters and they accomplished more through threat than they achieved in actual battle.

State-side newspapers reported the renewal of hostilities by the Indians on the western plains. Easterners visualized Fort Riley as under constant siege with huge stone walls encompassing the small garrison. It would have been more realistic if

18. Sometimes called Jeff Davis hat, Hardee, or Kossuth. Secretary of War Jefferson Davis insisted upon the adoption of this hat.

19. Reduced to $13.00 in 1872, with small increases after 3 years and "bounties" for reenlistments on the frontier averaging $30.00 to $140.00, depending upon location of station.

Courtesy Union Pacific Railroad *Photo by A. J. Russell*

Usually a shotgun or large caliber rifle hung over the door outside of the cabin. If a settler family laid claim to the land, built his sod house or log cabin, and planted his field, all within the year, he was then considered lucky he hadn't been payed a visit from "Mr. Lo." Pictured here is a Mormon family.

the newspapers had recorded continuation rather than renewal, for the sporadic warfare never altogether ceased. But at Fort Riley there were no huge stone walls. There were stables, five in number, a sutler's store, and billiard house for the officers, an express office and a post office. The quartermaster employees' houses were near the mess houses and sutler's residence. The chaplain's residence and chapel were surrounded by a white picket fence. The superintendent's house and ordnance building were situated in a group, away from the parade ground. Barracks included six large two-storied buildings, three were on each side of a hollow square, facing one another. Six double houses for officers' quarters were on the remaining two sides of the square. This square was the parade ground with a deep rich green lawn, in the center of which stood a cannon flanked by a flagpole. A carriage drive ran around the parade ground, and on windy days, clouds of Kansas dust never ceased to creep into the frontier-fashionable, neatly-kept quarters, irritating the officers' wives to extremity.[20]

This same Kansas wind played havoc with the ladies by upsetting their skirts, throwing hem after hem over their heads revealing white petticoats and dainty ankles beneath. The women soon learned that buckshot sewn into the skirts' lower hem-line would weigh down the outer skirts, hindering the wind from upsetting them. As soon as this problem was solved, curious soldiers had little more to hope for in the windswept future.

The establishment of Fort Riley was suggested by Colonel T. T. Fauntleroy, of the 1st Dragoons, in July, 1852. In a letter to General T. S. Jessup, then quartermaster general of the army, Fauntleroy urged that a post be located at a point where the Republican fork unites with the Kansas River. After careful deliberation, the secretary of war appointed a board of officers to locate a new post in the vicinity of the forks of the Kansas River. Escorted by Capt. Robert Hall Chilton of the 1st Dragoons, the board surveyed the area and approved the site. A report was submitted November 10th, 1852, and endorsed by Secretary of War Charles Magill Conrad, January 7th, 1853. A picket was established on the selected site, and because it was found to be very near the geographical center of the United States, it was called "Camp Center." In May, 1853, three companies of the 6th Infantry arrived at Camp Center with orders to erect temporary buildings. After construction had begun, an order changed the name of the camp to Fort Riley, honoring Brevet Major General Bennet Riley, who died at Buffalo, New York, June 9th, 1853.

Appropriations were made by Congress in March, 1855, to prepare Fort Riley for a cavalry training post by building new quarters, stables for five troops, storehouses and whatever was needed. Most of the buildings were built of stone taken from a nearby quarry, with all work done by hand. In the East, contracts were let for window sashes, doors, framework, ornamental woodwork for officers' quarters, glass and hardware. This was shipped by boat to Fort Leavenworth and then by wagon to Fort Riley.[21]

The vast undeveloped empire lying between Fort Riley, Denver, the Platte River, and Red River, was unoccupied except by bands of Kiowas, Cheyennes, Arapahoes, and Lipans, dependent for food and clothing on the vast herds of buffaloes that roamed the plains. Across these hunting grounds passed annually hundreds of wagons, battering hubs and scraping their sides in slashing newly-cut trails toward the mineral regions of the Rocky Mountains and the Pacific Coast. How many failed to reach their destination was manifested by numerous neglected graves of victims of

20. "The History of Fort Riley," by W. F. Pride.

21. "The History of Fort Riley," by W. F. Pride.

starvation, disease, and occasional Indian attacks.

Friendly Indians urged upon the government their need for arms and ammunition for hunting the buffalo on which they depended for subsistence. Indian traders could see their need for breech-loaders to increase their production of furs and hides, but these weapons could also be used in warfare. A report submitted by Major H. Douglas, 3rd Infantry, commanding Fort Dodge, sums up the difficulties.

Fort Dodge, Kansas
January 13, 1867

General: I consider it my duty to report what I have observed with reference to Indian affairs in this country, so that such representations may be made to the Department of the Interior by the commanding general of division as he may think proper, also other items of information which may be useful.

The issue and sale of arms and ammunition — such as breech-loading carbines and revolvers, powder and lead, (loose and in cartridges,) and percussion caps — continues without intermission. The issue of revolvers and ammunition is made by Indian agents, as being authorized by the Commissioner of Indian Affairs, and the sale of them in the greatest abundance is made by traders. Butterfield, an Indian trader, formerly of the overland express, has the largest investment in Indian goods of all the traders. He has sold several cases of arms to Cheyennes and Arapahoes. Charley Rath, a trader, who lives at Zarah, has armed several bands of Kiowas with revolvers, and has completely overstocked them with powder.

Between the authorized issue agents and the sales of the traders, the Indians were never better armed than at the present time. Several hundred Indians have visited this post, all of whom had revolvers in their possession. A large majority had two revolvers, and many of them three.

The Indians openly boasted that they have plenty of arms and ammunition in case of trouble in the spring.

The Interior Department does not seem to appreciate the danger of thus arming those Indians. The evil of presenting a revolver to each of the chiefs of bands would hardly be appreciable, but when the whole rank and file are thus armed, it not only gives them greater courage to murder and plunder, but renders them formidable enemies.

The agents have no real control over the traders; in fact, they are accused by many, both Indians and white men, of being in league with them, and of drawing a large profit from the trade. Should such be the case, (and I think it highly probable,) it is a

Courtesy Union Pacific Railroad

Mormon emigrant train crossing the Platte River (painting).

Courtesy U.S. Signal Corps photo (Brady Collection)

A Sioux and Cheyenne Villege, "the calm before the storm."

natural consequence that the agent does not wish to control the trader.

The anxiety of Indians at the present time to obtain arms and ammunition is a great temptation to the trader. For a revolver an Indian will give ten, even twenty times its value, in horses and furs; powder and lead are sold to them at almost the same rate, and as the bulk is small, large quantities can be transported at comparatively little expense. This anxiety cannot be caused by a lack of such articles, because they have plenty to last for some time, but everything tends to show that the Indians are laying in large supplies, preparatory to an outbreak. When the outbreak occurs, we will see too late that we have provided our enemies with the means for our destruction.

A great deal of dissatisfaction seems to have been created among the Indians by the unequal distribution of presents.

The Kiowas complain bitterly of Colonel Leavenworth, their agent, stationed at Fort Zarah. Kicking Bird, a chief of the Kiowas, states that only a few small bands of Kiowas got any presents, the balance last year got nothing; that it had been represented to Colonel Leavenworth that most of the bands were bad in their hearts, and would not go in to get their presents; that he, Kicking Bird, sent runners to tell Colonel Leavenworth that his stock was poor and he could not move in there, but he would in the spring, if the agent would keep his share of the goods, but Colonel Leavenworth would not listen, and either gave all the goods to the bands then in, or sold them to other Indians, and told them they would get no goods that year.

How much of this is true I know not, but from all I can learn there seems to be at least some foundation for the story. Bad management, bad faith, and injustice are sure to produce the worst results. Kicking Bird says that all bad feeling in his tribe is owing to the injustice of their agent; that it required all his influence to prevent an outbreak, and he is afraid that they will commence hostilities in the spring.

The Arapahoes, Cheyennes, and a large band of Sioux, under the leadership of Big Bear, are now en route for the purpose of crossing the Arkansas into the Kiowa country. They move ostensibly to graze and hunt buffalo. A portion of the Arapahoes, under the general leadership of Little Raven, crossed the river about four miles below this point.

The Sioux and Cheyennes are encamped about 100 miles north of this post on the Republican, and are said to be hostile. They are to cross about eleven miles below here. They are all well mounted and well armed with carbines and revolvers, and supplied with plenty of ammunition.

Kicking Bird says the Sioux and Cheyennes asked his permission to cross the river, and that he refused it for fear of trouble, but that his men wish them to cross, and he believes that they will all cross the river, and that in the spring, when the grass comes up, there will be war. He had been treated kindly at Fort Dodge, or he would not tell us so, but we must look out for our lives and for our stock in the spring. He says, as they talk now all the tribes north and south of the Arkansas will be in the outbreak, his own tribe among them.

He also states that Santante or "White Bear" a principal chief of the Kiowas, is always talking of war; that they have already had a counsel at the Kiowa camp, in which the Cheyennes, Sioux, Arapahoes, Kiowas, Comanches and Apaches were represented, and it was agreed that as soon as the grass was old enough they would commence war; that he (Kicking Bear) had been kindly treated at Fort Dodge, and he wished to put us on our guard; that before spring the Indians might change their minds, but at present their intention was war; he said he would be backwards and forwards frequently to give us the news.

The chief (Kicking Bear) is known to General Sherman who talked with him last fall, and is believed at this post to be the most reliable of all the Indians.

I would respectfully state that it is my purpose to keep the district and department informed of all movements of Indians in large bodies as far as it is possible.

I am, very respectfully, your obedient servant,
H. Douglas
Major Third Infantry
Commanding Post.[22]

With the increased number of officers and soldiers being sent west, there seemed to be a lamentable ignorance in the East of the vast extent of the country even among "army people," and of the wants and requirements of those whose professions sent them there for an undetermined tour of duty. It seems that when an officer was sent to the plains it was only necessary for him to pack a small trunk or valise with a few indispensable articles and immediately proceed to his station, much in the same manner as if he were joining his regiment in the field. Totally unprepared for the frontier life they were obliged to lead, they accepted various opinions from people with lesser experience than themselves, as to what should be taken and what should not. "Everyone told us that it was unnecessary to bring anything with us; that officers on duty on the frontier have no need of anything save what they can get from the quartermaster," replied one young officer, somewhat disturbed with his predicament.[23]

Common ignorance brought one officer to the frontier with only two blankets for bedding, in the middle of December, with three inches of snow on the ground, and he was surprised that the surgeon could not furnish from hospital property everything he would require. In another instance a second lieutenant reported to his commanding officer without a uniform, and when asked what he proposed to do without a dress uniform, he explained that an older officer back east told him that officers never wore anything at a frontier garrison, except common soldiers' clothes. He was surprised that such was not the case. It was also supposed that while serving some distant garrison, or when on detached service, they would lose their quarters after being in the field for a number of weeks. Such false notions were often taken seriously because of the lack of information furnished from competent sources.

Quarters were furnished by the quartermaster with heating and cooking stoves; a plain table or two, a rough bunk or bedstead, and possibly a chair made of unfinished pine boards. Anything else that the officer should need, he must provide for himself. Surgeons are not in the habit of providing bedding or beds for the use of officers, and the quartermaster does not provide him with furnishings or blankets although he may purchase these items at government prices. Officers who have been on the frontier long enough to learn how to live, and who had any taste for living like gentlemen, usually furnished their quarters comfortably. Curtains and carpets were not altogether unknown, even in bachelor quarters. With the aid of a company carpenter, a few pine boards and empty hardtack boxes,

---

22. "Issue of Arms to Indians," Letter from the Secretary of War; (relative to the issue of a large number of arms to the Kiowas and other Indians) 39th Congress, 2nd Session; Mis. Doc. No. 41, 1867.

23. Army Navy Journal — January 11, 1868.

Courtesy The Kansas State Historical Society

Fort Harker, 1867. An army post established in 1866 to protect settlers and railroad construction parties.

chairs were built. Pictures and engravings hung in handsome gold frames along with stuffed birds and animals, adding a civilized appearance to these small quarters.

Officers in garrison generally wore the regulation uniform, even patronizing first-class tailors. It has been noted that officers on the plains were as well dressed as those who were on duty at Eastern stations. Officers prepared and well-advised as to what items were necessary for frontier duty were generally equipped with the following: A good mess chest, well-furnished for four or six persons, a good roll of bedding and a mattress, a few comfortable fold-up camp chairs, and a trunk filled with a good supply of clothing for at least one year. A wise officer will leave his measurements with a good tailor and bootmaker before leaving "the States," in order to replenish his wardrobe at any time by sending his order.

Books and weeklies offered relaxation during idle hours, and were often exchanged or passed on to someone else. Once the officer had established himself at a post, he found he was obliged to purchase what was available from the sutler at a cost of 100 or 200 percent more than he would have paid had he brought these items with him. Probably more than anything else, an officer would trade his most precious memento for a good mattress. A ticking filled with dry prairie hay was hard to get accustomed to. It constantly needed refilling, developed barbs and insects, and in a short time gave off a musty and offensive odor.

Even though these men lived in a frontier fashion, they always thought of themselves as gentlemen, and they lived as such. Their living habits may have been simple, but they were far from that of frontier ranchmen who ate fried bacon with their fingers and slept on the ground, a saddle for a pillow.

Women who accompanied their husbands to frontier posts generally complained of the great difficulty in getting food that was wholesome and nutritious. Laws passed by Congress allowed officers to purchase from the government such supplies as they could certify were needed for their own use; however, they criticized the limitations. A schedule of what items might be obtained was usually posted to keep everyone informed of their purchasing boundaries. An allowance for one month for each officer is as follows: Two cans peaches, one can oysters, one-half can jelly, one-half can jam, four cans of tomatoes, two cans corn, one can peas, two cans milk, three pounds soda crackers, two and a half pounds mackerel, one and a half pounds dried beef, two pounds Java coffee, two and a half pounds sperm candles, one-quarter pound officer's soap, one-quarter gallon syrup, one and one half pounds dried peaches, and two pounds lard.[24]

24. Army Navy Journal — August 24, 1867.

Art by E. L. Reedstrom

Typical cavalryman standing to horse at Fort Riley.

If the officer was lucky enough to have only a wife, he could get by replenishing his table with additional meat from a hunt. But for some, who had children and employed servants, the pitiful amount which they were allowed to consume each day was wholly inadequate. While many wives were willing to forego the privilege of delicious vegetables and sweet fruits and a comfortable home, to comfort and cheer husbands in their lonely and monotonous frontier life, other women returned to their eastern homes to wait for their husband's tour of duty to end.

Besides all this, what woman did not know was the frightfully exorbitant prices of the sutler and the great monopoly he exercised. Canned oysters, that they paid the government 29 cents for, were retailed by the sutler for one dollar, and nearly all canned vegetables sold for similar prices. Fruits in cans were higher still. There is no doubt that an officer's pay was inadequate if he were compelled to depend on the sutler, but if any major complaints were voiced by these frontier women it would probably be against the commissaries who told them that they could only have so much, and the rest of the time they lived on bacon, beans, beef, and flour.

ORGANIZATION OF CAVALRY, 1866-1876

July 28, 1866	*March 3, 1869*	*July 15, 1870*
1 colonel		
1 lieutenant colonel		
3 majors		
1 adjutant (extra lieutenant)		
1 quartermaster (extra lieutenant)		
1 regimental commissary (extra lieutenant)		no commissary
1 veterinary surgeon		
1 additional veterinary surgeon (not commissioned)		
1 sergeant major		
1 quartermaster sergeant		
1 commissary sergeant		
1 saddler sergeant		
1 chief trumpeter	1 chief musician added	chief musician continued
1 regimental hospital steward		no regimental hospital steward
12 companies each:		
1 captain		
1 first lieutenant		
1 second lieutenant		
1 first sergeant		
1 quartermaster sergeant		
5 sergeants		
8 corporals		4 corporals
2 trumpeters		
2 farriers and blacksmiths		
1 saddler		
1 wagoner		
78 privates	60 privates	60 privates

Acts of June 16 and 23, 1874; March 2 and 3, 1875; June 26, 1876:
no commissary sergeant
4 corporals in each company
54 privates in each company

Chaplains: 1 in each colored regiment (9th and 10th Cavalry), not commissioned in 1866. By the act of 1869, there were 4 in the 4 colored regiments and 30 post chaplains, to rank as captains of infantry.

Indian scouts to the number of 1,000 may be employed as cavalry soldiers under all acts, 1866-1876. There were 474 in service in 1869.

Surgeons were Medical Department, not a part of regimental organization. Acts of 1866-1870 provided 1 brigadier general, 1 colonel, 5 lieutenant colonels, 60 majors, and 150 first lieutenants who were promoted to captain after three years, and 5 medical storekeepers who ranked as captains of cavalry. The only enlisted men were hospital stewards, 459 in 1866; 365 in 1869; 297 in 1870. Acts of 1874-1876 increased commissioned ranks: 6 colonels, 10 lieutenant colonels, 50 majors, 74 captains, and 51 first lieutenants.

OFFICERS, 7TH CAVALRY, 1866-1876

Colonels	
A. J. Smith	28 July 1866 — 6 May 1869
S. D. Sturgis	6 May 1869 — 11 June 1886
Lieutenant Colonels	
G. A. Custer	28 July 1866 — 25 June 1876
Elmer Otis	25 June 1876 — 2 April 1883
Majors	
Alfred Gibbs	28 July 1866 — 26 December 1868
Wickliffe Cooper	28 July 1866 — 8 June 1867
J. H. Elliott	7 March 1867 — 27 November 1868
W. S. Abert	8 June — 25 August 1867
J. A. Thompson	25 August — 14 November, 1867
J. G. Tilford	14 November 1867 — 22 September 1883
Lewis Merrill	27 November 1868 — 21 May 1886
M. A. Reno	26 December 1868 — 1 April 1880
Adjutants	
W. W. Cooke	8 December 1866 — 21 February 1867 and
	1 January 1871 — 25 June 1876
Myles Moylan	21 February 1867 — 31 December 1870
G. D. Wallace	25 June 1876 — 6 June 1877
Quartermasters	
T. W. Custer	3 December 1866 — 10 March 1867
J. M. Bell	1 November 1867 — 31 March 1869 and
	26 October 1869 — 31 December 1870
A. E. Smith	31 March — 7 July 1869
J. F. Weston	1 January 1871 — 29 February 1872
H. J. Nowlan	1 March 1872 — 25 June 1876
W. S. Edgerly	25 June — 14 November 1876
C. A. Varnum	14 November 1876 — 31 October 1879
Commissaries	
T. B. Weir	24 February — 31 July 1867
H. J. Nowlan	30 October 1867 — 15 July 1870
No more until:	
S. R. H. Tompkins	1 July 1899

CHAPTER TWO

AN ACT OF WAR

Through the year 1866, the Kansas frontier was relatively quiet. Cheyennes in the North were helping Red Cloud's Sioux fight against traffic on the Bozeman Trail. They also took a leading part in the slaughter of Fetterman's command, and in 1867 they were back on the southern plains, restless and discontented. There were occasional encounters with overland travelers and settlers, but much talk of raids said to have been committed by Indians was reported to the military, with the threat of an uprising in the spring. The Government, seeking to do something to prevent this, sent an expedition to the plains under Major General Winfield S. Hancock, commanding the Department of the Missouri.

Prepared for war but intending to seek peace, Hancock left Fort Riley in April, 1867, with 1,400 men, cavalry, artillery, infantry, and a pontoon train. With a sometimes lagging supply train, the column presented a formidable appearance, and it is probable that the 'moral effect' served to awe the red man into good behavior for a time. General Hancock had reached Fort Riley, Kansas, from Fort Leavenworth by rail at the end of March; here four companies of the Seventh Cavalry and a company of the 37th Infantry joined Hancock's command. After leaving Fort Riley, the march continued to Fort Harker, some 90 miles. The command went into camp on the Smoky Bottom, just west of the post, drawing provisions and supplies for the expedition, and was reinforced by two more troops of cavalry. The troops then marched toward Fort Larned, near the Arkansas River, arriving there April 7. The command included eleven companies of the Seventh Cavalry, Lieutenant Colonel Custer; seven companies of the 37th Infantry, Captain Parsons; a battery of the Fourth Artillery and an Engineer detachment commanded by Lieutenant Micah Ryder Brown. General J. W. Davidson accompanied the expedition as inspector general. Brevet Major General Andrew J. Smith, colonel 7th Cavalry, also accompanied the expedition as commander of the District of the Upper Arkansas.

James Butler Hickok, commonly known as "Wild Bill," was attached as a scout. Greatness had recently been thrust upon him by publication of an article in the February, 1867, issue of Harper's Magazine. A

Courtesy Author's Collection

Major General Hancock

number of Delaware Indians accompanied the command as scouts, guides, hunters and interpreters. They had no friendship for their wilder brethren, and moved with the command in full battle array with faces painted for war. Their services were very valuable to General Hancock, as they served as the command's eyes and ears.

A grand "pow-wow" was to be held near Fort Larned, and arrangements with the chiefs of a Cheyenne village nearby planned to effect greater security and safety for those whose business compelled them to travel through or reside in the valley of the Smoky Hill. Runners had been sent by the agent of the Cheyennes, Arapahoes, and Apaches, inviting their head chiefs to a council on April 10. A blinding snowstorm struck April 9, lasting the full day until late evening. Horses suffered from the severe cold and officers ordered double rations of oats to the horses, and guards were instructed to pass along the picket lines, whipping the horses to keep them moving constantly so they would not freeze. Eight to twelve inches of snow prevented travel, and the council was postponed until the weather moderated.

One of the big attractions in the expedition's train was a six-year-old Cheyenne boy, survivor of Sand Creek, who was being carried back to his people, a recent treaty having stipulated the child's return. Colonel John M. Chivington's Colorado volunteers in 1864 attacked a camp of Cheyennes. While waving an American flag, and also a white flag of truce, Arapahoes and Cheyennes at Sand Creek were butchered brutally. Men, women and children tasted their own blood while pleading for their lives, trying to show the troopers that they were peaceful. The day after the battle, two soldiers found the boy concealed in a hole in the bank of a creek and rescued him. At the same time, two small Cheyenne girls were found, but only one girl returned with the boy.[1]

1. The Cheyenne boy and girl were exhibited in the Wilson and Graham Circus. After the Indians had demanded these children be returned, the government detailed an officer to trace them. Through some confusion, only the boy was secured. The girl disappeared with the showman, never to be heard of again. After the boy was returned to the Indians, it was said by some that the

Art by E. L. Reedstrom

Custer in parley with Indians.

Art by E. L. Reedstrom

One of the Cheyenne Chiefs.

The boy lived in the United States[2] for four years, showing an increasing amount of willingness to learn the white man's way. When troopers teased him, saying he would have to live with his savage uncle, the boy would draw a jack-knife of formidable dimensions and announce that if he didn't like his uncle, or if he was mistreated, he would kill him without notice. Civilization had little effect on the boy; through violent and ungovernable temper, signs of his savage ancestry became visible many times. The boy had lost whatever Cheyenne tongue he knew, which was probably very little when captured, but he could speak English far better than some white boys his age. Full realization of his immediate future with his new Cheyenne family and their barbaric way of outdoor living weighed heavily on the boy as the days grew closer. General Hancock manifested great interest in the youngster, keeping him at his quarters and treating him with favors and kindness.

In the late evening of April 12, a band of warlike Indians, mainly Cheyennes, appeared in Hancock's camp. Among them were two chiefs of the "Dog Soldiers" ready to parlay after a meal and the customary smoke. The Indians were magnificently dressed in gorgeous crimson blankets, their faces streaked with war paint, and buckskins embellished with fine designs of beads and porcupine quills. After the meal all were comfortably seated around a huge fire. General Hancock addressed the Indians:

> I told your agent, some time ago, that I was coming here to see you, and that if any of you wished to speak to me, you could do so. Your agent is your friend. I don't find many chiefs here; what is the reason? I have a great deal to say to you, but I want to see all the chiefs together. I want to say it all at once. But I am glad to see those chiefs that are here. To-morrow I am going to your camp. I have a boy, said to be a Cheyenne, whom the Cheyennes claim. We have made a promise, in which we pledged ourselves, if possible to find this boy, and girl, who were somewhere in the United States. We have found the boy, and here he is, ready to be delivered to his nearest relatives, who may call for him. I will leave him at Fort Larned with the commander. He will deliver him up to them. The girl is in Denver. We have written for her, and she will no doubt be sent here, either to your agent, or to the commander at Fort Larned, for delivery to her relatives. You see, the boy has not been injured; the girl will be delivered by us, also uninjured. Look out that any captives in your hands be restored to us equally unharmed. I tell you these things, now, that you may keep your treaties. Now, I have a great many soldiers; more than all the tribes put together. The Great Father has heard that some Indians have taken white men and women captives. [These prisoners were taken by Kiowas in Texas. The Cheyennes had nothing to do with them.] He has heard, also, that a great many Indians are trying to get up war to try to hurt the

Courtesy Herb Peck, Jr.

Osage Scout for Custer.

---

boy was an Arapaho, son of Red Bull. The circus people named the boy Tom Graham, but army officers dubbed him Graham Wilson. "Life of George Bent," by Geo. E. Hyde, pg. 257.

2. East of the Mississippi was always referred to as "back in the states," or "state side."

white man; that is the cause of my coming here. I intend not only to visit you here, but my troops will remain among you so that the peace and safety of the plains is preserved. I am going also to visit you in your camps. The innocent and those who are truly our friends we shall treat as brothers. If we find hereafter that any of you have lied to us, we will strike you. In case of war we shall punish whosoever befriends our enemies. If there are any tribes among you who have captives, white or black, you must give them up safe and unharmed as they are now. I have collected the evidence of all outrages committed by you, so that your agents may examine into the matter, and tell me who are guilty and who are not. I have heard that a great many of Indians want to fight. If so, we are here and prepared for war. If you are for peace, you know the conditions. If you are for war, then look out for its consequences. Your agent is your friend, but he knows his friendship will not save you from the anger of your Great Father, if we go to war. If we find any good Indians, and they come to us with clean hands, we will treat them as brothers, and we will separate them from the malcontents, and provide for them if necessary. This we will do, that the innocent may escape the war which will be waged against the guilty. We are building railroads and military roads through the country; you must not let your young men stop them; you must keep your men off the road. These roads will benefit the Indian as well as the white man, in bringing their goods cheaply and promptly to them. The steam-car and the wagon-train must run, and it is of importance to the whites and Indians that the mails, goods and passengers carried on them shall be safe. You know very well, if you go to war with the whites, you will lose. The Great Father has plenty more warriors. It is true, you might kill some soldiers, and surprise some small detachments. But soldiers came here to be killed — that is what they are for; we have plenty more, and as soon as one is killed, we have another in his place. If you take a passenger train, and kill women and children, you will be exterminated. If there are any good Indians that don't want to go to war, I shall help them and protect them. If there are any bad chiefs, I will help the good chiefs to put their heels on them. I have a great many chiefs with me that have commanded more men than any of you ever saw, and they have fought more great battles than you have fought fights. My chiefs cannot derive any distinction from fighting with your small numbers. They are not anxious for wars against Indians, but they are ready to make a just war. Let the guilty then beware. Stick to your treaties and let the white man travel unmolested. Your Great Father is your friend, as well as the friend of the white man. If a white man behaves badly or does a wrong to you he shall be punished, if the evidence ascertained at the trial proves him guilty.

[With this, the Indians began to stir, look at one another, with a great sensation passing among them.]

We can redress your wrongs better than you can.

[Grunts, groans of "wagh, ugh" rose above the crackling of embers from the council fire.][3]

Hancock noticed that the Indians were somewhat restless, and with a certain eagerness to hear their side, he shortened his speech.

I have no more to say. I will await the end of this Council, to see whether you want war or peace. You ought to be the white man's friend. Come to the white man, and he will take care of you. I would advise you to cultivate their friendship. That is all I have to say.

During Hancock's speech it was noticed that the Indians were entranced with the uniforms and sabers that flashed in the fire light, often fixing their eyes on the red horsehair plumes of the artillery officers swaying to and fro at each nod of the head. Some chiefs seemed puzzled in determin-

3. Army Navy Journal, "Hancock's Speech to Indians," Vol. IV, 1867, page 578.

Art by E. L. Reedstrom

Sergeant to horse.

ing whether they were confronted with "medicine men" or designated chieftains.

Tall Bull, pulling his blanket snugly around him, awaited his turn and said that his tribe was at peace and had no intentions of harming the whites. His brief response was noncommittal; chiefly he declared a pacific intent, but, "Your young men must not shoot us, whenever they see us they fire, and we fire on them . . . Whenever you want to go to the Smoky Hill, you can go. We are willing to be friends with the white man. If you go to the village tomorrow, I won't have any more to say to you than I have now. . . ." Hancock answered that he intended going to their village the next day, and hoped to see all the chiefs there.

The next day Hancock started for the village on the Pawnee Fork as planned. After traveling twenty-three miles from the fort, the command encamped for the night. At approximately 11 a.m. the next day the march was resumed. Only a few miles were covered before scouts raced back with hands held high, signaling a halt. It was obvious why the scouts returned so quickly. Before the troops, stretched across the prairie, was an Indian line of battle. An estimated 400 mounted warriors and chiefs bedecked with their brightest colors showed a number of breech-loading Sharps rifles in addition to sinew backed bows and quivers filled with arrows. Some rode double; others, scattered between ponies, were on foot. Far to the left of their line a white flag was seen, where some 30 or 40 chiefs assembled. Hancock lost no time in issuing orders to his aides. Commands echoed between the columns of the expedition and bugle after bugle sounded. Infantry moved out in advance of the reserve columns, and the forward line knelt loading their new transition Springfield breech loaders. Sabers, drawn, flashed in the morning sun. The artillery was somewhat slow in following up closely, but finally formed a line of battle, with the cavalry on their flanks. The only other sounds heard from both sides were the nervous horses snorting the frigid air and pawing the ground.

As the warriors sat upon their ponies, black, white, spotted and bay, their chiefs were riding back and forth, gesturing and talking, trying to keep the hot-blooded braves in order. The bright colors of shields painted with sacred symbols blended with war bonnets flopping in the sharp wind. War paint streaked bronze faces and decorated ponies awaited the white man's first move.

Edmund Guerrier, scout and interpreter, with Wild Bill Hickok, rode boldly forward signaling peace, and invited the chiefs to

Courtesy National Archives

Custer began to adopt buckskins in the field, much like the frontiersmen he had seen lingering about the post.

meet them halfway, for the purpose of a council. Roman Nose accepted, and spurred his pony forward. He was accompanied by several other chieftains carrying a white flag of truce at the end of a pole. Guerrier signaled for Hancock and his officers to approach. Arriving in the circle of horses, Hancock was somewhat hesitant in shaking hands with Roman Nose and the other chiefs, but interpreter Guerrier lessened the tension by conversation in Cheyenne.

Hancock, through Guerrier, questioned the hostile attitude displayed. "If you desire war," said he, "I am ready here and now to gratify your wish." The chiefs answered that they did not desire war, but were peacefully disposed. They were told that the command would continue toward the village and camp with the promise that soldiers would not approach their village or disturb them. Roman Nose grew angry; he had told Bull Bear earlier that he intended to kill Hancock before all his troops, but Bull Bear argued that this would endanger the families in camp. Looks and behavior of the warriors, with bows strung, rifles and pistols ready to fire, seemed to indicate they were awaiting a signal to fire upon the troops. Hancock ended the talk by telling the chiefs it was too windy to hold council in the open, that he would receive them at camp that night. Roman Nose and the other chieftains promised they would be there, and started back to their village. Only Bull Bear remained with Hancock's officers, trying to convince them that a further march toward the village would alarm the women and children. The general did not agree with the idea. The troops, taking up the line of march behind Roman Nose and his warriors, traveled until mid-afternoon, continuing until the command came within three hundred yards east of the Indian encampment. In the village there were 300 lodges, generally averaging eleven persons per lodge, including warriors, women and children, or an estimated three thousand Indians. Situated on the banks of the Pawnee Fork, with an abundance of wood, water, grass, it was an ideal encampment from which any approaching enemy could be spotted.

Shortly after tents were pitched, Hancock was told by prominent chiefs of the Cheyennes that many women and children had fled upon seeing the approaching column, fearing a second Chivington massacre. On hearing this, Hancock became angry and insisted they all return, promising good treatment to all.

The chiefs asked for two horses in order to pursue the fleeing women and children and try to bring them back. Guerrier was to be sent into the village to report every two hours whether any remaining Indians were leaving. The half-breed remained in the village only a few hours, reporting that the Indians were saddled up and moving out. At 11 p.m. Custer, who had just retired, was ordered to surround the village and prevent anyone from leaving. It was some time before all the troops in Custer's command were aroused and assembled. Verbal orders were to be administered and no bugle calls were to be sounded. Anything loose upon the saddles such as cups or sabers was tied down to prevent noise during their movement. Upon surrounding the village, Custer reported to Hancock that it appeared to be deserted but it was feared that the Indians were up to their old tricks by remaining silent, to decoy the troopers into a trap. There were only a few hundred cavalrymen surrounding three hundred lodges,[4] forming a human circle about the village with a radius of about a half mile. The unbroken silence was becoming unbearable. Finally, Custer organized a party of six, including an interpreter, to reconnoiter the village more closely. Nothing was seen indicating that any Indians were within the village. Examination of the lodges revealed that the Indians had departed swiftly, abandoning

4. My Life on the Plains, G. A. Custer; Sheldon and Company, N.Y., 1874, page 27.

nearly all household goods. There were enough trophies lying about to satisfy the intruding soldiers, almost forgetting the important mission they had set out upon. So great was the haste of the Indians in leaving that in some lodges kettles filled with meat still hung bubbling over the fire. Like the shadows of night, the Indians had stolen away, leaving their dogs asleep in the lodges, when the troopers peered in. Plundering committees were formed and the men ran from one lodge to another, picking up relics, carrying away as much as their arms and pockets could hold.

Hancock, upon learning of the deserted village, dispatched several companies of infantry to replace the cavalry and protect the village and its contents from any further looting, until its final disposition could be determined. Custer and his troops returned from the village after being relieved by the infantry, and reported the full particulars to General Hancock. Outraged by the Indians' movements, Hancock ordered Custer to take eight troops of cavalry and start in pursuit of the Indians at early dawn, April 15. There was no sleep for the command that night, as preparations for the march occupied the entire night and part of the morning.

About 2 a.m., April 16, General Hancock summoned his officers to his tent and informed them that he had decided to burn the village and everything within it the next morning; that he considered the Indians had acted treacherously towards him, and that they deserved punishment. Most of the officers and Edward W. Wynkoop, Indian agent, were against this, and urged the General to ponder well upon such a course. The village was not burned that day, but in the morning a courier from Custer arrived informing Hancock of the killing of two white men and the destruction of Lookout Station, on the Smoky Hill. Enraged by the dispatch, Hancock issued final orders that night for the burning of the Indian village, to General A. J. Smith, to take place the morning of April 18.

Headquarters Department of the Missouri, in the field
Camp No. 15 Pawnee Fork, ~~Fort Leavenworth~~ Kansas, April 18th 1867.

Special Field Orders
No. 13

1. ... As a punishment for the bad faith practised by the Cheyennes & Sioux who occupied the Indian Village at this place, and as a chastisement for murders and depredations committed since the arrival of the command at this point by the people of those tribes, the village recently occupied by them which is now in our hands will be entirely destroyed.

All property within the village, such as tools, camp Equipage &c, will be preserved and taken up as captured property by Capt. G. W. Bradley A.Q.M., Chief Quartermaster of the Expedition.

Brevet Major General J. W. Davidson, Major 2d U.S. Cavalry, Acting Inspector General of this Department will take an accurate inventory of all species of property in the village, previous to its destruction.

Brevet Major Genl A. J. Smith, Colonel 7th U.S. Cavalry, Comdg Dist of the Upper Arkansas, is charged with the execution of this order.

By Command of Major Genl Hancock
W. G. Mitchell
Capt. &c A.A.A. Genl.

W G Mitchell

Courtesy Dr. Elizabeth Lawrence

Document ordered by General Hancock may be classified as a Declaration of War against the Indians.

Headquarters Department of the Missouri, in the field, Camp No. 15, Pawnee Fork, Kansas, April 18th, 1867. Special Field Orders No. 13.

1 . . . As a punishment for the bad faith practiced by the Cheyenne and Sioux who occupied the Indian Village at this place, and as a chastisement for murders and depredations committed since the arrival on the command at this point by the people of these tribes, the Village recently occupied by them which is now in our hands will be entirely destroyed. All property within the village, such as tools, camp Equipage etc., will be preserved and taken up as captured property by Capt. G. W. Bradley, AQM, (Assistant Quartermaster) Chief Quartermaster of the Expedition.

Brevet Major General J. W. Davidson, Major, 2nd U.S. Cavalry, Acting Inspector General of the Department will take an accurate inventory of all species of property in the village, previous to its destruction.

Brevet Major General A. J. Smith, Colonel, 7th U.S. Cavalry, Commanding District of the Upper Arkansas, is charged with the execution of this order.

By Command of Major General Hancock
Signed: W. G. Mitchell
Captain and Assistant Adjutant General

Official Copy
W. G. Mitchell
Captain and Assistant General.[5]

The next day fire was set to the village and everything was burned excepting forty lodges, selected by General Hancock to be carried away as trophies. An old Sioux and a little girl, probably no more than ten years old, who had been atrociously outraged by Indian braves of the village, were found and taken to Fort Dodge. It has been charged that the girl was assaulted by troopers, but Custer reported that she was found badly injured. Within a few days after the troops left the fort, both captives died.

It was widely held then and now that Hancock was wrong in burning the Cheyenne village. The Cheyennes charged that the destruction of their lodges on the Pawnee Fork was the cause of the war that followed. In "My Life on the Plains," Custer quotes only the first paragraph of Hancock's field order, and comments, ". . . This act of retribution on the part of General Hancock was the signal for an extensive pen-and-ink war, directed against him and his forces . . ." In the Philadelphia "Press," October 26, 1867, Colonel Wynkoop is quoted: "The Cheyennes had given me to understand recently that the destruction of the village by Hancock *was the cause of the war*. The Cheyennes have burned the plains all around us."

Conflict of opinion between the agents of the Indian Bureau and military officers continued. Wynkoop wrote to Washington that, ". . . Since the Indians of my agency have not yet retaliated for the wrongs heaped upon them, it may be possible, if proper action be taken by the Department of the Interior, to prevent the military from forcing trouble, that a general Indian war may be prevented." To make his case stronger against General Hancock, Wynkoop sent a list of articles destroyed in the Cheyenne village and the Sioux camps.

5. My Life on the Plains, G. A. Custer, Sheldon and Company, N.Y., 1874, page 42. (Original document in Dr. Elizabeth A. Lawrence collection.)

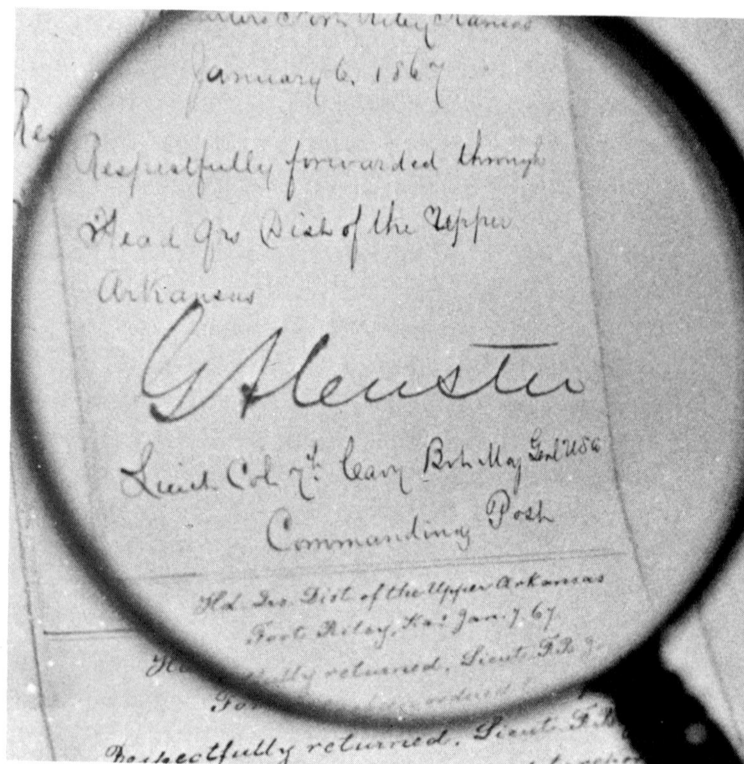

Courtesy Author's Collection

Custer's free scrawled signature was always predominant on written orders, autographed books, and letters to friends.

Map showing the scene of General Hancock's operations in the Indian Country, the Forts, Military Stations, Pacific Railroads, etc.

The Baltimore Gazette, Wednesday, June 5, 1867, published an item dated Washington, June 4:

> The Commissioner of Indian Affairs has just received a dispatch from Superintendent Murphy, at Fort Leavenworth, Kansas, stating that the American Express Company have given the following instructions to their employees on the Smoky Hill route to Denver City: 'Every Indian that comes within shooting distance, shoot him. Show them no mercy. They will show none to you.' He also states that General Hancock has ordered his post commanders to shoot every Indian found north of the Arkansas and south of the Platte rivers. Superintendent Murphy calls the attention of the Commissioner to these orders, and says that the Cheyennes, Arapahoes and Sioux, by stipulations of treaties with the United States, have the privilege of roaming in this country until assigned to other reservations, and the consequences of these measures will be to inaugurate an interminable war with these tribes that will cost the Government hundreds of lives and millions of dollars to bring to a final adjustment.

Hancock's Kansas Expedition was estimated by the government at approximately $1,000,000.00 for active campaigning against Indians. With fourteen hundred men in the field for four months their accomplishments were: Burning of one empty Cheyenne village, and the killing of two Cheyenne Indians[6] at the Cimarron crossing. The absence of Custer's cavalry caused Hancock to give up any move across the Arkansas. The command marched by way of Fort Hays to Fort Hooper, the force was broken up and units sent to Forts Lyon, Dodge, Hays and Larned. A strong fort, well manned, would be built at Monument Station.

General Hancock planned a demonstration of military force in the spring of 1867. Actually his expedition had an effect which was opposite to the one that he intended. The Indians, further aroused and angered, fled the field to avoid another Sand Creek affair. In spite of the fact that Hancock engaged in no hostilities, his expedition left the plains in a fairly open state of war.

---

6. One Bear and Eagle's Nest — "Fighting Cheyennes," Grinnell, page 258.

FROM FLAMING PLAINS TO A WINTER CAMPAIGN

After General Hancock retired from the field with his troops, Indian agents each asserted that his own tribe was innocent of any attacks on the overland stage routes, that it was others who burned the stations and killed the men in charge. All joined in denouncing Hancock for bringing on a general Indian war, and a pen and ink war developed between the two departments of the government that were dealing with Indians.

During the next three months, May, June and July, Custer led the Seventh Cavalry through Nebraska and Kansas, covering a thousand miles of scouting, purposes of which were to see what the Indians were doing; to hold parleys with chieftains in hope of a peaceful settlement; and to identify which bands were off raiding and who was leading them. Custer used much diplomacy with Indian councils, and the chieftains respected his methods. As time went on they also respected his bravery and the keeping of his word.

On the morning of June 26, 1867, Indians were reported running off stock from the

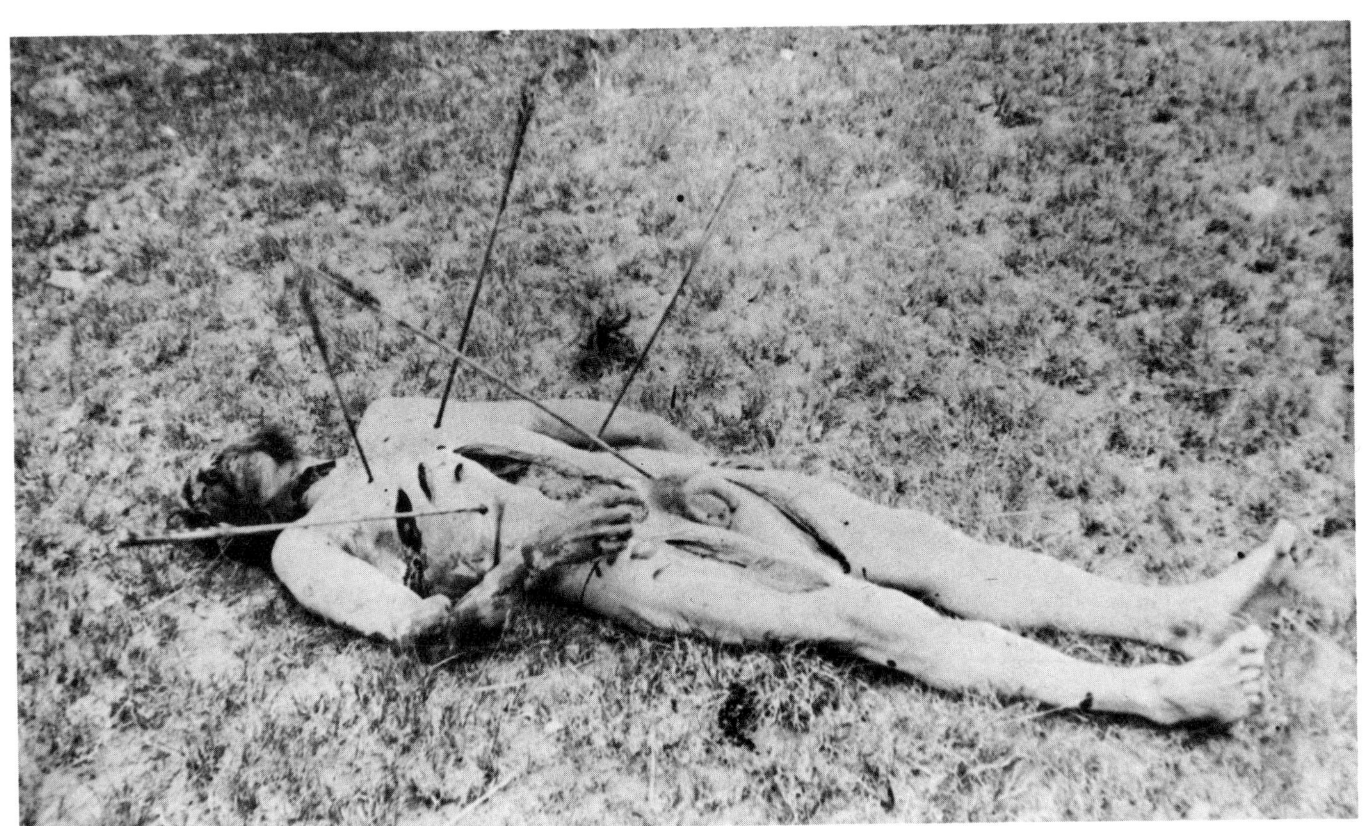

Courtesy Kansas State Historical Society

Typical example of Indian revenge. Sergeant Frederick Wyllyams, Company G, 7th U.S. Cavalry, was one of seven killed near Pond Creek Station, several miles from Fort Wallace, on June 26, 1867. Scalped twice, brained, throat cut, heart cut out, and body slashed. He was completely stripped of clothing.

Pond Creek Station, several miles from Fort Wallace. Troop G, 7th Cavalry, was sent to repulse the attack by Indians on the station and were soon caught up in a sharp fight. A description of the fight, from the Leavenworth Daily Conservative, July 10, follows:

GEN. WRIGHT'S EXPEDITION
THE ENGINEERS ON THE MARCH
They See "Lo" and "Lo" Shows His Hand
A Sharp Fight and the Indians Victorious
Out of 45 Men, 7 Killed and 5 Wounded
A Sergeant Scalped Twice, Brained, Throat Cut, Heart Cut Out, and
Body Slashed to Pieces!

(From Our Special Correspondent.)
Camp No. 18, Ft. Wallace, Kansas
June 30, 1867

We arrived here on the 24th inst. . .
On the 26th they (the Indians) attacked Pond Creek Station, two miles from and in full view of the Fort (Wallace), and commenced running off the stage stock. Our cavalry escort went out in pursuit of them and soon got into a sharp little fight. Out of 45 men engaged we lost seven killed and five wounded. Our cavalry were driven back, the dead fell into the hands of the enemy, and the bodies were stripped entirely naked, and some of them horribly mutilated. Sergeant Wyllyams, Co. G, 7th Cavalry, was amongst the killed, he fought bravely, and out of revenge the savages cut him up terribly. He was scalped twice, and his brains knocked out, his throat cut from ear to ear, his heart cut out and carried away to be eaten, and his arms and legs slashed and gashed to the bone.[1]

Courtesy Custer Battlefield Museum

Greyhounds tied up outside Custer's tent near Fort Dodge in 1868. The sibley tent was adopted after the Indian tepee and used by Custer many times in the field, as compared to the wall tent. Note pet pelican at far right.

Roman Nose and his band suffered heavy casualties, and early reports had Roman Nose killed, but this proved untrue. Soon after the fight, William A. Bell, a fellow countryman of Wyllyams, arrived and photographed the mutilated body. Only a few hours earlier, Sgt. Frederick Wyllyams had expressed a desire to help Bell print copies of photographs he had taken the day before. Bell had accompanied the expedition which was surveying a route west for the K.P. Railroad. The "greenhorns" who filled the ranks of the 7th Cavalry learned quickly that Indian warfare was serious business, and the sight of mutilated bodies would become a common experience.

During the hot summer of 1867, the Seventh Cavalry had another important fight with Indians, missed by Custer, to his regret. The command scouted the dusty plains for several weeks, subsisting on moldy hardtack, rancid bacon, beans and coffee, supplies drawn from Fort McPherson. When the rations became low, Custer sent a train of twelve wagons to Fort Wallace to draw supplies to sustain a lengthy scout. A mounted escort of forty-eight men, two officers, and a scout accompanied the wagons. On the way to Fort Wallace they encountered no Indians, but on the return trip with loaded wagons they were attacked by an Indian war party estimated at five

---

1. Leavenworth Daily Conservative, July 10, 1867, p. 1, c. 4; Kans. State Hist. Soc.

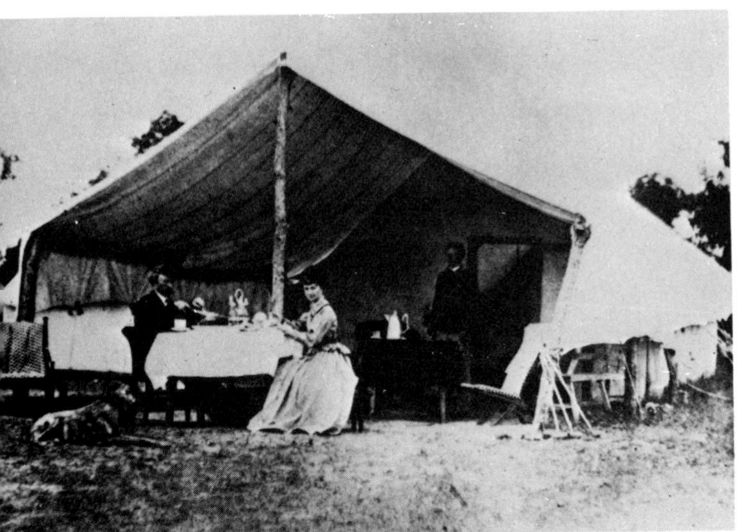

Courtesy Custer Battlefield Museum

There was plenty of game on the Kansas Prairie. Here on Big Creek, Custer is carving a prairie chicken. One of the greyhounds was constantly begging for scraps from the table.

hundred. Custer reported the attack by telegraph to Lieutenant General W. T. Sherman, Headquarters Army of the United States, as follows:

Headquarters Seventh U.S. Cavalry, Riverside Station, 40 miles west of Fort Sedgwick, July 6, 1867.

Lieutenant-General W. T. Sherman:

On the 24th inst., forty-five Sioux warriors attacked a detachment of this regiment under Captain S. M. Hamilton, near the forks of the Republican. Captain Hamilton's party, after a gallant fight, defeated and drove off the Indians, killing two warriors and wounding several others, his own party losing but one horse wounded. On the 26 inst., a war party of Sioux and Cheyenne combined, numbering between five and six hundred warriors, attacked and surrounded forty-eight men of this regiment, who, under Lieutenants S. M. Robbins and W. W. Cooke, Seventh Cavalry, were escorting my train of supplies from Fort Wallace. The Indians surrounded the train for three hours, making desperate efforts to effect its capture; but after a well-contested fight upon the part of Lieutenant Robbins, the Indians were repulsed with the loss of five warriors killed, several wounded, and one horse captured. Our injuries were but two men slightly hurt. The Indians were under the leadership of Roman Nose, whose horse was shot in one of the attempts to charge the train. At daylight on the morning of the 24th, a large band of Sioux warriors surrounded my camp, and endeavored to stampede my animals. My men turned out promptly, and drove the Indians away without losing a single animal. One of my men was seriously wounded in the melee by a carbine shot.

To Captain Hamilton, Lieutenants Robbins and Cook, as well as their men, great praise is due for the pluck and determination exhibited by them in these their first engagements with hostile Indians.

G. A. CUSTER, Brevet Major-General[2]

Custer scouted in Kansas and Nebraska during the rest of the summer and longed to have his wife Libbie near him. Sherman granted approval of allowing Libbie Custer join her husband at a fort nearer to him. Custer had written to his wife suggesting she join a party going to Fort Wallace, and wait there till a wagon train could bring her the rest of the way but the letter miscarried. When Custer's supply train reached Fort Wallace, Lieutenant Cooke, who had been ordered to see that Libbie returned with him, found that she was not there but at Fort Hays. Cooke hurriedly rode to Fort Hays under escort, but General Hancock insisted that Mrs. Custer remain at Hays, fearing a possible attack on the wagons. His refusing Custer's young wife permission to leave the post possibly saved her life.

The wagon train, to Libbie's keen disappointment, left without her. Several months later Lieutenant Cooke told her that had she been with the train when the Indians attacked, it would have been his duty to shoot her, as directed by Lt. Col. Custer. Not believing Cooke at first, she asked whether she would have been given a chance for life. The tall slender Canadian explained that Custer had given all his officers instructions, should ever Mrs. Custer be under their escort when attacked by Indians, it was their duty to kill her immediately, taking no chances that she would fall into the hands of the Indians.

On June 29, 1867, Second Lieutenant Lyman S. Kidder, 2nd Cavalry, with a detail of 10 men from Company M, was given dispatches to deliver to Custer, believed

---

2. Army-Navy Journal, July 20, 1867; pg. 758.

camped at the forks of the Republican. Red Bead, a Sioux, was guide for the command. Kidder, inexperienced in Indian fighting, was twenty-five years of age, and a veteran of the Civil War. The 10 men under his command were mostly young boys, and about half of them foreign-born. Not knowing the fate in store for them, they set out on what was later termed as a "suicide mission."

Custer, meantime, had given chase to Pawnee-Killer, leading a band of several hundred warriors. An attempt to follow the Indians failed, as the Indian ponies outran and outdistanced the heavily burdened cavalry mounts. The command halted at the North Republican riverhead, near the South Platte in Colorado. Men dropped from their saddles under a hot July sun, and the animals groaned painfully for want of water. During the ordeal, many dogs, which accompanied the command as pets, died from thirst and exhaustion.

Custer telegraphed Fort Sedgwick for further instructions from General Sherman. He was told that Kidder had long since been sent by the Division Commander with letters of instruction. Custer reported that nothing had been seen of Kidder's detachment, and requested telegraphic copies of the messages. General Sherman ordered Custer to march his command southward from the Platte to the Smoky Hill River, at Fort Wallace.

Temptations of mining towns and their saloons and the nearness of the overland route induced wholesale desertions from Custer's command, forty men leaving in one night. The deserters, knowing the country was infested with blood-thirsty hostiles, took their chances blinded by temptation of newly discovered gold fields. Their plot had been devised only the evening before, after orders had been issued to march at daylight. That morning, at 5 a.m., the column started out retracing their steps. There was no time to pursue the deserters and try to effect the capture of possibly a few. Chances were that Mr. Lo would have a few scalps before the day ended.

Custer's command marched southward until noon, having covered fifteen miles, then halted to rest and graze their horses. A group of men who plotted to desert with arms and horses had assumed that the halt was for the remainder of the day, and planned to slip away that night into the mountains. When orders were given to repack

Courtesy Custer Battlefield Museum

While the soldiers are preparing for another inspection, officers and civilians lounge on the Parade Grounds discussing the next field expedition. Near Big Creek, 1868.

Courtesy Custer Battlefield Museum

At either Fort Hayes, Kansas, or in camp near Big Creek, 1868. General Custer, Elizabeth Custer and Captain Tom W. Custer.

and prepare to march in an hour, thirteen soldiers were seen leaving camp in the direction from which they had come. Six were dismounted and seven were riding off at a gallop. The boldness of this daylight desertion was a shock and a surprise to everyone. Desertion such as this, with their immediate officers watching, had never been heard of before.

Custer, seeing the fleeing men, shouted to Lieutenant Henry Jackson, Officer of the Day . . . "follow those men and shoot them and bring none in alive."[3] While Jackson was mounting his horse, Custer shouted orders to brother Tom, and Lieutenant W. W. Cooke, to follow suit. Major Joel Elliott swung into his saddle and took the lead, leaving Cooke and Tom some distance behind. Elliott was first to come within shouting distance of the men on foot, and ordered them to halt and lay down their weapons. Two of the deserters did so promptly and raised their arms. The third, Trooper Charles Johnson, swung about making a move with his carbine as if to fire. Elliott, a few yards off, thought the gesture to be threatening, spurred his horse to a gallop and rode into Johnson knocking him down, the weapon flying into the air. Cooke and Tom Custer arrived, jumped from their saddles and opened fire on the unarmed men. Johnson was hit twice, at least once while on the ground. Elliott galloped past, in pursuit of the mounted troopers. Shots from Cooke and Tom Custer found their marks on Bugler Barney Tolliver and Private Alburger. The bugler received one wound in the arm; Tolliver two wounds, one in the shoulder, the other in his side.[4] The fourth man flattened himself on the ground as the firing commenced and was not hit. Two other troopers moved out of the way of Elliott's horse as he raced by, but were later captured by a guard who accompanied the Officer of the Day.

Elliott and Jackson discontinued their pursuit of the mounted party of deserters, as they had gained too much ground to be captured. After returning, Elliott sent back for a wagon which arrived 45 minutes later and the wounded were loaded into it. When they returned to the column, men broke ranks and rushed to the wagon to see their wounded comrades. Custer ordered the gawking troopers to return to their places and form companies and prepare to move out. As the command resumed its march, the wagon with the wounded was ordered at the rear of the column in charge of Lieutenant Jackson. During the ten mile march, several men dropped from ranks to take their overcoats and blankets to the wounded men. Surgeon Coates testified at Custer's court-martial that he looked in on the wounded during the march and administered an

3. The Custer Court Martial, by Robert A. Murray (pg. 2) — Reprint, Wyoming State Historical Society.

4. Ibid.

opiate,[5] but Lieutenant Jackson, in charge of the wagon, insisted that he did not.

At night the command halted and tried to get water from a dried creek bed by digging deep into the sand. Coates said that he and Custer visited the injured men, and after examining their wounds, administered more opiates. He further states that Custer did not want anyone to know that he accompanied him. It was learned later that the wounds were not dressed until two days later, and Coates accepted full responsibility for this error.

Custer learned that more desertions were probable and he reacted swiftly by placing every available officer on guard duty with strict orders to shoot anyone who appeared outside the limits of his tent, after failing to answer a hail. The next morning, at roll call, everyone was present; in fact, from that moment on any thoughts of desertion were abandoned during the continuance of the expedition.[6]

Nothing had been learned of Lieutenant Kidder and his men, and no one could be sure which route he had taken. With concern growing day by day, Custer's officers consulted their scout, William Comstock. "Wild Bill" was frequently sought out by everyone, including Custer. With many years of experience in Indian fighting, he was the only one who might give some encouragement as to the possibilities of Kidder still being alive. Comstock gave his opinion to the concerned officers, "I'm told that the lootenint we're talkin' about is a new-comer, and that this is his first scout. Ef that be the case, it puts a mighty onsartain look on the whole thing, and twixt you and me, gentlemen, he'll be mighty lucky ef he gits through all right. To-morrow we'll strike the Wallace trail, and I kin mighty soon tell ef he has gone that way."[7]

Courtesy Author's Collection

John Baird poses in Scouts costume, typical of the 1860 period. He cradles a Hawken .53 caliber rifle.

After Custer's column hit the Wallace trail, it was only a few miles before Comstock and the Delaware scouts discovered tracks by shod horses. "Well, what do you find, Comstock?" was Custer's inquiry. "They've gone toward Fort Wallace sure," Comstock reported. "The trail shows that twelve American horses, shod all around, have passed at a walk, goin' in the direction of the fort; and when they went by this p'int they were all right."[8]

5. Opiates; Medicines which procure sleep. (Sedatives) Reece's Med. Guide by Richard Reece, M.D.; Albert Colby & Sons, Baltimore, Md. (1873)

6. Life on the Plains, G. A. Custer; Sheldon & Company, N.Y., 1874, Page 73.

7. My Life on the Plains, G. A. Custer; Sheldon & Company, N.Y., 1874, Page 74.

8. Ibid., pg. 75.

As Custer's column rode on, something huge and strange looking appeared in their path, a mile ahead. A closer observation found it to be a dead horse. Further down the trail, another horse was found, also stripped of saddle and equipment. Continuing further, the scouts discovered shod tracks and pony tracks moving at a gallop. It was surmised that the Indians had gained no advantage over the small group and a running fight for life was most evident. The tracks led the scouts from the high plateau into a valley of tall grass and a shallow stream. Within a mile of the stream, the bodies of Lieutenant Kidder and his men were found.

Stripped of their clothing, mangled, brutally hacked and disfigured beyond recognition, lying in irregular order within a very limited circle were the remains of the men of Company M. Several bodies were lying in a bed of ashes, where the Indians had burned some of the troopers to death. Each was scalped, their heads bashed in, and the nose of each man was hacked off. All the bodies were pierced with many arrows (from twenty to fifty were counted). Empty cartridge shells were everywhere, and it was evident that Kidder and his little band of inexperienced Indian fighters had fought to the end. Custer thought it fitting that the remains should be consigned to a common grave, and so a single trench was dug nearby and the grim task of burial proceeded in silence.

Arriving at Fort Wallace, Custer and his exhausted column found that the fort had been attacked several times, with casualties on both sides. All travel over the Smoky Hill route had ceased; stage stations were abandoned and stages were taken off the route. Mail and couriers had ceased to reach the fort, and communication seemed impossible. The fort and the immediate area was considered as undergoing a state of siege. As if the garrison did not have enough problems, cholera made its appearance, and death was a daily occurrence. Supplies were exhausted except for rancid bacon and hard-tack, left over from the Civil War. Fresh provisions were essential if the cholera epidemic was to be curbed. There were no supplies nearer than Fort Harker, two hundred miles away, to supply the garrison with the much needed fresh provisions.

At sunset, July 15, 1867, Custer left Fort Wallace with one hundred of the best mounted men to open the way to Fort Harker. Following the Smoky Hill stage route east, Custer planned to cover the 150

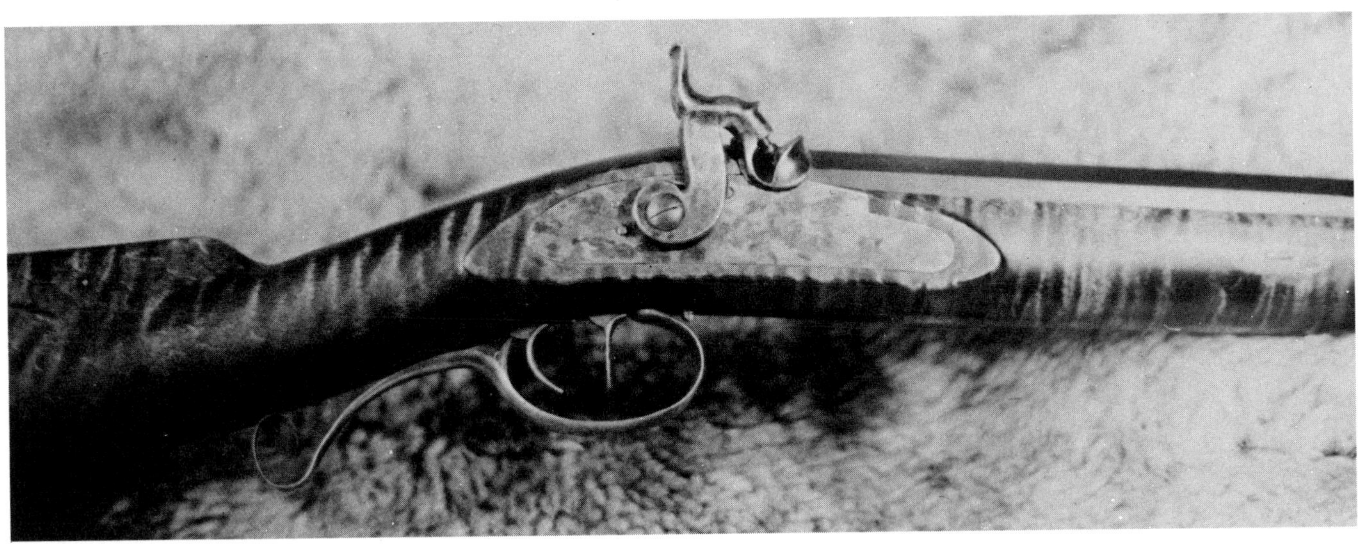

Courtesy John Baird

Close-up of Hawken "Big .50" half stock rifle.

miles to Fort Hays as rapidly as possible. After crossing this most dangerous route, he would continue to Fort Harker with a half dozen troopers, leaving Captain Hamilton to follow with the rest of the command. Because of the heavy marching of preceding weeks, the horses were generally in an unfit condition, yet serviceable. Custer hoped to have a train loaded with supplies at Fort Harker, and be ready to start back to Fort Wallace by the time Hamilton arrived with the rest of the column.

As cholera spread to Forts Larned, Harker and Riley, the death toll climbed rapidly. No one could pin-point the cause of this dreaded disease. Mass burials were many; coffins were make-shift and, toward the end, blankets were used to wrap the dead. The cholera epidemic was attributed to three causes: first, overcrowding; second, the accumulation of debris from recent great floods; and, third, bad whiskey. Along the Smoky Hill River and its tributaries were drifts, full of "rotten animals" and this, the Surgeons asserted, had affected the water which the men had to drink and use in their cooking. Modern medical science would agree that contaminated water would be a main cause.[9]

Cholera generally starts with noises in the head, vertigo, sickness, nervous agitation, colicky pains, discharge from the bowels, sickness of the stomach, slight cramps and decreased pulse. Sometimes these symptoms lasted for hours, at other times the patient would be struck down almost lifeless, without premonitory signs. When the disease is at its worst stage, there are cramps commencing at the fingers and toes, rapidly extending to the body. Eyes are sunken into their sockets, surrounded by a dark circle; there is vomiting and purging of a fluid resembling whey or rice-water; there is a wild and terrified expression on the face, which assumes a peculiar blue or

Courtesy U.S. Signal Corps photo (Brady Collection)

California Joe

Courtesy Nebraska State Historical Society

A rare tintype of Moses E. Milner, "California Joe," taken in Pioche City, Nevada in 1873. Pioche was a wide-open, roaring mining camp, shootings being so frequent "a man for breakfast" was a common expression.

9. Army Navy Journal—, Aug. 10, 1867.

leaden tint. Nails and fingers are the same color. The skin is cold, and the patient rolls about incessantly, as no position seems to relieve him. His voice has a peculiar sound and is almost gone, uttering a few words at a time. Breathing is sometimes short and wanting of air, but the mind is generally undisturbed. His only wish is to be left alone to die.[10]

Few garrisons had medical books or knowledgeable surgeons to cope with the situation. Folk remedies were at times administered, such as putting the patient's feet in hot ashes and water. Other remedies were taking ten grains of calomel and one of opium and covering up in bed with boiled ears of corn and hot bricks to induce sweating.[11]

The most effective way to check the epidemic was to catch it in its early stages. One belief has it that as nature has been aroused for its own protection, let no one interrupt or suppress this salutary process by administering such fluids as astringents, tonics, stimulants, and, above all, opium, brandy or wine. However, salt water fluids seemed best in most cases. With enough salt water (a pint of salt and water) swallowed, the patient will vomit the contents of his stomach; follow with 15 grains of calomel, and after four hours, an ounce of castor oil. By applying a hot bottle of water to the feet

10. Reece's Medical Guide, pg. 345 — Albert Colby & Sons — 1873.

11. Doctors of the American Frontier; Doubleday; pg. 189 (by R. Dunlop).

Courtesy Colonel Brice C. W. Custer

Custer's four trusted scouts, left to right: Will "Medicine Bill" Comstock, chief of scouts; Ed Guerrier, a half-blood Cheyenne; Thomas Adkins, a courier; "California Joe" (Moses E. Milner), chief of scouts, prospector, and Indian fighter.

and keeping the patient well covered with blankets, a gentle perspiration is started. With nothing in the stomach except cold water, the promonitory symptoms would pass, and all hazards of attacks are removed.[12]

When Custer became aware of the disease circulating among the forts, he became anxious to go to Fort Harker, where he assumed Libbie might be exposed to cholera. On July 19, 1867, at 2 A.M., Custer with his companions, brother Tom, Lieutenant Cooke and two troopers, reached Fort Harker, a ride of sixty miles in less than twelve hours. After telegraphing Fort Sedgwick, reporting the fate of Lieutenant Kidder and his group, Custer reported to Colonel A. J. Smith, telling him of the expected arrival of Captain Hamilton's column and the need for supplies for a return trip to Fort Wallace. There was no reason for Custer to await the train and escort, so he asked and received authority from Colonel Smith to visit Fort Riley, where he heard that Libbie had gone.

12. Reece's Medical Guide, Glossary of Medical Terms, Albert Colby & Sons, 1873, pg. 348.

Courtesy Author's Collection

McClellen saddle. Oil and lamp black helped to prevent rawhide from cracking but had to be constantly replenished.

Custer boarded the train for Fort Riley on the morning of July 19. Shortly after his arrival there, a telegram from Colonel Smith ordered him to rejoin his command immediately. Return by train was delayed for several days because of the Kansas Pacific Railroad's erratic schedule. Libbie Custer used what time they had together to enjoy every minute of her husband's stay. The torment of cholera and floods that had burdened their hearts were forgotten momentarily.

When Custer returned to Fort Harker, he reported to Colonel Smith as ordered, and found himself under arrest. The charges against him were: leaving Fort Wallace without permission, ordering his officers to shoot deserters, marching his men excessively, and abandoning two soldiers who were killed by Indians near Downer's Station. The charges made by Colonel Smith were instigated by General Hancock on the basis of complaints against Custer. Captain Robert M. West, 7th Cavalry, filed additional charges, based on the treatment of the deserters. Captain West had been ordered in arrest by Custer at Fort Wallace on charges of being drunk on duty and, for this, his actions may have been prompted. The most serious of the charges faced by Custer was that accusing him of ordering the shooting of deserters, one of whom, Private Charles Johnson, died of his wounds. Custer chose the religious Captain Charles Carroll Parsons, of the 4th Artillery, to assist in his defense. Custer felt justified in ordering his officers to shoot deserters, because of possible loss of many of his command while facing hostile Indians. Putting the fear of death into the men succeeded in stopping further desertions.

The court convened on Sunday, September 15, 1867, at Fort Leavenworth, Kansas. It was frequently interrupted by absences and illnesses. The active sessions totaled eleven days, and the findings were issued on October 11, 1867. Custer was found guilty on all charges but with exceptions to some of the specifications. He was sentenced to one year's suspension from duty with forfeiture of proper pay. It was considered that the lenient sentence was because of Custer's previous outstanding services.

Hancock was transferred in September, 1867, to General Sheridan's post in the South, and Sheridan became commander of the Department of the Missouri. When he arrived at Fort Leavenworth, he found Libbie and his old friend "Jack"[13] troubled as to their future. Sheridan turned over his quarters to the Custers in courtesy to his subordinate from the war days. Here the Custers spent the winter in idleness and quiet. Cold weather had put an end to hostilities, and the winter of 1867-68 was quiet.

Libbie and Autie entertained a circle of friends, some from war days, others within the command. Card games and piano playing accompanied with singing were evening entertainment. Tactics were often discussed by the men while the women impatiently looked on. Custer would select several atlases and with pencil outline the campaigns of Wellington and Napoleon, or discuss his own Civil War strategy. When talking of these matters, his thoughts and speech were so rapid that sometimes Libbie would be confused and interrupt, "General, is that an order or a request?"[14] While campaigning, Custer allowed himself the same rations as his men, adding nothing to the daily diet of hard-crackers, bacon and coffee. Autie's choice of food while in quarters was never a problem for Libbie and their black servant Eliza. His favorite was roast beef and horseradish, with a side order of stuffed apple dumplings. Even at "stateside" restaurants, he would never tire of the same dish.[15] When spring came, they visited Libbie's home in Monroe, Michigan, renewing old acquaintances and visiting forgotten haunts.

While the Custers settled down to civilian life in Monroe, General Sheridan was already planning to beat the Indians at their own game. It was certain that the coming spring would bring a fresh campaign. "Little Phil" faced the threat of large scale outbreaks, even though the Medicine Lodge peace treaty had been signed the preceding fall. The treaty had set aside reservations south of the Arkansas River for the Cheyennes, Comanches, Kiowas, Arapaho and Lipan Apaches, clearing the way for railroad construction crews to lay track through the area bordered by the Arkansas and Platte rivers. Young blood was up, especially with the Cheyennes. They said the white man's treaties were worthless, that they had no right to take away their old lands. Perhaps a majority of the Cheyennes accepted the treaty, but chiefs did not have the right to speak for the minority group of the fraternity of Dogs who rejected any peace proposal. It was during this absence that many Cheyenne warriors fled north to join their Sioux allies harassing travelers on the Bozeman Road.

In the spring, when the grass was green and the ponies fat, the young warriors threatened to unleash a reign of terror against the whites for driving their families from their former hunting grounds. Telegraphs and dispatches were soon flashed from one command post to another. The warriors kept their word by striking the Saline and Solomon valleys, attacking wagon trains, burning homes, murdering men and ravishing women. The hostiles achieved what they set out to do, as scattered ranches and settlements were soon abandoned, and others fearful for their lives discontinued any travel in that immediate area.

General Sheridan held a series of command conferences at Fort Leavenworth in

---

13. The nickname "Jack" was given Custer by his close officers. It derived from his initialed luggage — "G.A.C."

14. E. B. Custer, Micro-film (Reed 4), Custer Battlefield, Mont.

15. Ibid.

early March. Companies and detachments of the 7th Cavalry, with enlisted replacements, were ready to go out to patrol stage routes, guard stations and scout areas around settlements. Winter rest and strict discipline brought the troopers into the field with new energy and anxiety for a long awaited patrol duty or scout. They all had a strong feeling of impending campaigning for the duration of the summer months.

Fort Larned, originally designed for the protection of the Santa Fe Trail, was located close to the Arkansas River. Here most of the peaceful Comanches and Kiowas assembled to receive the annuity goods promised them by the Medicine Lodge Treaty. Indian Agent E. W. Wynkoop, addressing the councilmen, told them that he could not issue the goods until the other tribesmen arrived. A large number of Cheyennes were still in the hills and not accounted for. The delay irritated the tribes and they became angry and restless. As Fort Larned housed only four companies of troops, the situation could become explosive. Agent Wynkoop was warned that if the annuities were not issued promptly, the so-called peaceful Indians would help themselves. Orders for a forced march reached the 7th Cavalry camp in mid-July. Leaving their tents standing, expecting a short absence, the command moved out for Fort Larned.

The 7th reached Fort Larned and went into a temporary camp near the post. Nearby the cavalrymen saw thousands of lodges, with Kiowas and Comanches shuffling about paying little attention to the arrival of the troops. Cheyennes and Arapahoes began to dribble in during the night, and Indian dogs kept a constant barking well into the morning. The arrival of a band of Cheyenne late-comers was heard from one end of the fort to the other, with their loud cries of lament for those of a war party who had not returned alive from a sortie against the Utes. That evening they held a scalp dance, honoring those who had shown valor against the enemy Utes. Dancing around a ritual fire council, the warriors enacted their battle as well as displaying captured relics adorned with fresh scalps.

Agent Wynkoop finally decided that his Indians were all in, and started to issue the eagerly awaited arms and ammunition to the supposedly peaceful plains dwellers. Food, tools, blankets, cooking gear, and hundreds of assorted items were distributed, much to the disapproval of army officers watching. It was seemingly senseless for one department of the government to give weapons to Indians who were potential enemies of another department. The Indian Bureau could explain that these people were hunters, and the weapons were needed to hunt buffalo and other game for food.

Army officers often asserted that the Indians were better armed that the soldiers. It is true that a few hostile Indians had standard weapons that the Army issued, but only after capturing them in skirmishes with the soldiers. Such captures were few, and ammunition for the newer models was hard to come by. What the Indians received from the Indian Bureau annuities were outmoded weapons, muzzle-loading rifles such as the Lancaster, manufactured in England in 1857; the Hawken percussion rifle, or the "St. Loui' Big .50"; early Springfield models; muskets with British proof marks, and a host of what is now known as "the Plains Rifle," a percussion gun either in a half or full stock. The flintlock was most useful to the Indian who might be far from trading posts. While percussion caps were not readily available, a flint could always be improvised for hunting or warfare.

The Indian gave little attention to the maintenance of his weapon. He left it neglected in the rain, dust, mud, and rarely cleaned it. When the stock was badly cracked or broken, he wrapped it with wet rawhide which when dried shrunk to a strong and usually satisfactory repair. Indians commonly used various sizes of brass tacks, making designs on both sides of the stock and forearm to induce good medicine. Mirrors were sometimes imbedded in the stock and might be used for sun signals.

After the big annuity issue, the Indians broke camp and disappeared, leaving the fort to its isolation. It was not long afterwards that the Cheyennes took to the warpath, raiding settlements on Walnut Creek and the Solomon River in Kansas. Indian chiefs and headmen protested they had no way to control the young headstrong warriors, and as the leaders disclaimed responsibility for the raids, they were charged by the Army with "practicing their well-developed act of cunning, deceit and deviltry."

Brevet Brigadier-General Alfred Sully moved out of Fort Dodge shortly after dusk on September 1, 1868, with an expedition including eleven companies of the 7th Cavalry, under the immediate command of Major Joel Elliott, three companies of the 3rd Infantry, several medical personnel and three citizen guides. Determined to punish the hostile Indians, he marched his punitive expedition south, deep into Indian territory. Marching the command out after dusk, Sully hoped to elude the eyes of any Indians who might be watching his movements from a distance. The General commanded his force while riding in an ambulance, a conveyance which everyone joked about after his defeat hastened him back to Fort Dodge.

With considerable success, Sully had fought plains Indians before, deep in the heart of Sioux country in Dakota, during 1863-64-65. Owing to this previous experience, the whole command looked forward to catching the perfidious warriors and whipping them soundly. Sully marched south and west with his cavalry and wagon-borne infantry, crossing the Arkansas River, into Indian territory toward the Cimarron River, where they halted several hours before dawn. Pushing further on, in a southerly direction, with no Indians in sight, Sully believed he had succeeded in deceiving them. But when a small herd of buffalo was sighted, and several eager young officers went after the herd, they found themselves not alone in the hunt. A lone Indian, chasing the same herd, was equally surprised seeing the soldiers and sped away, dodging a few futile shots. The surprise the General had believed he had achieved by his stealthy approach had vanished as quickly as the fleeing warrior's pony.

Several days later, the command encamped at the confluence of Crooked Creek on the south side of the Cimarron River, unaware they had been surrounded by Indians. The next day, as the command was preparing to pull out, Captain Louis McLane Hamilton rode up to two soldiers who were some distance from the advancing column. Hamilton, who commanded the rear guard, reminded them of Sully's firm orders against stragglers. After leaving the two soldiers, Hamilton rejoined his own command for only a few moments, when screams from both stragglers were heard. Racing to the rear of the column, officers and a company of troopers saw both men scooped up by mounted Indians and carried off in the opposite direction. Gaining ground on the raiders, the company pressed forward, compelling the Indians to drop one of the wounded troopers. But before the pursuing soldiers could overtake the escaping foe, a mounted messenger caught up with the little troop with orders from General Sully to abandon the chase and return immediately to the forward command. The troopers halted in disbelief. To allow one of their men to be carried off by the enemy without any chance to rescue him was not soldier-like. From that day on, any regard for the General was expressed with salty comments, and the respect for all high ranking officers in general fell to a degrading level amongst the soldiers in the command. Later that day, after a halt, both men were allowed to be buried with full honors.

From September 11, and for five days afterward, Indians used hit-and-run tactics against the column, sniping from ambush during the day and showering the camp with arrows at night. During one of these engagements, Captain Keogh's horse was grazed by a bullet from a Comanche warrior. Keogh, impressed with the animal's steadiness under fire, decided to purchase the seven-year-old buckskin for himself, giving him the name of "Comanche."

The Indians that Sully faced were thought to be a mixed force of Kiowas, Comanches, Cheyenne Dog Soldiers and Arapahos, who were constantly aggravating the command with concentrated fire from behind one sand hill to another. Sully decided that it was useless and dangerous to pursue the warriors any longer. He would return to Fort Dodge and refit for another expedition. The wounded were cared for and the two men killed in the day's fighting were buried at the picket line, where the horses could trample down any signs of a grave being dug there. If found by Indians, the bodies would be dug up and scalped.

Sully's failure with the expedition, and the loss of respect by his men, had embittered General Sheridan, not only because of the abandoning of the two soldiers, but the overall supervision of the expedition. Sully's strategy lacked a great deal in planning, striking against the Indians when the grass was green and ponies able to outdistance the cavalry horse, demonstrated once more that any chance of combating the hostiles and bringing them to bay during the spring or summer campaigns was practically impossible. What Sheridan wanted was an experienced leader, with the energy and initiative to "bring the red fox in." After considering the records of several officers, Sheridan decided on Custer. He sent a telegram to Monroe, Michigan, which read:

> General Sherman, Sully and myself and nearly all the officers of your regiment have asked for you and I hope the application will be successful. Can you come at once? Eleven companies of your regiment will move about the first of October against the hostile Indians, from Medicine Lodge Creek, toward the Wachita Mountains.
>
> P. H. Sheridan, Major General Commanding.

Custer did not wait for official orders from Washington, relieving him from the court-martial suspension. He immediately wired Sheridan that he would be on the next train to take command of the 7th. With a farewell kiss to Libbie, Custer boarded the train westbound with his luggage and his usual stag hounds. After ten months of forced vacation, Custer was eager to get back into action. Knowledgeable to the situation on the plains, Custer may have seemed puzzled with Sheridan's wire asking for him. Since winter was coming, either Sheridan was going to catch the Indians napping during the winter, or something else was in the breeze. Regardless what was before him, he was ready to accept anything just to be in the saddle again, chasing Indians.

On October 6, 1868, Custer rejoined his regiment as its field commander at camp on Bluff Creek near Fort Dodge. A freezing wind blew from the northwest, a forecast of coming wintry cold. Custer found the same low morale that he had to deal with a year before at Fort Wallace. Major Elliott, who had commanded the regiment since Custer's departure, was looked upon as a far less experienced leader. The men were poorly mounted and in shabby uniforms, and the failure of the summer campaign had left them disheartened.

Sheridan told Custer that he planned a winter campaign when heavy snows would slow down the warriors and their ponies would be too weak to travel. If the villages were hard hit and their supplies destroyed, the Indians would have to come into the reservations or starve. Sheridan's scouts deemed it impossible for the troops to survive such a winter expedition, but Custer approved the plan and was eager to march against the enemy.

Hostiles plagued the 7th's encampment by firing into tents and trying to scare off the horses. They were met with Spencer carbine fire, which sent the warriors off beyond carbine range. Late that night four columns left camp to scout the frozen upper streams, hoping to find the warriors' lodges. They turned up nothing, due mainly to the conduct of a whiskey-soaked scout called California Joe.

California Joe came into enduring fame through the writings of General Custer and his wife, Elizabeth. In "Life on the Plains," Custer described his first meeting with the scout near Fort Dodge in October, 1868, prior to the Washita Battle. A number of scouts were attached to the cavalry, each available separately to accompany detachments. One of their number, in this case California Joe, was designated Chief of Scouts.

In Custer's "Life on the Plains," he writes about the scout:

> Being unacquainted personally with the merits or demerits of any them (referring to the scouts) the selection of a chief had necessarily to be made somewhat at random. There was one among their number whose appearance would have attracted the notice of any casual observer. He was a man about forty years of age, perhaps older, over six feet in height, and possessing a well-proportioned frame. His head was covered with a luxuriant crop of long, almost black hair, strongly inclined to curl, and so long as to fall carelessly over his shoulders. His face, at least so much of it as was not concealed by the long, waving brown beard and moustache was full of intelligence and pleasant to look upon. His eyes were undoubtedly handsome, black and lustrous, with an expression of kindness and mildness combined. On his head was generally to be seen, whether awake or asleep, a huge sombrero, or black slouch hat. A soldier's overcoat, with its large circular cape, a pair of trousers, with the legs tucked in the top of his long boots, usually constituted the make-up of the man whom I selected as Chief of Scouts. He was known by the euphonious title of "California Joe"; no other name seemed ever to have been given him, and no other name appeared to be necessary.

Custer seemed confident in California Joe on short acquaintance, but the mountain man was as much shocked by the appointment as the other scouts were in learning of his acceptance. Many were confident of their own appointment because of friendly association with officers close to Custer. After the official interview had opened, California Joe thought it proper to seek more intimate acquaintance. He frankly addressed Custer with a few questions of his own: "See hyar, Gineral, in order thet we hev no misunderstandin', I'd jist like ter ax ye, first, are ye an am'blance man or a hoss man?" Professing ignorance to the meaning of the question, Custer asked him to explain. "What I mean, do yer b'lieve in catchin' Injuns in am'blances or on hoss-back?"

"Well, Joe, I believe in catching Indians wherever we can find them, whether they are in ambulances or on horseback."

Courtesy U.S. Signal Corps photo (Brady Collection)

Nude Kiowa Girl

Changing position in his chair, California Joe inhaled deeply from his ash-caked briarwood pipe, which was in full eruption and belching smoke that seemed to bring tears to the General's eyes . . . "Thet ain't what I'm a-drivin' at. S'pose you're after Injuns and really want ter heve a tussel with 'em , would yer start after 'em on hossback, or would yer climb inter an am'blance and be hauled after 'em? Thet's ther pint I'm a headin' fer!"

Custer answered that he would prefer the first method, on horseback, providing he really desired to catch the Indians, but if he wished them to catch him, he would adopt the "ambulance system" of attack. "You've hit the nail squar' on the head!" said Joe, shaking a finger at the commander. "I've bin with 'em on the plains whar they started out after Injuns on wheels jist as ef they war goin' to a funeral in ther States, an' they stood 'bout as many chances uv catchin' Injuns ez a six-mule team would uv catchin' a pack uv thievin' Ki-o-Tees, jes as much."[16]

California Joe's occupation as Chief of Scouts lasted about as long as a bottle of eastern whiskey would to a thirsty soldier.

Only weeks before the Battle of the Washita (November 27, 1868), four separate detachments were ordered to move on an all-night ride in search for indication of an Indian rendezvous. Each detachment numbered about one hundred cavalry, well mounted and well armed, with guides who knew the country well assigned to each. California Joe was assigned as Chief of Scouts. Ol' Joe, for the first few hours in the saddle, entertained his riding partner with tales of personal experiences with Indians, and episodes in mining life. Joe had a fondness for his canteen and was drawing upon it more than usual. Unknown to the officers riding with him, the canteen was filled with

16. Research Review; Vol. IV, Summer, 1970, No. 2, "Moses E. Milner or California Joe."

Courtesy Custer Battlefield Museum

Custer and his Osage Indian scouts camped near Fort Dodge in 1868. Pet pelican in front of guidon.

the worst brand of whiskey attainable on the frontier.

Perhaps Joe did not intend to indulge to that extent which might depose him from properly performing his duties, but he, like many other good men whose appetites for whiskey were stronger than their resolutions, failed in his reckoning. As the liquor took effect, Joe's independence increased until his mule, no longer restrained by his hand, slowly moved him away from the troops until the only part of the expedition which he recognized as important was himself and his mule. As the troops continued forward, none took notice of the disappearance of their Chief of Scouts. The troops had been marching constantly since leaving camp and some were almost sound asleep in their saddles when the column was halted shortly before daylight and the word was passed along that the advanced guard had discovered signs indicating Indians nearby. Every member of the command came alert, and any vestige of sleep disappeared. The advanced guard, consisting of a non-commissioned officer and a few privates, had reached a crest, and below them, in the heavy darkness, they could see several flashes of light. A party was chosen to crawl close to the enemies' camp and gather all information available. The Chief of Scouts was nowhere to be found. A search was made for him along both flanks of the column, but it was discovered he had not been seen for several hours. As the group of men was being selected to approach the supposed Indian village, a single rifle shot broke the stillness, followed by a most powerful howling and screaming, as if a terrible battle was taking place. Every carbine in the column was advanced and positioned for action. Charging wildly toward the column, now visible by the first rays of the sun, was California Joe. Shouting at the top of his voice, now almost hoarse in tone, he began striking wildly to the right and to the left as if beset by a whole tribe of warriors. It was good fortune alone that prevented him from receiving a volley before he was recognized. It took four men to pull California Joe from his mount and take from his hands a breech-loading Springfield[17] musket, from which he was inseparable. A Remington revolver and hunting knife were lifted from his waist belt. All efforts to quiet or suppress him proved unavailing until an officer ordered him bound hand and foot, and in this condition tied him to the back of his mule. In this sorry plight, the Chief of Scouts continued with the troops until their return to camp, where he was transferred to the guard house as a prisoner, for misconduct.

Sheridan was confident that his winter campaign would catch the Indians off guard. The cold weather would most certainly hold them in their villages. Their ponies would be thin and weak for lack of grass, and a surprise attack would have every chance of success. Sheridan's plan involved the operations of three columns: Colonel Andrew W. Evans with six troops of the 3rd Cavalry and two companies of the 37th Infantry were to march from Fort Bascom, New Mexico, and establish a supply depot at Monument Creek, then continue a scout along the Canadian and the North Fork of the Red River until they reached Red River, which was the boundary of the Department of the Missouri.

Seven troops of the 5th Cavalry under the command of Major Eugene A. Carr were to march southeast from Fort Lyon, Colorado, and make contact with Captain William H. Penrose and his column of five troops of cavalry, then scout toward Antelope Hills, along the North fork of the Canadian River.

The third column was to march from Fort Dodge under the command of General Sully, and move southward, establishing a cantonment at the fork of Beaver Creek and Wolf Creek. This column was made up of

17. This term was still being used — reference made to the 50/70 1866 Mdl. converted.

eleven troops of the 7th Cavalry and five companies of the 3rd Infantry. The 19th Kansas Volunteer Cavalry which was organized at Topeka, Kansas, was ordered to join the column at Camp Supply. The time set for all the columns to march was November 1; however, owing to many delays in getting supplies, the departure date was changed to November 12.

Several hundred recruits had recently joined the 7th, as well as a large number of green horses. This meant intensive training and drill to prepare the regiment for the winter campaign. Custer ordered target practice twice a day. He selected forty sharpshooters and placed them under Lieutenant Cooke.[18] Scouts, interpreters and couriers included a party of Osage Indians, led by their chiefs, Hard Rope and Little Beaver, many of whom had served with the cavalry on other expeditions. California Joe and Jack Corbin were employed as scouts, interpreters and couriers. Custer always referred to his scouts as the "eyes and ears" of the Seventh Cavalry.

Custer was anxious to catch the Indians napping. He called his scouts together and promised a bonus of one hundred dollars from his own pocket to the first man to lead the regiment to a hostile village. White scouts, hired by the government, were paid seventy-five dollars a month, and a bonus similar to the one Custer offered was not altogether an uncommon practice by officers.

In organizing his men for the winter campaign, Custer set about in assigning horses to companies by color, including gray horses for the band.[19] Winter clothing was issued and Custer equipped himself with special overshoes made of buffalo hide, heavy woolen underclothing, topped off with a buckskin shirt and trousers. A heavy buffalo overcoat and a beaver cap hid any insignia of rank. With a rough scrappy beard beginning to show, Custer lost his usual dapper image. On November 12, 1868, General Sully's column of infantry, cavalry and four hundred wagons moved out, Custer's cavalry scouting ahead. On the sixth day Sully halted at a favorable camp site with an abundance of undisturbed pasture on Wolf Creek, at its confluence with the Beaver. A mile from this point, a site was staked out and named Camp Supply.

For the next few days the troops were busied in building stockades, construction of a blockhouse, and digging wells. Pits, four and one-half feet deep and walled with cottonwood logs, with a roof covering of logs, hay and earth, formed comfortable quarters for the men. The cavalry, working side by side with the infantry in construction of the camp, voiced no discontent. Their stay would be brief and their mission dangerous soon enough, without altercation amongst their own.

The expected arrival of the 19th Kansas Volunteer Cavalry to join the expedition provoked a dispute over rank between Custer and Sully. The Kansas regiment was raised by Governor Samuel J. Crawford, who took the field as its colonel. Both Sully and Custer were lieutenant colonels in lineal rank, but Army Regulations provided that brevet rank takes effect in commands or detachments "composed of different corps."[20] Sully, who had been serving in his brevet rank as brigadier general both as member of the Indian Peace Commission and as district commander, issued an order assuming command of the expedition. This order Custer disputed as he held the rank of brevet major general. When General Sheridan arrived at Camp Supply (escorted by

18. Expenditure for target practice did not come about for another 10 years or so, and was probably paid out of the officers' pockets.

19. Every man was furnished by Ordnance Dept. with a horse cover made from condemned canvas. — "Ten Years with Custer" by Capt. John Ryan, Newton Circuit, Mar. 19, 1909.

20. *Revised Regulations for the Army of the United States, 1861*, par 10, p. 10; Articles of War, Art. 61, p. 508. Sully had been commissioned major general of volunteers at the close of the Civil War but this rank became of no effect after discharge of Civil War volunteers. Custer had commissions both as brevet major general of volunteers and brevet major general. The second rank had permanent status in the Regular Army as had Sully's as brevet brigadier general.

two companies of the 19th Kansas), he settled the dispute by returning Sully to his district command at Fort Dodge (as brevet brigadier general) and appointing Brevet Major General George A. Custer to command the expedition. Ironically, the 7th Cavalry was almost immediately detached for the Washita expedition under command of Lieutenant Colonel Custer, and the expedition was not reassembled until the following spring.

From the diary of W. S. Harvey, blacksmith, Troop K, 7th Cavalry, the following:

> We were grazing the horses in the sand hills on that day when, in the afternoon, orders came to return to camp at once and prepare for thirty days campaign. It is my recollection that three wagons were assigned to each troop, this for convenience for picket line — one for troop mess, etc., one for officers' mess, extra ammunition, etc., and one for forage. Baggage was limited to necessities.
>
> November 23rd — Reveille at 3 o'clock. Snowed all night and still snowing very heavy. The darkness and heavy snowfall made the packing of the wagons very difficult, but at dawn the wagons were assembled in the train and daylight found us on the march, the band playing, "The Girl I Left Behind Me," but there was no woman there to interpet its significance. The snow was falling so heavily that vision was limited to a few rods. All land marks were invisible and the trails were lost. 'We didn't know where we were going, but we were on the way.' Then General Custer, with compass in hand, took the lead and became our guide.[21]

Courtesy Custer Battlefield Museum

Custer's dress at the Washita was buckskins, fur cap, and a full scrubby beard.

Much discomfort was felt by the men as large snowflakes fell lazily and melted almost immediately. All were wet to the skin. Luckily, there was no wind to drift the snow or freeze the wet clothing. The snow did create problems for the horses, however, as the snow balled on their feet, causing floundering and adding to the fatigue of travel. The column arrived at Wolf Creek about two o'clock with the wagon train far behind. Horses were unsaddled, and the men gathered fuel for fires. The valley was alive with rabbits, and soon all messes were supplied with rabbit stew. Everyone tried desperately to protect their rawhide McClellan saddles, partially soaked from the heavy snow. Unequal drying would warp the saddle trees, which would split at the seams, causing many sore backs on animals and raw buttocks on the troopers.

On the 24th, the skies cleared and the weather turned warmer. During the night the snow had ceased, but it had accumulated to a depth of eighteen inches, sagging many tent roofs, covering everything in sight. During the march of approximately eighteen miles, many of the men became snowblinded because of the reflection of bright sunshine glaring on the snow. Many deer were seen, but they were too swift to bag. A few buffalo were killed along with

21. "Some Reminiscences of the Battle of the Washita" —; Gen. E. S. Godfrey — Cav. Journal — Oct., 1928.

many rabbits. They camped that night on Wolf Creek.

November 25 found the column marching up Wolf Creek, then turning in a southerly direction toward the Canadian. The peaks of Antelope Hills loomed up before them and served as their marker for the rest of the day. Camp was made late that evening on a small stream about a mile from the Canadian. Tired men slid from their horses and bedded down almost immediately, some forgoing their warm meal. Others dried out socks and clothing before small camp fires. Wood was becoming scarce. Many soldiers making a trip to the quartermaster sergeant's wagon for an armful of wood were turned away. The lookout for fuel on the march had been neglected and wood for tomorrow's camp would be even more scarce. A number of horses and mules were brought in late that night, totally exhausted from the day's march, and if they would not show any improvement by morning, they would be destroyed.

At daybreak, November 26, troops G, H and M, commanded by Major Elliott, found an Indian trail distinctly marked in the snow, estimated as made by a hundred war-

Courtesy Herb Peck, Jr.

Kiowas and Cheyennes. Left to right: Kiowa — Cheyenne and two Kiowa braves.

riors. Although some snow had fallen on the trail, it was calculated that the tracks were scarcely twenty-four hours old. A scout was sent to Custer, reporting the Indian tracks. Custer sent the scout back to Elliott with a hasty message, ordering Elliott to follow the trail until 9 P.M. and then wait until the rest of the command could catch up. In the meantime California Joe was given the task of finding a ford along the Canadian for the wagons to cross, as the river was rising rapidly with swift currents and floating ice. The cavalry crossed first, then the wagons rushed through without halting, to avoid bogging down in quicksand.

While the wagons made the cross over, Custer and a number of officers went to the top of the hills to view the surrounding countryside. Suddenly they were caught up in a cloud of frozen mist, and looking up in astonishment, they saw the sun surrounded by three ellipsoids with rainbow tints, the axis marked by sundogs, except for the third or outer ellipse, which seemed to hover below the horizon. This glorious sight was not visible to the troops below.

Soon after the courier's hasty departure to Elliott, Custer ordered Officer's call and reported the news. Eighty men were to be left with the wagons and the rest were to march at once. One wagon was assigned to each squadron (two troops); another to Troop G and the teamsters, and one to headquarters. To the quartermaster, Lieutenant James M. Bell, one ambulance was assigned. Every trooper was ordered to carry one hundred rounds of ammunition, coffee, hard bread, and overcoat, but no blankets. The men were to bivouac in the snow with just these bare necessities. The troopers were armed with Spencer metallic cartridge magazine carbines and the Colt revolver taking paper cartridges and caps. The men seemed to take on a different attitude as they prepared for the march. Old "Iron Ass" Custer had caught something in the wind. He was moving around camp faster than he did on any normal day, and it was obvious with the additional rounds of ammunition assigned that a scrap wasn't too far off.

Weak horses were selected to pull the wagon train, commanded by the Officer of the Day, Captain Louis M. Hamilton, a grandson of Alexander Hamilton. Horses with more stamina would be able to stay with the attacking force. Hamilton was distressed because he would be left behind with the wagon train. He pleaded with Custer to change his assignment but was refused unless he could find an officer to exchange with him. Lieutenant E. G. Mathey, suffering from snowblindness, agreed to take Hamilton's place.

The weather turned warm as the regiment moved forward to intercept Elliott's trail. Horses slipped in mud and slush, almost toppling at times. Dogs accompanying the command strayed off the muddy trail, yapping and barking at fleeing rabbits. Custer was disturbed by the racket the dogs were making and sent orders to have it stopped. The noise would surely start up the Indian dogs and alarm the camp. According to the narrative of John Ryan (a trooper who accompanied the march), Custer had to destroy two of his own staghounds because of their persistent barking.

> One dog in my company, of whom the men were very fond, was a little black dog called Bob, and as harmless as a kitten. We had to part with him, and one of our men drove a picket pin into Bob's head and he was left for dead. After that engagement was over and several days had elapsed, that dog joined us and the men cured him and brought him back to Kansas.[22]

The snow was now a foot deep on the plains. The horses were beginning to tire from breaking the hard upper crust of frozen snow. At 9 P.M., the regiment overtook Elliott who had halted near a stream in a timbered area. Horses were unsaddled, fed

22. The Newton Circuit; April 2, 1909; "Ten Years with Gen. Custer," by Capt. J. Ryan.

and rubbed down; fires were lighted but concealed as much as possible. Coffee was soon bubbling, and the men commenced breaking 'hardbread' with the butts of their pistols. After an hour's rest, orders were given to saddle horses with as little noise as possible. No matches were to be struck by smokers, and loud talking was forbidden. Little Beaver dismounted and with another tracker led out, followed by Indian and white scouts, with Custer riding near the advance. The cavalry trailed a half a mile behind, plagued with the crunching noise of frozen snow that could be heard a considerable distance away.

After several hours of tracking, the scouts hurried back to the command and a halt was ordered. Little Beaver had smelled smoke. Custer ordered the scouts to advance cautiously, carefully examining the area, while the cavalry slowly followed. A small camp fire was soon found still smouldering, and it was deduced by the Indian scouts that small boys had been trying to keep warm while herding and grazing the ponies. It was estimated that the Indian village was ahead two or three miles, and the scouts took up the trail once more. By now, the moon had risen, illuminating the surroundings, making it fairly easy to follow the trail. Above the steady crunching of ice and snow beneath shod hoofs an occasional cough from a trooper or a muffled sneeze broke the frigid air. Everyone tried to follow in the tracks of the one ahead, making the least noise possible. The wagons were still some distance behind.

Upon nearing a rise, an Osage tracker crawled to the crest to reconnoiter the area before him. On returning, he crouched close to the ground and rejoined the others to report what he had seen. On a return trip from one crest, Little Beaver reported to Custer, "Heaps Injuns down there."[23] Custer was soon peering over the same crest, taking the same precautions as his tracker. Custer could only see what looked like a herd of animals off in the distance, and turning to Little Beaver asked him why he thought Indians were there. "Me heard dog bark,"[24] was the scout's reply. As both listened intently for several moments, they heard the distinct bark of a dog, followed by the tinkling of a bell, indicating a pony herd, and then the distant cry of an infant.

Custer was satisfied that the Indian camp lay before him, he was also satisfied that the troops were still undiscovered. It was past midnight when Custer assembled his officers. He asked each to remove his saber, so its rattling would not attract attention, and join him at the crest where the situation could be studied and action planned. Upon returning to the troops awaiting less than a mile from the crest, Custer explained his plan of attack and assigned squadron commanders their duties and positions.

Major Elliott was to take Troops G, H and M, and march around to the rear of the village, approaching from the northeast as determined by the lay of the land. Captain William Thompson with Troops B and F was to strike well to the right of the trail, approaching from the southeast, and connect with Elliott. Captain Edward Meyers, with E and I, was to approach from the southerly direction. Lieutenant Bell's wagons, along with Captain Frederick W. Benteen and his squadron, were to halt several miles down the trail to await the outcome. Soon Captain Benteen and his squadron were instructed to join the forward command and Lieutenant Bell was told to hold the wagons at that point until he heard the attack, which would commence around daybreak.

Custer and his four companies, A, C, D and K, moved silently into place, with Lieutenant Cooke's sharpshooters dismounted and close in advance. The four troops were divided into two squadrons, Captain Robert M. West on the right of the

23. "Life on the Plains" — Custer — pg. 158.

24. Ibid.

standard and guard, and Captain Hamilton on the left. Directly behind Custer and his staff was the regimental band, mounted on horseback and ready to sound off as the troops charged into battle. Many of the scouts, including California Joe, feared that the village was larger than estimated, and that the chances of a surprise attack were slim. There was no firm knowledge of the enemy's strength or the size of the village, as trees along the river bottom hid much of the encampment. How far along the frozen Washita[25] did the village spread? Custer did not know, but he had followed the trail of a war party to this village, and he had caught them napping.

The Osage scouts put on death paint, as was their custom before charging the enemy, using "fire paint" which is red. It was applied with the left hand all over the face. They chanted prayers, "As the fire has no mercy, so should we have none." Mud was then applied on the cheek, below the left eye, as wide as two or more fingers. Then each pony was painted with some of the same mud, on the left cheek, shoulder, and thigh. The war chant continued in low tones among the Osages as the white scouts looked on.[26]

Custer's strategy during the Civil War had been based on surprise attack, often regardless of numbers. Here, as well as at the Little Big Horn, eight years later, he divided his command to attack simultaneously from different directions. The village was partially surrounded, and no alarm had been given. As the dogs below continued their furious barking, it seemed possible that the village had been abandoned. The night was bitter cold, the men huddled in whatever shelter they could find, throwing the capes of their overcoats over their heads to shield them from the sharp winter breeze. Orders were issued for the men not to stamp their feet or swing their arms to step up circulation because of the possibility that the noise would be heard and attract the dogs. Some troopers kept active by checking their weapons, bridles and saddle girths several times to occupy the dragging hours till dawn. As the dawn broke through a wintery mist, orders were passed along to remove overcoats and haversacks, leaving one man in each company to load them into the wagons when Lieutenant Bell came up. At a little before sunrise, Custer ordered his men to mount and take their formation. Slowly the command marched over the crest of the ridge, hoofs breaking the snow crust at a walk, and advanced some distance toward a lower ridge. The dogs in the village continued their furious barking.

Suddenly an Indian emerged from one of the lodges, ran to the bank of the Washita, looked about and then fired his rifle into the air. It was later stated that the Indian had seen a trooper raise his rifle to take aim, beginning the Battle of the Washita. Upon hearing the rifle report, Custer turned to his bandmaster and shouted, "Give us Garry-Owen."[27] The first few notes of that rollicking march sounded across the valley and echoed back from opposite sides, but by the time the band had played one strain from GarryOwen, their spittle froze the instruments. Only the bugles sounding the charge and cheers from the entire command filled the air.

As the Indians ran from their lodges, terror stricken, some escaped toward the upward creek bank, others took refuge behind trees and logs. The Spencer carbines boomed, the pistols cracked, and the terrified pony herd thundered past lodges intermixing with warriors and racing past the bluecoats. It was hard to determine whether

25. In Cheyenne, Washita means "Lodge-pole" (O-Ke-a-a): Thirty-three Years Among Our Wild Indians, by Col. R. I. Dodge; Archer House, Inc., N. Y.

26. Annual Report of the Bureau of Ethnology; J. W. Powell, 1888-89, pg. 632. (Government Printing Office, 1893.)

27. "Life on the Plains" — G. A. Custer; Sheldon & Co., N. Y., 1874 — Pg. 163. Custer cites the title as "Garry Owen." See Boots & Saddles, E. B. Custer; N.Y., one word "Garryowen." "Of Garryowen in Glory," Lt. Col M. C. Chandler; 1960, we find "GarryOwen."

an Indian was knocked over by one of the ponies or had fallen from a wound received from the troopers' fire. Custer could hear his sharpshooters discharging their rifles with deliberate accuracy. The Indians began to return the fire with bullets and arrows from every direction. From sink holes and depressions warriors grouped to stand off the charging soldiers. Their raking fire was both deadly and accurate. Custer ordered his sharpshooters to clean them out, and, within a short time, seventeen warriors were killed in one depression. Those who sought only freedom raced toward the scattering pony herd trying to mount for a hasty exit. Only a few were successful. The screams of Indian women and children fell on the troopers' ears, and yelping hounds seemed everywhere and in everyone's way. The wild rush of charging troopers through the village was met by the defiant war cry of half-naked Cheyennes, as they leaped from their lodges, evidently awakened from a sound sleep. Those who fell wounded were at the mercy of steel shod hoofs spattering everything with mud, slush and human blood.

Lieutenant Bell, upon hearing the firing, rushed his teams forward to join the command. While loading the overcoats and haversacks into the wagons, he was attacked by a superior number of Indians and the greater part of the duffel was abandoned, but his arrival with the reserve ammunition was warmly welcomed. Custer noticed that Captain Hamilton had disappeared. Tom Custer was seen having his hand bandaged while holding a pistol in the other. While the fighting was still going on, Custer detailed men to round up the pony herd. A field hospital was established among the lodges with Captain Henry Lippincott, Assistant Surgeon, in charge. The surgeon had his own problems. He stumbled about with his hands over his eyes, suffering intense pain from snowblindness.

Major Elliott spotted a group of dismounted Indians escaping downstream and asked for volunteers to overtake them. Regimental Sergeant Major Kennedy and nineteen others responded,[28] and as the detachment swung into their saddles, Major Elliott turned and waved his hat to Lieutenant Owen Hale, standing nearby, and called, "Here goes for a brevet or a coffin." That was the last Hale saw of Elliott and his party.

Custer dismounted and entered the make-shift hospital to check on the wounded. Dr. Morris J. Asch was bending over and administering first aid to a trooper who was seriously wounded. Custer was soon advised of the death of Captain Hamilton, shot through the back. Custer was about to leave when he saw four troopers carrying another troop commander in a blanket into the hospital. It was Captain and Brevet Colonel Albert Barnitz, shot through the body near the heart with a rifle bullet, and in serious condition.

Custer's orders were to avoid killing of any but fighting men,[29] but the women were as dangerous an adversary as the warriors, and young boys between the ages of ten and fifteen were expert in the use of weapons and determined to count coup. Captain Benteen, after trying to take a youngster prisoner, was shot at by the lad several times, wounding the officer's horse in the neck. Benteen had no alternative but to kill the boy to save himself. An elderly woman bolted for a depression to hide with a captured white boy, but before any soldiers could snatch the boy from her, she drew a butcher knife and disemboweled the youngster. Before she dropped the gasping lad, several troopers shot at her, taking half her face away.

Lieutenant E. S. Godfrey, of Troop K, wrote in his reminiscences, "With Custer at the Battle of Washita":

---

28. There has been some doubt as to the number of men for this detail. See "Life of G. A. Custer"—by Jay Monaghan—footnote, Pg. 320, Chap. 23.

29. Life on the Plains, G. A. Custer; Pg. 164; Sheldon and Company, N. Y., 1874.

> After passing through the village, I went in pursuit of pony herds and found them scattered in groups about a mile below the village. I deployed my platoon to make the roundup and took a position for observations. While the roundup was progressing, I observed a group of dismounted Indians escaping down the opposite side of the valley. Completing the roundup, and starting them toward the village, I turned the herd over to Lieutenant Law who had come with the second platoon of the troop and told him to take them to the village, saying that I would take my platoon and go in pursuit of the group I had seen escaping down the valley . . . I discovered a lone teepee, and soon after two Indians circling their ponies. A high promontory and ridge projected into the valley and shut off the view of the valley below the lone teepee. I knew the circling of the warriors meant an alarm and rally, but I wanted to see what was in the valley beyond them . . . Arriving at and peering over the ridge, I was amazed to find that as far as I could see down the well wooded, tortuous valley there were teepees — teepees. Not only could I see teepees, but mounted warriors scurrying in our direction.[30]

Godfrey and his platoon were charged by the hostiles, but by deploying his men as skirmishers, he fought off the warriors. After the Indians left, Godfrey and his platoon raced back to the village where mop-up actions were diminishing, and reported to Custer. When the words "big village" were mentioned, Custer exclaimed . . . "What's that?"[31] and put Godfrey through a series of questions. At the end, Godfrey indicated that he had heard firing in one of the valleys during his return to the village which continued long after he had arrived back with the remainder of his platoon. At first the shots seemed to indicate a constant battle, and then, after a short lull, the firing became heavier, lasting nearly all day.[32]

Godfrey was again questioned by Custer about the Indian village. At the end of the inquiry, Godfrey mentioned that he had heard that Major Elliott had not yet returned and suggested that the firing may have been an attack on Elliott's party. "I hardly think so," Custer said slowly, as he thought for a moment . . . , "as Captain Meyers has been fighting down there all morning and probably would have reported it."[33]

Custer called Romeo, his scout, to question the women prisoners concerning the village reported by Godfrey. He ordered Troop K to destroy all Indian property with no carrying off of loot. Many soldiers had already gone through the lodges and come up with unusual items. Daguerreotypes of family groups and portraits were among the loot found, along with letters, clothing, mirrors, bits of flat metal, weapons and colorful cotton quilt bedspreads from farm settlements. Brims from the crowns of eastern felt hats and been cut away, and saved for making a war bonnet or other headpiece.

Custer was saddened by the report that his staghound 'Blucher' was found dead, shot through with an arrow, near the place where Lieutenant Bell was attacked and forced to leave some overcoats and haversacks captured by the hostiles.[34] Libbie would also be saddened and Autie would tell her of this brave dog chasing after the enemy while the command was attacking the village. He had been with Custer on many expeditions, and his loss was almost like that of one of the family.

Meanwhile Indians from the other camps down the river had begun to display a menacing front. Low in ammunition, the command must not be cut off from their main supply at the wagon train. Custer asked Romeo to assemble the captured women and children, some sixty in all, and place them in view of the gathering antagonists, with the hope that the hostiles would not fire endangering their own people. Custer realized that it would be but a matter of hours before the warriors from the farthermost villages would join the attack.

30. E. B. Custer microfilm, Reel 6 No. 6088; Custer Battlefield Hist. Museum. This account was written long after the battle by E. S. Godfrey for the Cavalry Journal.

31. "Some Reminiscences of the Battle of the Washita," by Gen. E. S. Godfrey, Cavalry Journal, October, 1928.

32. Ibid.

33. Ibid.

34. "Life on the Plains" — G. A. Custer — Pg. 173.

Custer abandoned the idea of saving all the ponies he had captured. He allowed the women to choose ponies to ride in retreat from the village. Each commissioned officer was allowed two ponies from the herd, and captured mules were hitched to the wagons to replace the ones played out. Lieutenant Godfrey was ordered to kill all ponies except those authorized for use and those given to the scouts. Godfrey and his troop tried to rope the animals and cut their throats, but the ponies were so frightened that this was almost impossible. Godfrey asked for help to shoot the ponies as his men tired of fighting the vicious animals. Four or five companies surrounded the herd to shoot them. During the killing of the eight hundred ponies, the hostiles, who had been watching from the furthest hill slopes, had disappeared. Apparently they realized that any shooting might endanger the women and children.[35]

John Ryan, of M Troop, noticed that his $14 overcoat which he had kept with him was covered with blood from an Indian scalp he had taken. He tore the scalp away from the saber hook it hung from and threw it to the ground. Ryan had taken the first Indian scalp for M Troop along with another trophy, a muzzle-loading buffalo gun made at Lancaster, Pennsylvania, of the style issued to Indians for hunting purposes. Lieutenant Owen Hale, company commander for M Troop, asked Ryan why he discarded the Indian scalp. Surely, after going through what he did to get it, it was considered an honor on that occasion. The trooper growled about his ruined overcoat, turned and marched away.[36]

Trumpeter John Murphy, while pursuing the Indian ponies with Troop M, saw a lone Indian fleeing and gave chase. Suddenly, the warrior stopped in his tracks, turned, and let fly an arrow at the trooper. Murphy threw himself to one side of the saddle to escape the arrow, but not being quick enough, it struck him in the right side, entering in an upward position and penetrating several inches. If Murphy had stayed erect in his saddle, the wound would have

35. Reminiscences of the Battle of the Washita, Godfrey, Cavalry Journal, October, 1928.

36. Ten Years with Gen. Custer Among the Indians; J. Ryan, Newton Circuit, April 2, 1909.

Courtesy Custer Battlefield Museum

Cheyennes, mostly women and children, captured during the Battle of the Washita, and concentrated at Fort Dodge, Kansas.

been fatal. The arrow was withdrawn quickly by a comrade, possibly saving the trumpeter's life. An arrow shot into the body must be withdrawn immediately, or the head will remain. Steel points were usually glued to the tips of war arrows by the warriors to prevent the extraction of these points. When the arrow enters the body, the glue, becoming softened with blood, readily detaches the head from the shaft.[37]

A detail from each company was assigned to destroy the Indian lodges. Lodge poles were hauled down and the hides fell to the ground. As most of the lodges had fires inside, the hides would start burning almost immediately. There were many explosions from stores of black powder inside the lodges. General Custer and several other officers selected trophies for personal collections, while the remaining stores were destroyed. Colorfully decorated bridles, saddles and beaded moccasins were among items taken by the officers. A dispatch case with orders from General Sheridan was found and given to Custer.[38]

Romeo assembled the prisoners so that Custer could speak to them with the scout acting as interpreter. The 'big chief,' as Indians referred to all officers, assured them of kind treatment, but they must accompany the command as prisoners. Custer gathered much valuable information from the women as to what chiefs were in command and which band of hostiles he had attacked. A middle-aged woman then told Romeo that she wished to speak to Custer on behalf of herself and her companions. Her name was Mah-wis-sa, and she was Black Kettle's sister. She told Custer that Black Kettle was one of the first to fall under the guns of 'the big chief.' On the preceding night war parties had returned from the settlements, and the entire village danced and sang of their achievements until the late hours of the morning. It was because of this the soldiers had been able to steal as close to the lodges as they did without arousing the Indians. Then, as a petition for peace, she brought forth a young Indian girl no more than seventeen years of age, and began a marriage ceremony. Custer, who had no knowledge of what was happening, turned to his scout and asked him what she was preparing to do. Romeo grinned and explained, "Why, she's marryin' you to that young squaw!"[39] Custer interrupted Mah-wis-sa and told her that in all due consideration of her kindness, he could not accept the girl in accordance with the white man's laws, at the same time assuring them of his acknowledgment and gratitude. Finally, Romeo and the 'big chief' turned away and attended to more urgent business.

Custer, fearing an attack from the other villages, had already extended his position around the burning lodges. The Quartermaster at the wagon train had sent the ammunition wagon in, barely evading the encircling warriors. The guards, who were left with the haversacks and overcoats, also came in, leaving both clothing and food to the Indians. Search parties were sent to find the dead and wounded and bring them in to the hospital. The loss to the command was two officers and nineteen enlisted men killed or missing.[40] The wounded were three officers and twelve enlisted men. The enemy had one hundred and three warriors dead and an undetermined number wounded.[41]

Custer was later blamed by some officers for his lack of concern regarding the disappearance of Elliott's party, and some felt that he should have made more effort to locate the missing men rather than to abandon the field not knowing their fate. In

37. Report of Surgical Cases, Circular 3; from 1865 to 1871, War Dept., Surgeon General's Office.
38. Life of G. A. Custer; J. Monaghan, Pg. 318.

39. Life on the Plains, G. A. Custer; Pg. 172.
40. Hamilton, Elliott and his party.
41. Returns from the Regular Army (Cav. Ret.), Sept. 1866-Dec. 1873; Roll 71.

Godfrey's narrative,[42] he states that a scout had reported seeing Major Elliott and party, in pursuit of some escaping Indians, disappear down the right side of the valley. Captain Meyers rode down that valley for about two miles, but found nothing. Custer had experienced an extraordinary display of Indian force, a much greater opposition than he had anticipated. It is easy to understand Custer's anxiety to rejoin his wagons carrying subsistence stores and tents for the command, left miles away. The loss of overcoats and rations seized by the hostiles left the men without protection from the elements. The loss of the wagon train and the eighty men who guarded it could mean disaster in the icy wilderness. The safety of the entire command was a first consideration rather than accounting for the loss of a small part of it. Elliott's long absence and the reports of lengthy firing left little doubt as to the fate they had met.

42. Reminiscences of the Battle of the Washita, Godfrey; Cav. Journal, Oct. 1928.

Courtesy Herb Peck, Jr.

Sly Fox, Kiowa — (1873)

Immediately after dark, Custer ordered the command to form column of fours, throwing out a strong force of skirmishers. There was no attempt made to conceal the column or its direction of march. The prisoners were in rear, mounted on ponies, under sufficient guard. The chief trumpeter sounded the advance and the band began playing, "Ain't I Glad to Get Out of the Wilderness." Custer's first thought at observing mounted warriors on the ridges was that they would harass the column. The Indians seemed uncertain what to do at first, because of the direction the command was taking, directly toward their villages. Considerable confusion was apparent and chieftains raced their ponies from one end of the ridge to another as if in last minute consultation. The Indians did not fire into the column, probably fearing to endanger the women and children. Later most warriors disappeared, leaving only a few to observe the march. The column reached the deserted villages. Their occupants had swiftly departed during the battle at Black Kettle's village. After reaching this point, several miles below the site of Black Kettle's village, the command was ordered to face about and follow the earlier trail they had made in striking the village.

The command marched briskly until two o'clock in the morning, then halted and bivouacked until daylight. Most of the men had not eaten for twenty-four hours, and hard crackers and coffee were most welcome. Fires were kindled and wet clothing and equipment dried. Custer sent Colonel West's squadron forward to reinforce the wagon train. At daylight, the troopers were in their saddles again, rested after a somewhat hasty meal. At 10 o'clock, cheers rang out. The train was discovered safely in camp. Halting only to change teams, Custer pushed on to the point where they had at first struck the timbered valley, reaching there early in the afternoon. The men could now unsaddle, pitch tents, and cook up rabbit stew.

After dinner, Custer began writing his report to General Sheridan, to be carried by California Joe to Camp Supply that night. Officers were called to Custer's tent and each one questioned as to casualties and that of the enemy warriors, which totaled one hundred and three slain. Lieutenant Godfrey visited Captain Barnitz and told him California Joe would take mail. The wounded Captain asked Godfrey to write a note telling his wife of his injury, that he was improving from his serious wound, and not to worry as he was in good care.[43]

43. Captain Barnitz survived his injury from the Battle of the Washita and retired Dec. 15, 1870 — Heitman, Historical Register & Dictionary of the U.S. Army, 1789-1903.

Courtesy Herb Peck, Jr.

Kiowa Chief, one of the head tribesman with Black Kettle's Village.

Courtesy Custer Battlefield Museum

Cheyennes captured at the Washita, Fat Bear, Big Head and Dull Knife.

When California Joe reported at Custer's tent and found his commander busily penning a report to Sheridan, he was asked how many men he wanted to accompany him on the return trip to Camp Supply. California Joe replied, "I've just been talkin' the matter over with my partner, and him and me both concludes that as safe and sure a way as any is for him and me to take a few extra rounds of ammunition and strike out from here together the very minnit it's dark. As for any more men, we don't want 'em, because yer see in a case of this 'ere kind thar's more to be made by dodgin' an' runnin' than thar is by fightin', an' two spright men kin do better at that athan twenty; they can't be seen half as fur. Besides, two won't leave as much of a trail for the Injuns to find . . ."[44]

California Joe returned to his tarpaulin shelter and informed his partner, Jack Corbin, of their immediate trip. The two men prepared their mounts, stuffing food into their haversacks along with additional ammunition. By the time both scouts returned to Custer's tent the report to Sheridan was finished. Custer regretted the long hazardous journey, but stressed the importance of bringing the good news of Black Kettle's defeat to General Sheridan. As California Joe mounted his favorite mule, and Corbin his fine gray charger, Custer reached up and shook hands with both men, bidding them God-speed and a successful journey. Joe wiped his nose with torn piece of gunnysack and said in a loud tone, "Wal, I hope an' trust yer won't have any scrimmage while I'm gone, because I'd hate mightily now to miss anything of the sort, seein' I've stuck to yer this fur."[45] Spurring their horses, the two scouts melted into the darkness carrying Custer's detailed report of the Battle of the Washita.

44. Life on the Plains; G. A. Custer, Pg. 177.

45. Ibid., Pg. 178.

CAPTIVES, BUFFALO, AND THE YELLOWSTONE

Early Saturday morning, November 29th, California Joe and Jack Corbin, half out of breath, jumped from their mounts in front of General Sheridan's tent at Camp Supply. They had been on the trail for 36 hours, hiding during daylight hours and traveling only by night. After Sheridan read the dispatch from Custer, the word spread throughout the post that the 7th Cavalry had destroyed Black Kettle's Cheyenne camp on the Washita River. Sheridan sent both scouts back to Custer with dispatches thanking him and all the men in his command for their heroism during the hard, cold campaign against the Indians on the Washita River.

Shortly after breakfast, on December 1st, word circulated through Camp Supply that the 7th Cavalry was not more than 10 miles from the post and would arrive early that morning. General Sheridan advised his staff officers to join him outside the stockade to review the heroes as they came in. Most of the garrison followed suit and stumbled outside straining their eyes toward the horizon for the column. A sudden lull passed over everyone, only the garrison colors were heard flapping in the wind. As the assembly waited silently, movement could be seen in the southwest hills. A rifle report sounded across the valley, followed by another. The chanting of war songs could be heard as the moving forms were recognized. Attired in their best costumes and streaked with war paint were the Osage scouts, riding their ponies in circles before the marching command and firing their rifles overhead. Following the Indian scouts were California Joe and Jack Corbin riding in front of Lieutenant Cooke's sharpshooters. Directly behind them was the 7th Cavalry band playing the regimental song "GarryOwen." Between the band and the sharpshooters ambled Indian women and children riding their ponies and dressed colorfully for the occasion. Next came Custer, in fringed buckskin jacket with leggings to match, sitting erect on his spirited charger. Behind him followed his troopers, some displaying bandaged limbs and heads. And last, the wagon train, with its cargo of wounded and dead, creeping behind the command like a funeral procession.

News of the battle of the Washita flashed over the country while humanitarians with their sentimental feelings decried Custer's victory over the Indians. On December 2nd, the New York Herald headlined:

"DECISIVE BATTLE WITH THE INDIANS: ONE HUNDRED AND FIFTY CHEYENNES KILLED AND A VILLAGE DESTROYED: LOSSES IN GENERAL CUSTER'S COMMAND."

What Eastern readers did not know, they assumed. It was believed that the army had attacked friendly and peaceful Indians, not knowing to any limit or degree the dark side of the Indian question. Custer's prediction of this came true,[1] and the army's performance of duty was criticized as a vicious attack on a defenseless people. The blow Custer had struck was a hard one, and fell on the band that, without provocation, had massacred settlers on the Saline and Solomon, perpetrating cruelties too fiendish for recital.

December 7th found the 7th Cavalry back

1. Life on the Plains; G. A. Custer; (1874); page 183.

in the saddle, with the 19th Kansas Volunteer Cavalry reinforcing the column. The men were issued 30 days' rations and about one-quarter forage rations for the animals. General Sheridan accompanied the command this time, the destination being the site of the destroyed village on the Washita, where an effort would be made to learn the fate of Major Elliott and the 19 men who had disappeared on the morning of the battle just a week ago. In the early morning of December 10th, with the thermometer reading 18 degrees below zero, the expedition reached Black Kettle's village, now a charred battlefield. Half wild and spiritless Indian dogs cringed at the appearance of the column; crows flew, and wolves trotted away from grisly remains. Custer accompanied by Sheridan rode to a ridge where the movements of the battle could be reconstructed. Frozen bodies of Indians still lay where they had fallen during the battle, but those of Black Kettle, Little Rock and several other chiefs, had been removed before the hasty flight of the villagers.

Sheridan deployed a squadron to search the area that Elliott had covered when in pursuit of the escaping Indians. A little more than two miles from the village the bodies of Elliott and his men were found, stripped of all clothing and horribly mutilated, lying within a circle, not more than 20 yards in diameter. Empty cartridge shells scattered around each body were mute evidence of their resistance against overwhelming odds. The mutilations were sickening to those who handled the grim task of identifying the bodies, and among men who had never previously witnessed such scenes, there is no question as to the vomiting that occurred. Doctor Henry Lippincott, chief medical officer, examined each body, making a report on the character and number of wounds received by each, as well as the mutilations.

"Major Joel H. Elliott, two bullet holes in the head, one in left cheek, right hand cut off, left foot almost cut off . . . deep gash in right groin, deep gashes in calves of both legs, little finger of left hand cut off, and throat cut.

"Sergeant Major Walter Kennedy, bullet hole in right temple, head partly cut off, seventeen bullet holes in back and two in legs.

"Corporal Harry Mercer, Troop E, bullet hole in right axilla, one in region of heart, three in back, eight arrow wounds in back, right ear cut off, head scalped, and skull fractured, deep gashes in both legs, and throat cut.

"Private Thomas Christer, Troop E, bullet hole in head, right foot cut off, bullet hole in abdomen and throat cut.

"Corporal William Carrick, Troop H, bullet hole in right parietal bone, both feet cut off, throat cut, left arm broken.

Courtesy Custer Battlefield Museum

Major Joel H. Elliott, lead a handful of men at the Washita. They were ambushed and killed to the last man. Returning to the battleground a week later, the 7th Cavalry, accompanied by General Sheridan, located the bodies of Elliott and 19 men who disappeared on the morning of the battle.

"Private Eugene Clover, Troop H, head cut off, arrow wound in right side, both legs terribly mutilated.

"Private William Milligan, Troop H, bullet hole in left side of head, deep gashes in right leg . . . left arm deeply gashed, head scalped, and throat cut.

"Corporal James F. Williams, Troop I, bullet hole in back; head and both arms cut off; many and deep gashes in back . . .

"Private Thomas Dooney, Troop I, arrow hole in region of stomach, thorax cut open, head cut off, and right shoulder cut by tomahawk.

"Farrier Thomas Fitzpatrick, Troop M, bullet hole in back; head and both arms cut off; many deep gashes in back . . .

"Private John Myres, Troop M, several bullet holes in head, scalped, nineteen bullet holes in body . . . throat cut.

"Private Cal Sharpe, Troop M, two bullet holes in right side, throat cut, one bullet hole in left side of head, arrow hole in left side . . . left arm broken.

"Unknown, head cut off, body partially destroyed by wolves.

"Unknown, head and right hand cut off . . . three bullet and nine arrow holes in back.

"Unknown, scalped, skull fractured, six bullet and thirteen arrow holes in back, and three bullet holes in chest."[2]

An account of Elliott's fight was given later by Indians who had witnessed the fight and all agreed that the major could have escaped with all his men if he had turned back at the first sighting of the huge band of warriors approaching. Not realizing that these hostiles were afraid to follow him too closely because of the nearness of the main body of troops, Elliott waged his own battle.[3] It was estimated that the odds were one hundred to one[4] against the troopers, Elliott could have had no idea a force of this size was approaching, and of course, he had no knowledge of the other villages down the valley.

It was after dark when all the bodies were carried into camp and prepared for burial on a knoll close by. Under the dim light of torches, the bodies were consigned to a common grave, except the remains of Major Elliott, carried back by the column and interred at Fort Arbuckle.

There was some opinion that Custer's abandonment of Elliott and his party was deliberate. Captain Frederick W. Benteen, whose jealousy and hatred against his commander grew each day, determined in his own mind that Custer was responsible for the deaths of Elliott and his men. Benteen, in trying to discredit Custer, sought to get a statement from one of Custer's scouts, who had heard Elliott's call for volunteers and had seen him ride in pursuit of the fleeing Indians, to the effect that Custer had let Elliott ride to his doom without any effort on his own part to try to save the party or make any attempt to locate them later. The scout, Ben Clark, knowing the circumstances, declined, wanting nothing to do with it. Benteen was more determined than ever to lash out at his commanding officer regardless of consequences.

Several months after the Washita battle, an article appeared in the St. Louis Democrat, which was copied by the New York Times, February 14th, 1869, highly critical of the leadership during the battle. The writer was anonymous, but definitely a participant.

THE BATTLE OF THE WASHITA

Death and Barbarous Treatment of Maj. Elliott and His Band-Destruction of the Indian Camp and Property.

(New York Times, February 14, 1869)

---

2. Elizabeth B. Custer, microfilm, Reel 1, Item 0845; (Report submitted by G. A. Custer, Dec. 22, 1868) Custer Battlefield Museum. Also see *California Joe*, J. E. Milner and E. R. Forrest, pages 188-189; Caxton Printers, Ltd., Caldwell, Idaho, 1935.

3. Custer's Indian Battles; C. F. Bates, Bronxville, N. Y., 1936; page 15.

4. E. B. Custer, microfilm, Reel 1, Item 0844.

Courtesy Author's Collection

Personal items of an officer. Bible, ink bottle, mirror, folding knife and spoon, binoculars, folding cup (or telescope cup) matches, reading glasses, plug of tobacco, tin match container, razor, 10 inch blade hunting knife with bone handle. German imported playing cards.

Fort Cobb, I.T., Dec. 22, 1868

. . . On the 11th we camped within a few miles of our "battle of the Washita," and Gens. Sheridan and Custer, with a detail of one hundred men, mounted, as escort, went out with the view of searching for the bodies of our nineteen missing comrades, including Maj. Elliott.

The bodies were found in a small circle, stripped as naked as when born, and frozen stiff. Their heads had been battered in, and some of them had been entirely chopped off; some of them had had the Adam's apple cut out of their throats; some had their hands and feet cut off, and nearly all had been horribly mangled in a way delicacy forbids me to mention. They lay scarcely two miles from the scene of the fight, and all we know of the manner they were killed we have learned from Indian sources. It seems that Maj. Elliott's party were pursuing a well-mounted party of Cheyennes in the direction of the Grand Village, where nearly all the tribes were encamped, and were surrounded by the reinforcements coming to the rescue of the pursued, before the Major was aware of their position . . . As soon as Maj. Elliott found that he was surrounded he caused his men to dismount, and did some execution among the Indians, which added to the mortification they must have felt at the loss of the village and herds of their friends and allies, and enraged them so that they determined upon the destruction of the entire little band.

Who can describe the feeling of that brave band, as with anxious beating hearts, they strained their yearning eyes in the direction whence help should come? What must have been the despair that, when all hopes of succor died out, nerved their stout arms to do and die? Round and round rush the red fiends, smaller and smaller shrinks the circle, but the aim of that devoted, gallant knot of heroes is steadier than ever, and the death howl of the murderous redskin is more frequent . . . Soon every voice in that little band is still as death; but the hellish work of the savages is scarce begun, and their ingenuities are taxed to invent barbarities to practice on the bodies of the fallen brave, the relation of which is scarcely necessary to the completion of this tale.

And now, to learn why the anxiously-looked-for succor did not come, let us view the scene in the captured village, scarce two short miles away. Light skirmishing is going on all around. Savages on flying steeds, with shields and feathers gay, are circling everywhere, riding like devils incarnate. The troops are on all sides of the village, looking on and seizing every opportunity of picking off some of those daring riders with their carbines. But does no one think of the welfare of Maj. Elliott and party? It seems not. But yes! a squadron of cavalry is in motion. They trot; they gallop. Now they charge! The cowardly redskins flee the coming shock and scatter here and there among the hills scurry away. But it is the true line — will the cavalry keep it? No! No! They turn! Ah, 'tis only to intercept the wily foe. See! a gray troop goes on in the direction again. One more short mile and they will be saved. Oh, for a mother's prayers! Will not some good angel prompt them? . . . There is no hope for that brave little band, the death doom is theirs, for the cavalry halt and rest their panting steeds . . .

And now return with me to the village. Officers and soldiers are watching, resting, eating and sleeping. In an hour or so they will be refreshed, and then scour the hills and plains for their missing comrades. The commander occupies himself in taking an inventory of the captured property which he had promised the officers shall be distributed among the enlisted men of the command if they falter nor halt not in the charge.

. . . The work progresses! The plunder having been culled over, is hastily piled; the wigwams are pulled down and thrown on it, and soon the whole is one blazing mass. . . The huge fire dies out; our wounded and dead comrades — heroes of a bloody day — are carefully laid on ready ambulances, and as the brave band of the Seventh Cavalry strikes up the air, "Ain't I glad to get out of the Wilderness," we slowly pick our way across the creek over which we charged so gallantly in the early morn. Take care! do not trample on the dead bodies of that woman and child lying there! In a short time we shall be far from the scene of our daring dash, and night will have thrown her dark mantle over the scene. But surely some search will be made for our missing comrades. No, they are forgotten. Over them and the poor ponies the wolves will hold high carnival, and their howlings will be their only requiem . . .

> Two weeks elapse — a larger force returns that way. A search is made and the bodies are found strewn round that little circle, frozen stiff and hard. Who shall write their eulogy?[5]

Upon reading the article, Custer flew into a rage. He ordered officer's call and confronted his subordinates in his Sibley tent while slapping a leather rawhide whip against his cavalry boots. It was evident that some of the officers had read the article, but few knew who had written it. Custer had every reason to believe it was one of his own officers, someone who had participated in the battle. He "hoped that the officer in question would be gentlemanly enough to expose himself, as he deserves to be horsewhipped." Benteen pushed his way through the officers, at the same time shifting his holstered pistol to a handy position on his belt, "General Custer, while I cannot father all the blame you have asserted, still I guess I am the man you are after . . . , and I am ready for the whipping promised."[6] Custer was not only taken by surprise, but dumfounded at Benteen's bold movement. "Colonel Benteen," Custer barked, "I shall see you later, sir."[7] With that, Custer dismissed the officers, turned and left the tent.[8] Benteen later claimed that Custer, out of revenge, assigned him to Fort Dodge, during which period the Captain's child died and his wife lay seriously ill at Fort Harker.

The day after recovery of the bodies, the Sheridan-Custer column started down the Washita, following the Indian trail. The abandoned villages extended some 13 miles along the river, and from the appearance of cooking utensils, robes, provisions and other property lying everywhere, the Indians evidently had fled in great haste. Marching through the ravines and canyons was toilsome and the troops moved out onto the divide only to encounter a blinding snowstorm. Fearing that segments of the command might get lost, they returned to the banks of the Washita. The next day the march continued down the river, still following the Indian trail, but slowed down considerably by crossing numerous ravines, some of which required digging out and bridging by pioneer parties. By the 16th, the column came upon a Kiowa village, and before the Indians knew of their presence, the soldiers were upon them. As they cautiously approached the village, a group of warriors came to greet them under a flag of truce with a letter from General W. B. Hazen, military superintendent of the southern Indians and acting agent at Fort Cobb.[9] The leading warriors were Lone Wolf, a Comanche, and Satanta, a Kiowa, both leaders of bands encamped near Black Kettle's village at the time of the battle. It was later learned that Mrs. Clara Blinn, a white woman, and her small son, Willie, had been held captives in Satanta's village, and were found murdered after the warriors abandoned the villages. The letter brought by courier from General Hazen stated that *all* the Indian camps near Fort Cobb were friendly and had not been on any war party for months. After the chiefs found that the column was not going to attack them, they proposed that the warriors join the column and march with it to Fort Cobb, while their villages moved to the same point on the opposite bank of the Washita. This was a deception, as toward night, most of the warriors slipped off, leaving about 20 chiefs and principal men with the column. Early the next morning these leaders escaped, with the exception of Lone Wolf and Satanta.

Sheridan saw that he had been deceived, and ordered Custer to arrest the two remaining chiefs. After reaching Fort Cobb that

5. Full contents of this letter is found in The Custer Myth; by Col. W. A. Graham Stackpole Co., page 212; New York Times, Feb. 14, 1869, on microfilm, author's collection.

6. Custer's Indian Battles; Bates, page 16. Also see E. B. Custer microfilm Item No. 3088, Reel 11, Custer Battlefield Museum.

7. Glory Hunter; Frederick F. Van De Water.

8. Custer's Indian Battles; Bates, page 16.

9. Hazen was assigned this duty by Sherman.

evening, Sheridan and Custer found that the Kiowas, instead of moving to Fort Cobb as they had promised to do, were headed down the main Red River, west of the Wichita Mountains, in the opposite direction, as fast as their ponies would carry them. The fabricated proposition that Satanta and Lone Wolf made to Custer and Sheridan was only a decoy to get the villagers out of harm's way. The villagers had probably put 100 miles between themselves and the column.

Sheridan ordered Lone Wolf and Satanta be hung by the neck unless the villagers returned within two days and delivered themselves at Fort Cobb. The message was most effective. The villagers soon began appearing at a gait as fast as that of their flight, taking only two days after the order was issued. In Sheridan's military report of operations for that year, he writes, "I shall always regret, however, that I did not hang these Indians; they had deserved it many times; and I shall also regret that I did not punish the whole tribe when I first met them. The graves along the Santa Fe road, and along the northern border of Texas, of murdered men and women, would give evidence of the justice of such a course; but where there are so many authorities a person sometimes gets confounded as what is his duty."[10] Perfectly convinced of the white man's power and that of his determined government, the lawless activities of the Kiowa declined and the tribe remained on their reservation with the exception of a few reckless young warriors, under the leadership of Satanta. Their raiding parties in Texas each summer were almost impossible to curb. These young bucks were headstrong and impatient, and slipping away from the villages at Fort Cobb was just as challenging as the plunder they anticipated.

The problem of the Kiowas seemed settled, and Sheridan and Custer turned their attention to the hostile Arapaho and Cheyenne, and the possibility of rescuing two white women captives. Most of the Comanches and Apaches had hastened to the reservation at Fort Cobb, after the fight on the Washita and the destruction of Black Kettle's camp. Lieutenant Colonel A. W. Evans had also been operating against the hostiles from Fort Bascom down the main Canadian to Monument Creek, there establishing his depot. With commendable energy he struck off to the south, and at the headwaters of the Red River, surprised a group of Comanches who had refused to come in. Twenty-five warriors were killed and a large number wounded. The village was captured and burned to the ground de-

Courtesy Custer Battlefield Museum

General Custer and the Grand Duke Alexis of Russia, 1872. Custer is holding his 50/70 modified breech-loading Springfield rifle.

10. Report of the Secretary of war; Vol. I, 1869; Report written by P. H. Sheridan; pg. 49.

stroying a great amount of property. General Eugene A. Carr was scouting along the main Canadian, west of the Antelope Hills, forcing bands of Cheyennes into the eastern edge of the Staked Plains, where the Indians found game almost nonexistent. The supplies they had put up for the winter had mostly been lost at the Washita engagement. Little Raven, Little Robe and Yellow Bear along with the majority of the hostiles were forced to come in and surrender. The surrender was made by Little Robe for the Cheyennes, and Yellow Bear for the Arapahoes. They agreed to deliver their people at Fort Cobb as soon as possible, but because of the exhausted condition of their stock, it would take some time to get them in. The Arapahoes were faithful to Yellow Bear's promise, and came in under their head chief Little Raven. The Cheyennes, however, broke their promise and remained on the southern plains, challenging the army.

Sheridan left the Custer column February 13th, 1869 to return to Washington because of his promotion to lieutenant general. Marching off to Camp Supply, Sheridan found good company with Colonel Sam Crawford of the 19th Kansas who was succeeded in that command by Lieutenant Colonel Horace L. Moore. Custer was left to hunt the hostile Cheyennes, who were apparently moving north toward Camp Supply. On March 2nd, Custer and 1,500 men, the 7th mounted and the Kansas volunteers marching as infantry, struck out after the Cheyennes with limited rations. During the march, horses dropped in their tracks and died, leaving a third of the cavalry to continue on foot. Soon rations gave out and the men had to resort to mule meat, and with the loss of animals, many wagons had to be abandoned.

The soldiers, dog-tired and hungry, were ready to turn back but their tireless commander pushed them on. The Kansans, however, were determined to wreak revenge on the Cheyennes because of the white women captives, thus bolstering the stamina of the entire command.

Striking a trail, the command followed it to the north fork of the Red River, where in mid-March they came upon the Cheyenne camp. Custer rode ahead of the column with an orderly and reached the center of the valley within sight of the village. Riding his horse in a circle, which was a plainsman's signal for wanting a conference, Custer attracted the attention of the Indians. After a few moments, three pony riders galloped from the camp with others following at a distance. Custer extended his arm showing the sign of friendship, and the Cheyennes replied in sign talk. Having no knowledge of the Cheyenne tongue, Custer conversed in sign language, some knowledge of which he had picked up. This was the village of Stone Forehead,[11] the Arrow Keeper.

As the advancing troops reached the ridge, they halted while Custer's adjutant, Colonel Cooke, joined his commander and the orderly. Stone Forehead appeared, and invited Custer and his party to join him in his camp. Together they rode to the Medicine Arrow lodge, in the center of the Indian village. Dismounting, Custer entered the lodge with Stone Forehead. Among some of the 200 lodges that made up the village, the general noticed that a number were of the Dog Soldier fraternity, the most active of hostile bands. The Keeper of the Sacred Arrows lit a pipe and handed it to the white chief. Custer, not a smoker, puffed on it until the bowl was emptied. Self-educated in lodge procedures, he noticed that Medicine Arrow[12] did not share the smoking pipe, but continued to hold the pipe until Custer had finished it. Then it was filled again and passed among the council. Peace was the

11. Life of George Bent, G. E. Hyde; page 325, University of Oklahoma Press; the name Rock Forehead is mentioned, instead of Stone Forehead.

12. My Life on the Plains, G. A. Custer; page 238; he refers to the head chief of the Cheyennes as "Medicine Arrow."

topic of conversation, and yet Custer felt that if the subject of the two captive women was brought up and their release demanded, hostilities would erupt again between the forces, thereby endangering the women. The white chief proclaimed that his intentions were honorable and he desired a peaceful relationship with the tribe. Medicine Arrow claimed that Custer was a treacherous man and he had come there with a bad purpose, to do harm to the people. The Arrow Keeper then shook the ashes loose in the pipe bowl and scattered them on the toes of Custer's boots. This was, in their ceremonial custom, a malediction.[13] As they sat smoking, Custer was planning how to surround the village, attack and capture them.

Custer asked if a suitable campsite could be chosen for his command, and a bivouac area was selected by the Indians completely out of sight of the Cheyenne village. This did not deceive the Indian fighter, as he presumed the entire camp would attempt to slip away during the night. After having settled down on the site picked by the Indian delegation, Custer posted pickets at prominent points, to observe the Indian village three-fourths of a mile away. This precautionary measure would insure immediately knowledge of any attempt to escape by the Indians, and at the same time observe any trickery they might possibly try while the soldier camp settled for the night.

Later that evening, 50 to 100 chiefs, warriors and young men arrived at camp and settled themselves around a campfire. Custer greeted Medicine Arrow and through an interpreter, found that the Cheyennes were desirous of manifesting their friendship. As evidence of their good faith, they were joined by a group of Indian entertainers who were dressed in a most fiendish and fantastic attire. As they commenced their program, Custer received reports from his lookouts of movements in the village that

13. Life of George Bent; G. E. Hyde; page 325.

Courtesy Custer Battlefield Museum

A Buffalo Hunt, Fort Hays, Kansas — Custer is just above Buffalo's head.

seemed to indicate they were getting ready to slip away. Now he understood the object of the entertainment; it was another attempt to occupy the soldiers' attention so the rest of the villagers could pack up and take flight. While pretending ignorance of the situation, Custer continued to converse with the chiefs, giving attention at the same time to the ceremonies. A plan was devised by Custer to seize the chiefs after the entertainers left and hold them as hostages for the surrender of the two white girls, along with a promise of future good behavior. How to do it without causing any bloodshed can only be told in the gallant leader's own words. "Quietly passing the word to a few of the officers who sat near me around the campfire, I directed them to leave the group one by one, and in such manner as not to attract the attention of the Indians, proceed to their companies and select quickly some of their most reliable men, instructing the latter to assemble around and near my campfire, well armed, as if merely attracted there by the Indian serenade. The men thus selected were to come singly, appear as unconcerned as possible, and be in readiness to act promptly, but to do nothing without orders from me."[14]

Within a short time, 100 men appeared and intermingled with the Indians, laughing and pretending interest in the entertainment as they moved closer. The painted musicians apparently from exhaustion took their leave, informing Custer that they would return later that evening to repeat their performance. About 40 Indians were left, including a few chiefs that remained to continue their conversation with the commander. Custer indicated in a quiet manner the principal chiefs he wished to seize and hold hostage, but to do this without any loss of life was a problem.

He asked interpreter Romeo to say that the white chief wanted silence among the Indians as he was about to communicate something of great importance. Custer arose, unbuckled his revolver belt and threw his weapons upon the ground. He asked that they look about them and count

14. My Life on the Plains — G. A. Custer; (1874), page 242.

Courtesy U.S. Signal Corps photo (Brady Collection)

Scouts and Packers. A hundred and fifty pounds was more than an animal should pack. Sometimes a sturdier horse can haul up to two hundred pounds if evenly distributed. Army packers most generally loaded what they thought was enough and many times overloaded an animal. They were constantly trying to catch up to the command.

the armed soldiers that had cut off any avenue of escape. The Indians began to grow uneasy but Custer held their attention by talking. He demonstrated that he wanted no bloodshed by dropping his pistol belt but he stated that it was the Indians who came under false pretense to deceive the white chief while their camp was preparing to slip away.

An effort was made by the Indians to escape. Some of the younger men jumped to their horses, others pulled pistols and strung bows. For several moments it seemd as if Custer's strategy would fail. The older men counselled the young warriors not to provoke a fight. In the increased excitement the younger men made a rush for the village and although the armed soldiers could have easily picked the Indians off their mounts,

Courtesy Custer Battlefield Museum

Custer and scouts on the Yellowstone Expedition of 1873. Custer holds map, his scout, Bloody Knife (at left, kneeling), is pointing. Tent in rear was loaned by the N. P. Railroad.

Custer ordered them not to fire. All but four broke through and escaped, those remaining being the prominent chiefs that Custer had planned to hold as hostages.

The four captives were told to choose one of their number to return to the village with a message. Custer demanded the unconditional surrender of the two white girls held captive and that the entire Cheyenne village return at once to the reservation near Camp Supply, reporting to the military commander at that station. In case they failed to comply, the command would at once pursue them. Stalling for time, several warriors came close to camp seeking proof that the chieftains were still alive. When challenged and asked to come into camp, they refused. Custer had the chiefs call in loud tones that they were safe. After being convinced that no harm would come to them, the warriors came into camp and were relieved to find their chiefs were still alive. Satisfied with their fair treatment, the warriors returned to the village. After several days passed, Custer, tired of transmitting messages without results, called for a delegation of chieftains to hear his ultimatum. They came not knowing what the white chief intended to do, but soon learned that if the white women were not released by sunset of the next day, the lives of the three chiefs would be forfeited.

Custer knew that the Indians would not act promptly to his reply, and they would practice every delay possible before complying with the white chief's demands. The hostages became despondent as the sun began its descent in the west, and asked for a talk with Custer. One of the chiefs offered to go to the village and hurry things up, promising to return immediately with the white women. He emphasized his influential standing, saying that the others would respond to his demands. Custer replied, as he recalled it in *My Life on the Plains:*

"... if he was of such importance in his tribe as he claimed to be, he was the most proper person for me to retain possession of, as his people would be more likely to accede to my demands to save his life than that of a person of less consequence."[15]

Just before sunset, some 20 mounted figures appeared on the horizon to the west. Through a field glass Custer could not make out for certain their identity until he saw two figures dismount from a pony and advance toward camp. As they came closer they were seen to be the two white women he had been bargaining for. Daniel A. Brewster, brother to one of the women captives, who had accompanied Custer's column in hopes of finding his sister, now burst into tears and was the first to reach the girls as they feebly staggered toward camp. The story of their treatment, told by the captives, was of barbarous cruelties, and it was surprising any civilized persons could have endured it and survived.[16] Medicine Arrow now demanded the release of the three hostages, Big Head, Dull Knife and Fat Bear, but Custer refused until the tribe had completed the second part of the agreement by returning to the reservation. This Medicine Arrow agreed to do as soon as the grass was green for the ponies to travel.

Most of the tribe came to the vicinity of Camp Supply and communicated with the post commander. Only Tall Bull's band violated the promise made and rode north to the Republican, where they joined a party of Sioux. On May 13th, 1869, they were surprised and defeated with heavy losses, whereupon the tribe finally was assembled at Camp Supply.

Custer and the 7th Cavalry marched to Fort Hays with the 19th Kansas "foot-sore" volunteers. The cavalry would stay there most of the summer, but the Kansas volunteers, having found their captive women, were disbanded and returned home. The Indians who had plundered the Southern Plains were believed to be under control by the spring of 1869. The winter campaign was a total success. There had been a fulfillment of all the conditions that Sheridan had hoped for; namely, punishment of the hostiles, their property destroyed, and the Indians disabused of the idea that winter would bring them security from the army's long reach. Finally, the tribes south of the Platte were forced onto the reservations set apart for them by the government. There were a few wilder bands of Kiowas and Comanches remaining out on the Staked Plains who, feeling a strong lingering dis-

Courtesy Herb Peck, Jr.

Trooper (unknown) in early 1870's holding Sharp's carbine with homemade thimble "prairie belt."

15. My Life on the Plains; Custer, page 249.

16. Captives were Mrs. Anna Belle Morgan and Brewster's sister, Miss Sara C. White, both women captured the year before on the Kansas frontier.

content toward the whites committed intermittent raids on a small scale. The Cheyenne Dog Soldiers were still hanging onto their hunting grounds and each summer raided Texas and below the Rio Grande. There were no real major outbreaks until 1874 when the Indians were driven to open hostilities again by unjust treatment on the part of agents of the Indian Bureau. It was believed by Custer that peace could have reigned much longer than it did, with the use of proper diplomacy and treatment.

While the Indian problem in the Southwest seemed settled for the time being, headquarters of the 7th withdrew from the field to its station at Fort Leavenworth, most of its companies being scattered in various posts from which patrols were sent on escort duty, and other scouts and expeditions. While in garrison during the winter of 1869-70 troopers entertained themselves with amateur theatrical shows, horse racing and card playing. Buffalo hunts were staged for visiting celebrities and lavish dinners followed by hops gave Custer and his wife Libbie a reputation for hospitality. All of this could not fill Autie's life in garrison, and he resumed his writings of plains experiences. The now-famous Indian Fighter[17] would relive his past by setting down on paper the free life of a cavalryman.

When there were rumors that the 7th might be transferred to the Department of the South, Custer, afraid of leaving his beloved plains, applied for a transfer to another regiment that would leave him on frontier duty. He was denied this and assigned to a two-company post at Elizabethtown, Kentucky, some 40 miles south of Louisville for two years of routine duty. In March, 1871, headquarters was established at Elizabethtown. The regiment, in small detachments, assisted United States marshals in hunting illegal distilleries and in curbing activities of the Ku Klux Klan, hunting for moonshiners in Kentucky, Tennessee, and South Carolina.[18]

In January, 1872, the Grand Duke Alexis, third son of the Czar of Russia, arrived in the United States for an official visit. Because of the apparent friendship the Russian government had showed during the Civil War, he was received with governmental and public hospitality. Alexis, 22 years of age, was accompanied by Admiral Poisset, with whom he had been at sea since he was seven, and Vice Chancellor Machin. It was understood that the grand duke was to see everything possible, from manufacturing of goods, to schools, churches and prisons, but instead of being delighted with all this he seemed bored but acquiescent. Banquets were held in his honor with long speeches, salutes were fired, flags and banners raised, all in praise of the young Russian who responded with small dull speeches. Alexis spoke and understood English well, but did not enjoy American humor. He especially did not enjoy those who slapped his imperial back or dug an elbow into his royal ribs in emphasis. How could the public know that in Russia no one dared touch a person of royalty?

The banquet halls and torchlight ceremonies ended in Chicago, probably for the better, as the last hotel bill from the East came to $1,500 for one meal. General Sheridan had invited the grand duke to a buffalo hunt on the plains, his bored attitude changed to one of the greatest delight. Custer was summoned from his station in Kentucky to help conduct the hunt, and the special train, provided by the Pennsylvania Railroad, carried the party with General Sheridan and staff to their destination. All the way to Fort McPherson, Custer and Alexis acted like two small boys. They danced, sang, and wrestled in the aisles and

17. Although many will not agree to this statement of "Indian fighter," it was enough for hero-worshippers. Custer's rekindled fame after the Washita brought him back into public praise, and they watched him curiously.

18. See "Of GarryOwen in Glory," Lt. Col. M. C. Chandler; pages 35-38.

challenged each other to the Indian arm-wrestling game. At Fort McPherson, wagons awaited the party to take them 50 miles to Willow Creek, where their camp was laid out. Hospital tents, wall tents, and "A" tents had been erected. In an Indian village of 400 lodges, Spotted Tail, his braves and their wives, awaited the party's arrival. After eight hours of travel, escorted by two troops of cavalry, the party reached the camp where a band played at their entrance with the Russian national anthem. Dinner was served in flag-draped tents, and toasts from the officers wished the grand duke "a successful buffalo hunt."

At nine o'clock the next morning the first hunt began. Buffalo Bill Cody, who had tutored the grand duke the evening before, loaned him his trained horse, Buckskin Joe, and assured him that the animal was well trained for that purpose. At dawn, Spotted Tail's scouts had been out locating a herd, and upon finding the shaggy animals grazing, sent word back to Custer and Cody. Hasty preparations were made and the royal party, following the scout back to the location of the herd, formed in a gully and prepared for the charge. The grand duke was given the first shot. He fired six shots from his pistol while only 20 feet away from the buffalo, flinching each time, and failing to hit anything. Cody rode alongside the duke and handed him another loaded revolver, and six more shots were fired without dropping the animal. Cody, upon seeing that the buffaloes might dash off in the excitment, handed Alexis his .50 caliber Springfield rifle and slapped Buckskin Joe on the rump, whereupon the horse bolted to within 10 feet of the snorting bull. A cloud of smoke erupted as the recoil almost knocked the duke from his saddle, more surprised from the report of the rifle and its kick than the now-sprawling buffalo that dropped before him.[19]

Courtesy Dr. Elizabeth A. Lawrence Collections *Art by E. L. Reedstrom*

General Custer in 1872 dressed in his usual field attire with fur cap, sporting a favorite 50/70 modified breech-loading Springfield rifle.

The grand duke reeled in his saddle, shouted and waved his hat to his comrades who were watching some distance back. They, too, cheered and applauded him, although the spectacle was more hilarious than rewarding. Later that day, the duke shot a buffalo cow with a revolver at the range of 30 yards, which surprised everyone, including the grand duke. All told, in that five-day hunt were eight buffaloes credited to the wild and inaccurate shooting of the Grand Duke Alexis. On the last day of the hunt, the Indians demonstrated their method of buffalo hunting, with bow and arrows and lance. The grand duke was thrilled by their expert horseman-

19. Newspapers back East reported Cody shooting the buffalo for the grand duke; in Lives and Legends of Buffalo Bill; Univ. of Okla., Don Russell, page 178, states that Cody may have held the duke's hand, but the duke pulled the trigger. I am more inclined to believe Russell's account. Also see, L. B. Custer microfilm (Reel 4) No. 3267 (letters) page 69, Custer Battlefield, states Custer held buffalo while the duke shot. It is possible they mean — Custer held rifle, not buffalo.

ship, and stated that the Indians were better riders than the Cossacks of Russia.

After the hunt, Custer accompanied the duke East, and at Louisville, Mrs. Custer joined the party which continued on to New Orleans, where a Russian warship awaited the grand duke. Newspapers ran complete details of the buffalo hunt and of the grand ball given later at Louisville, and the event gave socialites and army officers something to wag their tongues about for some time to come.

Wedding bells rang for Margaret Emma Custer, the general's only sister. Her marriage to Lieutenant James Calhoun, newly-assigned to the 7th Cavalry at Custer's request, assembled the family in Monroe, Michigan, the first week of March, 1872. Boston Custer, Autie's youngest brother, expressed a desire to join the regiment in any capacity, and hoped that his influential brother could do something about it. Boston had been a consumptive for a number of years and believed that he would benefit from life in the open air of the plains.[20] Autie promised Boston that as soon as he and Libbie returned to Elizabethtown, an effort would be made to establish some sort of position for him in the 7th.

There were several vacancies in the regiment, and if he went through the proper channels, it might take some time to process, and again the chances of refusal were great. Custer decided to contact his political and influential friends and ask as a favor to him that his brother be appointed to the 7th as a second lieutenant. He would surely champion his young brother and help him in every way to become a credit to the cavalry corps. A letter to a close friend and superior officer is as follows:

Galt House
Louisville, Ky.
March 14, 1872.

My dear Genl.*

I want to ask a great favor of you. There are three or four vacancies in my regiment (7" Cavalry) in the grade of second lieutenant. These I presume will be filled by appointment. I am extremely anxious to obtain an appointment from the Secretary of War for my youngest brother Boston Custer as second Lieutenant in the 7" Cavalry. My brother is in every respect admirally adopted to perform the duties of a cavalry officer. He is nearly twenty four years of age, of excellent habits and character and I think would be a credit to the service. I would be under great obligations to you if you would interest yourself in my behalf with Genl. Belknap and endeavor to secure this appointment. If you can ascertain anything definitely regarding the prospect of obtaining it I would be glad if he received a note from you — I would write to Genl. Belknap, but to send through the regular channel would result in no benefit to my application considering delays, etc.[21]

20. E. B. Custer; microfilm. Reel 6, item 6295, Custer Battlefield Museum.

*General's name unknown. Possibly Lt. Gen. P. H. Sheridan.

21. Reproduced from the collections of the Manuscript Division, Library of Congress. (Record Group 11700). Copy in Author's collection.

Courtesy Dr. Elizabeth A. Lawrence

Buffalo Bill Cody served with Custer. He and the Grand Duke Alexis of Russia became favorite hunting companions.

Hoping you may find it consistant to grant me this favor,

I am Truly yours,
G. A. Custer

The letter is endorsed on first flap:

Genl. G. A. Custer
Louisville, Ky.
In relation to his brother's application for a Lieutenancy in the Army.
Answd. Mar. 27/1872
No appointments now being made.

The brief endorsements message in answer, "No appointments now being made,"[22] ended that effort. However, Boston was employed as a forage master from June 5th, 1875 to March 3rd, 1876, at a monthly compensation of $75. Later in 1876 Boston was employed as a civilian guide by the 7th Cavalry quartermaster, at $100 per month, His short career with the army ended when he followed his brothers to their doom at the Little Big Horn.[23]

Regulations observed in the examination of candidates for appointment to second lieutenant in the Army of the United States were published in the Army and Navy Journal, August 16th, 1873, as follows:

G.O. No. 81, Washington, Aug. 1, 1873:
1. No person shall be examined who has not a letter authorizing the same from the War Department.
2. No candidate will be examined who is under 20 or over 30 years of age; who, in the judgment of the Board, has not the physical ability to endure the exposure of service; who has any deformity of body, or mental infirmity, or whose moral habits are bad.
3. The Board being satisfied of these preliminary points, will proceed to examine each candidate separately:
First. In his knowledge of English grammer, and his ability to read and write with facility and correctness.
Second. In his knowledge of arithmetic, and his ability in the application of its rules to all practical questions.
Third. In his knowledge of geography, particularly in reference to the northern continent of America.
Fourth. In his knowledge of history, particularly in reference to his own country.
Fifth. In his knowledge of the Constitution of the United States, and of the organization of the Government under it, and of the general principles which regulate internation intercourse.
4. The Board will consider eight as the maximum of the first, fourth, and fifth heads, and ten as the maximum of the second and third heads; and no candidate will be passed by the Board who shall not have received at least half of the number of maximum marks on each head or subject of examination.
5. In addition of such Boards of Examination as may be appointed by the Secretary of War, a Military Division or Department commander, upon notification from the Adjutant-General of the Army that a candidate has been authorized to report to him, will convene, at division or department headquarters, a Board to consist of four commissioned officers, including a medical officer; the duties of the latter to be confined to the medical examination. The proceedings of the Boards will be forwarded to the Adjutant-General of the Army.
By order of the Secretary of War. (W. W. Belknap)
Thomas M. Vincent, A.A.-G.[24]

In the spring of 1873, the 7th Cavalry was reunited for the first time since the Washita campaign in 1868 when the restless and threatening mood of the Sioux made it necessary to send the regiment into the Dakota Territory. The Northern Pacific Railroad had asked the government to protect its survey west of the Missouri River from hostile Indian attacks. A considerable amount of Indian resistance was expected, so a large force of infantry, artillery, and cavalry, was sent to quell any attempted uprising.

After the regiment had assembled at Memphis, it was sent by steamboat to Cairo, Illinois, where horses, men, and luggage changed to railroad cars for another lengthy trip to Yankton, Dakota Territory. At Yankton the 7th went into camp on a low plain several miles from the city. Officers' wives stayed in a hotel in town except for Mrs. Custer and Maggie Calhoun (the General's sister) who took over a vacant house midway between town and camp. After several days, a typical Dakota blizzard struck,

22. Ibid.
23. Biographies of the 7th Cavalry; by Ken Hammer, Old Army Press, 1972, page 18-19. Also see Men with Custer; Hammer, Old Army Press. Also, in "The Custer Story" by M. Merington; shows "Bos" employed in the forage Dept. of the 7th Regiment in 1871; letter to Libbie from Autie; page 232.

24. A.N.J.; Aug. 16, 1873, page 4.

isolating everyone. Shelter was sought for the horses, as it was feared that they would be frozen if left out of doors. The snow was so blinding that it was impossible to see further than 20 feet. During the storm, which lasted four days, Custer was incapacitated by one of his brief illnesses,[25] but was nursed back to health in a short time by Libbie and Maggie. In the camp, tents had split from the heavy weight of snow and many cases of frozen fingers and frostbitten toes were reported. When the horses were brought back to camp, they were a sorry-looking lot, gaunt from hunger and thirst, and many were without their tails and manes. Crammed together in close quarters, they had nibbled at each other in efforts to obtain a little nourishment.

As the snow thawed, the camp seemed isolated in a vast lake. Movement to and from town was exhausting for both man and animal, as mud clinging to hoof and boot taxed muscle and energy. Custer was well enough to inspect the camp and make preparations for the last phase of their trip, a march of 350 miles up the Missouri to Fort Rice, where they would join the Yellowstone expedition of more than 1,500 officers and men under Colonel D. S. Stanley. On June 10th, 1873, Custer and his 10 companies arrived at Fort Rice. For the next 10 days the 7th practiced drill formation topped with a grand review and inspection by the department commander, Major General Alfred H. Terry.

Libbie and Maggie bade farewell to their husbands, and with an escort went on to Bismarck where they boarded a train to St. Paul, and then home to Monroe, Michigan.

The expedition, when completely gathered on the bank of the Missouri, at Fort Rice, was composed as follows:

Ten companies of the 7th Cavalry, Lieutenant Colonel G. A. Custer, commanding;[26]

Four companies of the 8th Infantry, and six companies of the 9th Infantry, Lieutenant Colonel L. P. Bradley, commanding;

Five companies of the 22nd Infantry, Senior Captain C. A. Dickey, commanding;

Three companies of the 17th Infantry, and one company of the 6th Infantry, Major Robert E. A. Croften, commanding;

Five scouts from Fort Totten and five from Fort Wadsworth;

Seventy-five Ree Indian scouts under Lieutenant Daniel Brush, 17th Infantry, and

Two Rodman guns, manned by Company E, 22nd Infantry, Lieutenant John McAdam Webster, commanding.

Major Henry Lazelle, 8th Infantry, an officer of fine scientific attainments, was in charge of the scientific party to accompany the expedition. The scientists were: Mr. Allen, zoologist, mineralogist, and paleontologist; Mr. Powell, photographer; Mr. Kempitski, artist; Dr. Retter, geologist, and Mr. Bennett,* general assistant. These men were all provided with the necessary instruments and equipage, all highly skilled in their professions and anticipating some important discoveries. As long as the government was footing the bill, it stands to reason that they should be the first to know what resources lay in the path of the expedition.

On July 20th, 1873, the column moved west to the Yellowstone River with Custer and two companies of cavalry at its head selecting the route of travel. A herd of 700 cattle trailed with the troops, furnishing fresh beef, slaughtered as the need arose, at a rate of five days' fresh meat to two days' salted bacon. The forage ration was five pounds of oats per day to each animal. To carry forage, rations and equipage, 300

25. Conversation with Dr. Laurence Frost, Monroe, Michigan; the doctor believes this illness was more than a touch of pneumonia (March 21, 1974).

26. Custer also arranged to have Mr. Baliran, sutler, accompany the column with two wagonloads of liquor and trade goods, much to the dislike of General Stanley.

*First names unknown.

mule-drawn wagons accompanied the expedition. A number of these mules were new to the harness, and it was believed that they would give a great deal of trouble before they were properly broken to drive. The steamer "Far West" would take supplies up the Missouri and Yellowstone rivers to a planned location, and junction with the column, taking a direct route across the plains.

The orders governing the expedition were somewhat rigid, and marching allowances for officers and men were reduced to the lowest possible amount. One overcoat per each enlisted man, one blanket, two pairs of drawers, four pairs of socks, and two pairs of shoes were allowed to be carried on the body and in the knapsack. In addition, one pair of shoes for each enlisted man was carried in the wagons. The allowances for officers were one "A" tent for each field officer or captain, and one for each subaltern; one field desk for each battalion commander and one ordinary mess chest of cooking utensils for every four officers. Before the expedition got under way, an inspection was made to see that officers complied with the order. One officer was fortunate enough to be overlooked, and managed to bring his small cooking stove with him. However, it wasn't long before the stove came to grief due to peculiar circumstances.

A card game at the cavalry camp had continued into early morning hours, contrary to a rule that all games cease at midnight. Reveille was at 3, breakfast at 4, and advance sounded at 5 in the morning. The poker players were late at breakfast, and when the column moved out, leaving them behind, an officer of the guard rode up to see what the delay was. The iron cook stove was too hot to load in the wagon, and until it cooled enough so it could be handled, they had to wait. As the column moved further away, the officers became more and more concerned, and eventually loaded the hot stove into the wagon regardless of several pairs of blistered hands.

The surveyors had driven their stakes into the banks of the Yellowstone, impatiently waiting the column that was to protect them. Rains and a heavy hailstorm slowed the column's movements to a snail's pace, and during the first six days it was able to travel only 45 miles. Bloody Knife, Custer's most knowledgeable scout, had predicted that they would come upon hostiles in the vicinity of the Tongue River. On August 4th, Custer, with Bloody Knife and a squadron of cavalry, was detailed by General Stanley to go in advance of the wagons and survey the road. When eight or nine miles ahead, they halted and picketed their mounts in a grove of trees near the river to wait for the train to come up. During this wait, six Indians were seen moving in the direction of the picketed horses. The alarm was sounded, and Custer formed a line of dismounted skirmishers, driving the Indians off. They proved to be the decoy of a larger party lying in wait in a grove of woods to ambush the cavalry. Seeing that their maneuver had failed, the Indians, numbering up to 300, rode boldly out and advanced on the grove occupied by the cavalry. Custer threw his dismounted skir-

Art by E. L. Reedstrom

Taking a water break on the trail.

mishers out again. His total strength was a squadron of 80 men, commanded by Captain Myles Moylan, with Lieutenant Charles A. Varnum leading one company.

The Indians dismounted and moved in a semi-circle around the soldiers who had the river at their backs. Rapid firing commenced at a distance of 400 yards. While the largest group engaged Custer in front, another party crawled along the river bank and tried to stampede the cavalry horses. When this failed, they set fire to the grass in several places. After three hours of continued fire, ammunition began to run low. Moylan and Varnum suggested a charge to scatter the Indians but Custer delayed, hoping that the main command would come up and assist in capturing the Indians. When ammunition for the .50 caliber Sharps was almost gone, Custer ordered a charge. The Indians precipitately fled, dropping much equipment, and headed toward the Bad Lands.

In this engagement one man was slightly wounded in the arm, and one horse was injured from a rifle ball. The Indians' loss was two killed and several wounded. At the beginning of the fight, a group of Indians had left the war party in search of stragglers. Coming upon Dr. John Honsinger, veterinary surgeon, and Augustus Baliran, the cavalry sutler, who were about a mile from the column, the Indians killed them, taking their valuables and horses. Private John Ball of the cavalry, while out hunting, strayed too far and met a similar fate.

Four days after the Tongue River engagement, the column came upon the site of an Indian village whose people had abandoned a considerable amount of property in hasty withdrawal. General Stanley ordered Custer and 450 troopers to follow their trail. Custer led his men out and marched all night and most of the next day. At sundown, on August 9th, after covering some 40 miles, he arrived at the Yellowstone River where Indians had crossed 24 hours earlier, taking their families in bull boats and rafts. The next day the troops attempted to cross at the same point, which was 450 yards wide, but the current was too swift and deep to swim horses and men. Late that evening, Custer's camp was discovered by a small party. The next morning at dawn, he was attacked by 800 Indians, who came down to the river and began firing on his camp. Skirmishers were deployed on the bluffs, their carbines answering the Indians' fire. After two or three hours of firing, it was seen that 300 Indians had crossed the river above and below the cavalry camp, and were endeavoring to gain the bluffs at the rear. Custer ordered a mounted charge and pursued the Indians for eight miles. About this time, the main column arrived dispersing the Indians with artillery fire. In this fight, within two miles of the Big Horn, Custer and Adjutant Ketchum had horses shot from under them; Lieutenant Charles Braden was seriously wounded in the upper left thigh;[27] Private Tuttle, Custer's orderly was killed, and 20 troopers were slightly wounded. Four cavalry horses were killed and three were wounded. The Indian loss was estimated by Custer at 40 killed and wounded. The Indians were armed with heavy rifles and had plenty of ammunition. The band was mainly Hunkpapa Sioux, said to be led by Sitting Bull, supplied from Fort Peck[28] on the Missouri, a trading post, and Camp Cooke.[29]

An appropriation was made by Congress the previous year for making the trading post at Fort Peck a military post. A large quantity of arms and ammunition was shipped to this post marked "hardware," as a report to the Department of the Missouri clearly states:

---

27. The bullet was from a Henry rifle, fired at a range of not over 50 yards, went clear through the leg, badly shattering the bone and splitting it down to the knee. The story of transporting the wounded lieutenant 62 days after the fight on an improvised four-wheel stretcher is found in the U.S. Cavalry Journal, October 1904.

28. Fort Peck, near mouth of the Poplar River, Montana.

29. Camp Cooke, at mouth of the Judith River, Montana.

"The commanding officer of a military post on the Missouri, 1,500 miles from St. Louis, officially reports that the steamer which passed up the river laden exclusively with Government annuity goods had on board a number of boxes marked hardware, an inspection of which showed them to contain 2,000 Sharp's rifles, with abundance of ammunition. General Sheridan in forwarding this report says that if it is the policy of the Government to furnish Indians with firearms the muzzle-loader will answer every purpose for hunting or the chase; but if it is to put them on an equality with the Army, and make them superior to the frontier settlers, the purpose of the latest approved patterns of weapons is probably the proper thing to do."[30]

It was seriously felt that these agencies sadly needed investigation before the whole Indian question would once again erupt into a "total war" situation.

The Yellowstone Expedition arrived at Pompey's Pillar August 15th, and reached the Musselshell on the 19th, homeward bound. The geological survey and accompanying discoveries were important. The expedition had traveled 935 miles and completed the tour in 66 days. Custer was assigned to command Fort Abraham Lincoln for the winter, arriving there September 23rd with the 7th Cavalry. The health of the command was good, and Lieutenant Braden was getting on well.

30. A.N.J.; August 16th, 1873; page 4.

CHAPTER FIVE

THE LAND OF PROMISE

For the next three years, Fort Abraham Lincoln was home for the Custers, and the 7th Cavalry had a post of its own with room for half of the command assigned to duty there. The garrison was an answer to a growing demand for mounted troops to restrain hostilities by the Indians while the Northern Pacific Railroad was pushing for completion. Indian hit-and-run tactics left foot soldiers powerless to pursue and punish them, and the cavalry was the only solution to this problem.

Fort Lincoln had been built with quarters for six companies, having three barracks, seven detached officers' quarters, a granary, office and dispensary, guardhouse, commissary storehouse, quartermaster storehouse, laundresses' quarters, quartermaster stables, six cavalry stables, accommodating 600 horses, and an ordnance depot. All buildings were of frame structure, except for a few built from logs. The exteriors of the buildings were painted a dull drab slate color, but colors might be varied according to the choice of the commanding officer who had the buildings painted differently every year or two. Some distance from the laundresses' quarters (dubbed "Suds Row") were the log huts of the Indian scouts and their families.[1] It was said that the scouts lived more outside the buildings than within, as huge kettles were constantly bubbling over a campfire, while hungry Indian dogs lay nearby awaiting their chance to snatch a portion.

Off by itself was the sutler's store, with a billiard room attached. This was patronized by officers who sought recreation in a few games of pool or cards. A citizen from Bismarck was permitted to establish a barber shop near the sutler, keeping beards and mustachioed soldiers in full fashion with stateside "dudes." Soon afterward a cabin built of cottonwood with a canvas roof made its appearance. Here a photographer took up quarters charging soldiers one dollar for tintypes and three dollars for a cabinet photo.

On the bluffs, 270 feet above Fort Abraham Lincoln, was a sister garrison first occupied by infantry during the summer of 1872. This post was called Fort McKeen, established June 14th, 1872, by the 6th Infantry, Companies "B" and "C", under the command of Lieutenant-Colonel Daniel Huston, Jr., in compliance with Special Order No. 77, Headquarters Department of Dakota.[2] Fort McKeen was soon renamed Fort Abraham Lincoln, and thereafter that name designated both the infantry post formerly Fort McKeen, and the cavalry post nearby which was authorized by act of congress of March 3rd, 1873, with construction nearly completed that year.[3] After arrival of the 7th Cavalry in the fall of 1873, Fort Abraham Lincoln was expanded into a nine-company post by 1874, with detachments from the 6th and 17th Infantry regiments added to its garrison. The total strength was 655.

Life was not without hardships, especially during the winter months. Snow sifted beneath doors, windows and wall corners, piling in drifts outside, making any

1. Boots and Saddles; E. B. Custer; Harper & Bros., N. Y., 1885; page 98-99.

2. The Historical Significance of Ft. Lincoln State Park, A. O. Goplen; reprint from N. Dakota History — Vol. 13, No. 4 — 1946; page 183.

3. Ibid.

form of travel impossible. Water barrels behind the barracks and officers' quarters, froze to a depth of several inches and it was necessary to hack through the ice with an ax to get water. Usually the water was unpleasant tasting during extremely cold weather and snow was often scooped up and melted. Unseasoned lumber warped the buildings and firewood usually had to be dried for several days before it could be used. Frostbitten hands were a constant danger, often the swelling of fingers beyond their proportions caused losing the nails. Everyone was plagued with hordes of mosquitoes that seemed to be able to penetrate blankets. Fort Lincoln was notorious as the best breeding spot in the United States for these pests. Soldiers and civilians gave battle to them daily and ate and slept with them as well. "If these little devils are hell-bent on sticking with the Army," complained one disgruntled sergeant, "they should be sent to chase Indians, where there is more of him exposed." Cattle and horses were sometimes driven mad by these pests, and dogs sought temporary relief in holes which they dug into the sides of hills.

Hunting antelope, deer, buffalo, and rabbit not only gave the garrison a change of menu from government beef, but also gave the men sport and recreation. Eggs, often packed in barrels filled with oats, were shipped from St. Louis and on one occasion were received by the Custer family with the greatest delight. Libbie thought how fortunate folks were back in the states where eggs were plentiful, whereas on the frontier an egg was considered a supreme luxury. Company gardens grew a variety of vegetables. Men with experience in farming were designated to work the gardens each day, while not letting their daily duties go unattended. Although not included in rations issued to soldiers, the officers realized that to avoid scurvy, a substantial amount of fresh vegetables must be contained in their diets. Soldiers were encouraged to raise vegetables in post gardens, and not always were they successful with this project. Even with the abundance of fertilizer at cavalry posts, some gardens sprouted weeds, while others flourished.

Many diversions broke the monotony of garrison life for the women. Visiting went on among cavalry wives and infantry wives, and many of the "social get-togethers" seemed like a sorority meeting. Included were sewing clubs, recitals of poetry, read-

Courtesy Custer Battlefield Museum

Fort Lincoln, D.T., in an evening winter panorama. Officers and their ladies took full advantage of winter sports, with sleigh rides almost an every day occurance.

ing sessions for the children, and book clubs. Planning a ball or hop at one of the company barracks was undertaken with enthusiasm by the women in making up decorations, arranging the menu, and choosing the entertainment for the evening. Theatricals were always favored, and considerable talent was sometimes displayed on an improvised stage with hand-painted canvas scenery. Occasionally, a professional would be found in the ranks, delighted with the opportunity to perform. Theatricals were attended by citizens from Bismarck, and in turn, a group from Lincoln would perform at Bismarck. The 7th Cavalry band was an added attraction at these social affairs, and commanded a large audience at each performance when it wasn't attending the numerous maneuvers and drills.

Baseball games were played between companies, and drew cheering crowds. Fort Rice sent teams to Lincoln,[4] contesting for supremacy. The presence of officers and their ladies cooled violent and abusive partisanship. Soldiers who had no sporting blood sought entertainment by frequenting saloons and gambling houses at the "Point" across the river from the post. Saloons were numerous in Bismarck, and payday brought a rush of soldiers to bars and card tables. Games such as poker, Honest John, Keno, and Rush Rheuben took most of the pay from the soldiers' pockets.

The Black Hills Expedition was organized to explore the uncharted territory in the western and southwestern portion of Dakota and the eastern portion of Wyoming, with the intention of discovering practicable military routes between Fort Lincoln and Fort Laramie. It was said if more knowledge was learned of the resources in that particular area, military posts could be established with a better selection of suitable sites. Some believed that another purpose was to substantiate rumors that gold was to be found in the Black Hills. The government would, however, be pushing into this unexplored and sacred domain of the Sioux, violating the Treaty of 1868.

The original plan was to start the expedition off June 20th, 1874, but this was postponed to June 25th, because of awaiting the arrival of new arms. When these came, they were the latest improved pattern of Springfield carbines, calibrated for the 45/70 shell. Carrying these weapons in the field for experimentation and testing may have seemed a vital function to the government, but Custer would have rather kept the

4. Fort Rice's team was the "Athletes," and Lincoln had the "Actives." See *Custer's Gold;* Donald Jackson; page 84.

Courtesy Custer Battlefield Museum

Fort Abraham Lincoln, Dakota territory — The 7th Regimental Cavalry was the first to be garrisoned here.

Sharps improved .50 caliber carbine or retained the old reliable Spencer. Now, fully equipped with their new Colt. 45's and Springfield carbines, the command was ready to take to the field.[5]

The expedition left Fort Lincoln on July 2nd. It consisted of 10 companies of the 7th Cavalry,[6] Company I, 20th Infantry, and Company G, 17th Infantry. There was a battery of three Gatling guns, chambered for the .50 caliber and one-inch bore,[7] one three-inch Rodman gun, and a train of more than 100 wagons.[8] A detachment of 60 Indian scouts[9] were led by "Lonesome" Charley Reynolds and the Arikara-Sioux scout, Bloody Knife. Captain William Ludlow, chief engineer of the department, was assigned by the department commander as engineering officer. Unable to obtain funds for payment of salaries, Ludlow nevertheless secured the services of Professor N. H. Winchell of Minneapolis as geologist, and George Bird Grinnell, representing Professor Othniel N. Marsh of Yale College, who was to report on the paleontology and zoology of the region. Professor Winchell would also report on botany, assisted by Doctor J. W. Williams, assistant surgeon and chief medical officer. A photographer, W. H. Illingworth of St. Paul, went along to take pictures with the popular stereoscopic camera. Illingworth took along a wide variety of apparatus and chemicals in a spring wagon similar to one used on the Yellowstone Expedition in 1873. Ludlow had a

5. Black Hills Engineer; Nov. 1929; So. Dakota State School of Mines; page 230.

6. The 7th Cavalry left Fort Lincoln with six companies, picking up four more at Fort Rice.

7. The Gatlings could fire 250 rounds in one minute, and were good for 900 yards. In a two-column coverage of the Black Hills Expedition, the Army Navy Journal reported: "In case of a battle we shall also have the first opportunity yet presented, this side of the Atlantic, for testing the renowned Gatling gun in real action. In view of the contingency, Dr. Gatling hopes they will attack. For ourselves we are chiefly anxious for the scientific success of the expedition." (ANJ, Vol. XI, July 4th, 1874; page 745.)

8. This heavy train of supplies accompanied the troops with provisions for two months.

9. Rees, Santees, and a few Sioux.

Courtesy Custer Battlefield Museum *Photo by National Park Service, Department of the Interior*

General Custer's study at Fort Abraham Lincoln. Newspapers and journals are stacked high in left hand corner. To the far right are seen (left to right) an English .44 caliber Galand & Somerville revolver; two Smith & Wesson .38 caliber spur trigger tip-up barrel revolvers; and a Colt .45, 7½ inch barrel revolver.

detachment of engineer soldiers, consisting of two sergeants and four privates who were to keep two sets of notes of the route measured by prismatic compasses and odometers, while Ludlow's assistant, Mr. W. H. Wood, attended to the general topography and the astronomical observations for latitude and longitude.[10]

The expedition also included two practical miners, Horatio Nelson Ross and William T. McKay to study mineral deposits found along the trail. Brevet Brigadier General G. A. Forsyth and Brevet Lieutenant Colonel Fred Grant, President U. S. Grant's oldest son, also accompanied the expedition; Colonel Grant served as acting aide to Custer.[11] There was nothing to indicate that young Grant performed any vital service toward the expedition, but it did give the anti-Grant newspapers back East some material for editorial comment.

Newspaper correspondents included William Eleroy Curtis of the *Chicago Inter-Ocean,* Samuel J. Barrows, of the *New York Tribune,* who had been on the Yellowstone Expedition, and Nathan H. Knappen, of the *Bismarck Tribune,* had all one thing in common, to report officially the first findings of gold in the Black Hills.

Ahead of the ambulances and the artillery were 16 musicians astride white horses, playing the regiment's favorite tunes, "The Girl I Left Behind Me," and "GarryOwen." It was Custer's whim from time to time to ask the bandmaster to play while marching to stimulate the soldiers and take their minds off the long dull ride. Game darted out from time to time, and Custer's hounds were constantly baying and flushing birds and rabbits from brush and coulees. Buckskin-clad Custer, on his bay Dandy, was seen many times taking off alone after his dogs in hot pursuit, sometimes returning with small game or an antelope stretched across his saddle.

For all purposes, the expedition had been well fitted with equipment to carry out its plan. General Terry explained that the reason for the size of the expedition was to prevent any trouble with the Indians, and made no mention of any attempt to initiate strategy against them. The route was southwesterly toward the bend of the Heart River, across the north and south forks of the Cannonball and from there over the Belle Pierre Hills, and westward to Hiddenwood Creek where they camped the evening of July 8th. Wood for campfires was scarce and only found in river valleys. Water was not always in sufficient quantity, and some of it was impregnated with salts, making it disagreeable and injurious to drink. There was a fair amount of grass for the horses and the 300 beeves that were to be butchered when needed. The country bordering on the Heart River was reported good and that on the Cannonball as fair. Grand River country was poor, as well as that near the headwaters of the Moreau or Owl River.

10. A.N.J.; Ludlow's Report; Sept. 19th, 1874, page 91.

11. A.N.J.; Vol. XI; July 4th, 1874, pages 744-745.

Art by E. L. Reedstrom

"Bloody Knife," Custer's scout.

The route brought the troops in view of Slim Buttes and Bear Butte, and as they approached the Black Hills, they could well understand the reason for the name. The hills looked very high and dark under their covering of pine timber. On July 20th, they crossed the Belle Fourche. The character of the country changed considerably; there was now an abundance of grass, timber, fruit trees and flowers, and most appreciated, ice-cold water. Journalist W. E. Curtis reported: "The guides so far have proven trustworthy and competent. They have without exception led us to excellent camping grounds, have shown us better roads than were anticipated.[12]

Private John Cunningham of Company H, decided to go on sick report because he had been feeling rather poorly.[13] The medical officer believed that his diarrhea was not really serious and returned him to duty. After several days, his condition grew worse. Again he turned himself in to the first sergeant and was sent to the examining officer. He was returned to duty once more. The following day when the column resumed the march, Trooper Cunningham collapsed and fell from his horse. The medical officer, now convinced of his illness, placed the soldier on sick report and assigned him to ride in one of the better ambulances. Custer, however, had put "the best ambulance" to use carrying natural history collections of the expedition, and there was no room for Cunningham. (These new vehicles provided much more comfort than the other broken-down contraptions.) The ailing trooper was obliged to ride in one of the older and less comfortable ambulances. On July 21st, after the column descended into the valley of the Red Water, a branch of the Belle Fourche, Cunningham died in camp around midnight. Much blame was cast on Captain J. W. Williams, medical officer of the right battalion,[14] who had examined Cunningham and had refused to administer any drugs. He was accused of being drunk the night the trooper died.

Cunningham was wrapped in canvas and laid in an ambulance the next morning. As the men were saddling their horses at the picket line, gunfire was heard. Troopers rushed from their companies to the scene of the shooting, and found Private George Turner, of Company M, lying on the ground with a bullet wound in the abdomen. Private William Roller stood over the wounded trooper, a revolver still in his hand. The pair had quarreled for years, finally drawing on each in a typical showdown.

Turner was also wrapped in canvas and placed alongside Cunningham, and as soon

12. The Black Hills Engineer; Nov. 1929; published by The South Dakota State School of Mines; page 234

13. A.N.J.; Aug. 15, 1874; page 8.

14. The expedition had three medical officers: Dr. A. C. Bergen, assigned to the infantry battalion; Dr. S. J. Allen, Jr., assigned to the left cavalry battalion, and Capt. J. W. Williams handled the right battalion and was also chief medical officer of the command.

Courtesy South Dakota State Historical Society

Captain Smith, the Custer Expedition wagonmaster.

as the command went into camp on Inyan Kara Creek on July 22nd, both were buried as the companies lined up for funeral services. After the graves were covered, fires were set to conceal any sign of the burial plots from the Indians.[15]

After this camp near Inyan Kara, the route led in an irregular easterly direction along a tributary of Spring Creek. The valley contained a variety of wild flowers in almost incredible numbers. As the command waded through the meadows knee-high, soldiers scooped up handsful of flowers, decorating bridles and festooning their hats. From an elevated rock ledge the band played popular tunes of the day: "The Blue Danube," "Artist's Life," "The Mocking Bird," and "GarryOwen." The valley echoed with music in a weird and fascinating mood, echoing each note in double harmony, while the soldiers, in full enjoyment, absorbed the fragrant sweet air from the meadows. Custer, revelled with delight, and because of the abundance of flowers covering the valley floor, he named it Floral Valley.

15. It was common for Indians to dig up a grave and rob or mutilate the body.

Continuing up the valley, Custer wrote in one of his dispatches: "Favored as we had been in having Floral Valley for our roadway to the west of the Black Hills, we were scarcely less fortunate in the valley which seemed to me to meet us on the interior slope. The rippling stream of clear cold water, the counterpart of that we had ascended the day before, flowed at our feet and pointed out the way before us, while along its banks grew beautiful flowers, surpassed but little in beauty and profusion by their sisters who had greeted us the day before. After advancing down this valley about 14 miles, our course being almost southeast, we encamped in the midst of grazing, whose only fault, if any, was its great luxuriance. Having preceded the main column, as usual, with our escort of two companies of Cavalry, E and C, and Lieutenant Wallace's detachment of scouts, I came upon an Indian campfire still burning, and which with other indications showed that a small party of Indians had encamped there the previous night, and had evidently left that morning in ignorance of

Courtesy South Dakota State Historical Society

Custer's wagon train on the prairies, four columns near the North Dakota and South Dakota line.

our close proximity. Believing that they would not move far, and that a collision might take place at any time unless a friendly understanding was arrived at, I sent my head scout, Bloody Knife, and 20 of his braves to advance a few miles and reconnoitre the valley. The party had been gone but a few minutes when two of Bloody Knife's young men came galloping back and informed me that they had discovered five Indian lodges a few miles down the valley, and that Bloody Knife, as directed, had concealed his party in a wooded ravine, where they awaited further orders. Taking E Company with me, which was afterwards reinforced by the remainder of the scouts and Colonel Hart's company, I proceeded to the ravine where Bloody Knife and his party lay concealed, and from the crest beyond obtained a full view of the five Indian lodges, about which a considerable number of ponies were grazing.[16]

Custer sent an interpreter with a flag of truce, along with two Sioux scouts to tell the occupants of the lodges that the troops were friendly and meant them no harm. After this was done, a signal was given and Custer and his company surrounded the lodges. Dismounting, and entering the village, Custer shook hands with its occupants and invited them to visit his camp, where he promised to present them with flour, sugar, and coffee. The invitation was accepted. To the head men it was suggested that the Sioux should encamp with the soldiers for a few days and give information of the surrounding country, in return for the rations. With this understanding, Custer left the lodges, whose occupants numbered 27. Later that afternoon, "One Stab," the chief, and four others visited Custer's camp and asked for the rations, saying they would join the camp the following morning. Custer writes in his report of the incident, ". . . I ordered presents of sugar, coffee, and bacon to be given them; and, to relieve their pretended anxiety for the safety of their village during the night, I ordered a party of 15 of my command to return with them and protect them during the night. But from their great disinclination to wait a few minutes until our party could saddle up, and from the fact that two of the four had already slipped away, I was of the opinion that they were not acting in good faith. In this I was confirmed when the two remaining ones set off at a gallop in the direction of the village. I sent a party of our scouts to overtake them and request their return; not complying with this request, I sent a second party with orders to repeat the request, and if not complied with, to take hold of the bridles of their ponies and lead them back, but to offer no violence. When overtaken by our scouts one of the two Indians seized the musket of one of the scouts and endeavored to wrest it from him. Failing in this, he released his hold after the scout became dismounted in the struggle, and set off as fast as his pony could carry him, but not before the musket of the scout was discharged. From blood discovered afterwards, it was evident that either the Indian or his pony was wounded.[17]

One Stab was brought back to camp when it was found that the entire party had packed up and fled. The visit of the four Indians to obtain rations was a ruse to cover the flight of the rest. One Stab, who claimed to belong to both Red Cloud and Spotted Tail's agencies, protested, but remained with Custer for three days acting as guide. The chief said he had recently returned from the hostile camp on the Powder River, where a fight with the Bozeman exploring party had cost them 10 dead braves. One Stab was allowed to leave, as Custer had promised, and was reunited with his family.

After a further march of more than 10 miles, Custer went into camp early in the day, five miles from the western base of Harney's Peak. The following day, while

16. Army Navy Journal; Aug. 22nd, 1874.

17. A.N.J.; Aug. 22nd, 1874.

Courtesy South Dakota State Historical Society

Custer's permanent camp, French Creek (Golden Valley). Horses in foreground.

the command rested in camp, exploring parties set out in various directions. Horatio N. Ross and William McKay rode their wagon in and out of creek beds and up and over hills, prospecting for gold. Panning was the first step necessary to detect traces of gold in dry washes or creek beds but without water, little could be done. From dry washes, samples were brought to water and panned out there. In the dry washes, bedrock was reached by digging with a shovel, and a whisk broom, or a bristle brush was used to sweep around the imbedded rocks, collecting moist sand and placing it in a pan to be washed out. Gold generally runs with black iron granules in creek bottoms, imbedded between rocks and crevices. By working up the creek bed after color has been found, the prospector may find a larger deposit. The expedition did not stay longer than a day or two in any one area, so the findings were only traces of color here and there with an occasional showing of pinhead nuggets.

When a prospector was working a creek with an ample supply of water, his method of panning was as follows: After a scoopful of gravel or sand was dumped into the pan, it was covered with water and the pan was swirled around by hand, washing much of the mud away. The prospector then raised the pan from the water while continuing the circular motion accompanied by small jerks in and out of the water to wash away the lighter sand and cloudy water, leaving the gold-carrying residue. After the panner had eliminated rock and sand, leaving only the iron granules and the gold, the next step was to separate these two metals. A small magnet took out the iron, taking care not to carry off the few gold particles. This simple method is still used by prospectors searching for gold in the western mountains.[18]

Ross and McKay found likely looking

18. This author has spent six years prospecting in the West and has learned many tricks from older miners, using the same process the "forty-niners" were accustomed to use.

Courtesy South Dakota State Historical Society

Custer's permanent camp, French Creek (Golden Valley). Dead tree branch in foreground.

gold-bearing quartz and to analyze this, another process was used to separate the gold from the rock. An iron mortar and pestle was used to crush the rock and pulverize it to dust. This process was long and tedious. While one person ground the rock into small pieces, the other took notes and marked the outcropping from which the specimen had been taken. By keeping records of each specimen, a general assessment could be established for the area. After the rock was pulverized, it was put in the gold pan and the same process of washing it out was used. One of the easiest things to forget is to burn out a gold pan after it had been commonly used to wash hands and faces in. Film from soap will cling to the metal pan after the wash water has been thrown out. If this residue is not burned out, the result of any further panning will be negative. This is brought up because when a little gold was found in Custer Gulch, soldiers in their excitement tried to pan with tin plates and drinking cups, probably without success.[19] By observing Ross and McKay daily at their chore of panning the creeks, the soldiers had some acquaintance with the art.

Castle Valley was named for the castellated limestone ridges or precipices overhanging the route. The command camped there to examine the surrounding country during which time four surveying parties were sent out with shovels and pans to explore streams and tributaries. Beavers were seen in great numbers industriously making reservoirs of the streams with their dams. Springs were numerous and cold and pure. The soil was moist and fertile, and the vegetation fresh. Most of July 28th was spent in trying to find a way down Castle Creek. Custer had relied too heavily on an Indian

19. We are not assuming that this happened. Ross and McKay were experts in their field; however, the inexperience of a "greenhorn" panning some overlooked creek bed with a greasy pan or tin plate may have resulted in their total loss of interest.

guide, and an interpreter who misconstrued the guide's directions. The column wheeled about and made a second camp on Castle Creek, only a few miles below the previous one. The course on July 29th led southeasterly from Castle Creek up a small tributary, where was found heavy grass with wild oats and barley. A deeply worn Indian trail was followed up the creek, crossing a high prairie and passing boulders of red quartz. The wagon train in its slow and laborious fording of creeks and washes often dropped behind several miles but usually caught up in late evening.

July 30th, the command traveled most of the day through a pastoral scene of scattered woods and tall grass. Professor Winchell scribbled in his notebook, "The gold seekers who accompanied the expedition report the finding of gold in the gravel and sand along this valley."[20] The command went into camp on French Creek about three o'clock in the afternoon and remained there until the morning of August 1st. This allowed the animals to shed their burdens and rest their backs. Custer sent out surveying parties, and the gold hunters had the opportunity to prospect the area. While Custer and one company of cavalry attempted to climb Harney's Peak, the camp organized a baseball game which proved more exciting than the findings of a few glittering grains of gold. Up till now, the men were somewhat skeptical of any sizeable amounts of gold being found worth the taking in the Black Hills.

When the game was finished, the Actives scored 11 runs, the Athletes 6. Colonel Joseph G. Tilford, who had won a bet on the Actives, stretched a canvas between trees and gave a champagne supper for some of the officers. Illingworth, the photographer, was summoned with his equipment to photograph the posing officers sitting around the table filled with bottles. Colonel Fred Grant, notorious for his drinking parties, insisted on having his picture taken at the head of the table.

August 1st the expedition moved three miles down French Creek to give the animals fresh pasture. Custer announced that a courier would be sent to Fort Laramie within 36 hours, and mail would be taken.

Bloody Knife was summoned by Custer and asked for a scout to carry dispatches to Fort Laramie, 200 miles south of the command. Bloody Knife shook his head and replied, "My warriors are brave, but they are wise. They will carry a bag of letters to Fort Lincoln, but I cannot ask them to go through the Sioux country to Laramie." Bloody Knife knew that during this particular time of year, young Sioux braves were out hunting in parties so that the plains

Courtesy South Dakota State Historical Society *Photo by Illingworth*

After a company baseball game a champagne supper was given by Colonel Tilford. Colonel Fred Grant insisted on having the head of the table. Fred Benteen (middle of picture, sitting) looks on (1874).

20. Black Hills Engineer; page 245.

Courtesy South Dakota State Historical Society *Photo by Illingworth*

Custer's camp in Castle Creek Valley.

would be full of them. These scouts were Arikarees, hereditary enemies of the Sioux, and Bloody Knife was wise enough not to ask any one of them to undertake such a suicidal trip. Dispatches must be sent and Custer pondered the question of what to do. Charley Reynolds was sitting close by cleaning a revolver seemingly unattentive to the conversation. After a moment or two, Reynolds looked up and said, "I'll carry the mails to Laramie, General."

"I wouldn't ask you to go, Reynolds," said Custer.

"I have no fear," responded the scout quietly; "When will the mails be ready?"

"I was intending to send something tomorrow night," replied Custer.

"I'll go tomorrow night."

As Reynolds strode away, Custer remarked: "There goes a man who is a constant succession of surprises to me. I am getting so that I feel humble in his presence. Scarcely a day passes — and I have known him three years — that does not develop some new and strong trait in his character. I would as soon have asked my brother Tom to carry mail to Laramie as Reynolds."[21]

The next day Reynolds was seen leading an old bony, dun-colored horse to the farrier. The horse's shoes were taken off, the hoofs pared, and a set of leather shoes were fitted to buckle around the fetlocks. When asked what they were for, Reynolds explained that it was a little dodge of his to fool the Indians as they would make no trail. Reynolds expected the trip to take three to four days, no more than five. He packed as many days' rations as he thought he might need, and an ample supply of ammunition. He distributed most of the shells in his prairie belt so as not to off-balance him, and the rest were carried in saddlebags. After eating dinner, he lay down under a wagon

21. The Daily Grafic; N. Y.; July 10th, 1876.

and took a nap. Late that afternoon, an engineering party started off in the direction Reynolds was to take, and saddling his horse and strapping on a canvas bag containing the letters, he accompanied them. The party rode till 10 o'clock, and went into camp in a cluster of brush and trees near a brook. After a fire was lit and a pot of coffee made, the men gathered around the campfire watching Reynolds as he checked his saddle girth. Finding his gear in satisfactory condition, he mounted and spurred his horse lightly. "Lonesome Charley" turned momentarily in his saddle in the direction of the engineers, touched the brim of his hat with a farewell salute, and rode off into the darkness.[22]

Ahead of Reynolds lay a trackless wilderness, not a foot of which had the scout ever seen before. Because of the danger of hostile Indians, he traveled at night, guiding himself with a compass and the stars. Reynolds had never been to Fort Laramie, but he knew the general direction. After four nights of riding and three days of sleeping in the brush, he reached his destination with the mail and dispatches from Custer.

There has been considerable discussion as to the exact date when gold was first discovered during Custer's Black Hills Expedition. From the first moment after entering the Black Hills, Ross and McKay found gold-bearing quartz of potential value. When camped at Harney's Peak, color began to show with pinpoints of gold after panning a small creek bed. A sand bar yielded five to seven cents a pan; but had more water been available, better samplings might have been possible. At Custer Gulch, color was found in loose soil along the creek bed, netting 10 cents a pan. Ross, in his estimate of the area, doubted if gold would be found to yield more than $50 to $75 a day. It was thought that if the expedition had remained in one camp long enough to search further or follow up a potential "hot spot," a closer survey could have been conducted yielding better samples than that already found.

Dispatches from the three correspondents sent with Reynolds soon triggered newspaper reports with the finds of gold and silver, the "New El Dorado of America." The Bismarck Tribune, August 12th, was the first to publish news of the discovery, devoting the entire front page to the story. Meanwhile, in Custer's Gulch, soldiers waited for the general to return from his reconnaissance of the south fork of the Cheyenne. They had found what they were looking for and wanted to return to Fort Lincoln.

Base camp was broken on August 6th at 4:30 a.m. for the return trip to Fort Lincoln, 400 miles away. The trail was retraced for 30 miles, then turned eastward toward Bear Butte. After an advance party had located a

Courtesy Herb Peck, Jr. *Photo by Illingworth*

Sioux camp in Castle Creek Valley.

22. Some historians have dubbed this story of Reynolds' trip to Laramie pure legend, but it is reported in The Daily Grafic; New York, July 10th, 1876. It was signed "C," possibly written by William E. Curtis, correspondent who accompanied the expedition. D. Jackson's "Custer's Gold" says Reynolds had been chosen to carry the mails out of the Black Hills at the beginning of the expedition. See page 86.

Courtesy South Dakota State Historical Society *Photo by Illingworth*

First Black Hills Expedition, July 15th to late August, 1874. Custer's officer in camp. (Left to right), William Ludlow, Capt. of Engineers and Chief Engineer, Department of Dakota; Frederick D. Grant, Lt. Col. and Aide de Camp to Lt. Gen. Philip H. Sheridan; Lt. Tom W. Custer, 7th Cavalry; Lt. Donald McIntosh; Capt. Thomas H. French, 7th Cavalry, leaning on elbow; Lt. George D. Wallace, standing; Lt. James Calhoun (silhouetted), 7th Cavalry; Capt. George W. Yates, 7th Cavalry; unknown, sitting; unknown, sitting, unknown, standing; unknown, standing; Prof. George Bird Grinnell, with watch chain, standing; Maj. and Surgeon John W. Williams, sitting on ground; unknown, sitting in camp chair; Lt. Col. and Bvt. Major Gen. George A. Custer, 7th Cavalry, reclining. Prof. A. B. Donaldson, University of Minnesota, in shirt sleeves; Lt. Thomas M. McDougall, 7th Cavalry; Bloody Knife, Ree scout; Maj. J. G. Tilford, 7th Cavalry; Prof. N. H. Winchell, University of Minnesota (?), standing; Lt. E. G. Mathey, hands crossed on knee; Unknown sitting in chair; unknown, standing; unknown, sitting; Lt. Charles A. Varnum, 7th Cavalry, leaning on elbow; Capt. V. K. Hart, 7th Cavalry; Capt. Lloyd Wheaton, 20th Infantry; unknown, standing; Capt. Myles Moylan, 7th Cavalry; Lt. H. M. Harrington, in campaign hat, standing; Capt. Owen Hale, 7th Cavalry; unknown, standing (cap); Capt. F. W. Benteen, 7th Cavalry, campaign hat; Lt. Edward S. Godfrey, campaign hat; Lt. Francis M. Gibson, campaign hat.

campsite, Bloody Knife pointed out a large grizzly bear about 75 yards away, loping along the side of a hill. Custer reached for his Remington sporting rifle, .50 caliber,[23] and fired a shot that hit the animal in the thigh. The 800-pound grizzly wheeled around only to receive several more shots from Custer, Bloody Knife, and Ludlow, all firing at the same time. The bear dropped in his tracks, his huge form still quivering with life. Bloody Knife rushed upon the animal thrusting his hunting knife into the jugular vein dispatching him immediately. A close look showed the grizzly to be an old male, his teeth worn to stubs, his body riddled with scars. While the three hunters were trying to decide whose bullet had brought the animal down, Illingworth set up his equipment and took a photograph of the hunters and their prize. The subject of gold seemed to be forgotten for the moment, as the next day rifle fire echoed from hill to hill. The end results were 100 mainly white tailed deer shot by the soldiers.

On the afternoon of August 13th, Private James King of Company H died from a short and sudden illness.[24] It was ordered that King's body be sewn in a canvas and buried that evening. Colonel Tilford protested that no man in his battalion should be buried two hours after death and that a proper site for the burial should be picked and regular services held. Custer would not wait until morning, and said that if the left wing insisted on staying for the burial, they would be responsible for catching up with the rest of the command. The gray twilight of morning broke on August 14th, as Com-

23. Gun Report, Oct., 1968; Gen. Custer Favored a Remington, by L. A. Frost; page 13.

24. Custer's Gold; Don Jackson; page 96.

pany H prepared a final salute to their deceased comrade. Their faces wore the most solemn of expressions, as Colonel Benteen read the service, his gray hair tossing in a soft breeze. "We at death leave one place to go to another; he departs from a howling wilderness and goes to a heavenly paradise."[25]

The expedition passed a little to the east of Bear Butte on the morning of August 16th, the course lying nearly due north. After crossing the Belle Fourche River, Custer's scouts were met by four Indians en route to the Cheyenne Agency from their camp on Tongue River. Through sign language the scouts were told that Sitting Bull and 5,000 followers were lying in ambush to intercept the expedition at Short Pine Hills. The scouts reported to Custer what they had heard. Word was passed through the command, and everyone prepared for the expected ambush. The column marched northward passing between West Short Pine and East Short Pine Hills without seeing interceptors. It was decided that the report was a hoax, as no signs of pony tracks were seen. Custer later learned that the rumor was picked up by newspapers back East reporting that 4,000 Indians had jumped the column and a fight actually had occurred.[26] It was presumed that the Arikara mail carriers had passed the story on to the Fort Rice mail rider, who in turn reported the incident.

The draft horses and mules could scarcely keep pace with the rest of the column and they were constantly lagging behind. Camp was made the night of August 19th, near the northwestern base of Cave Hills where men and animals rested after the grueling march, averaging 30 miles a day. From this point, the route continued north and west, over a rolling prairie which the Indians had burned. The column avoided the charred prairie and sought the Little Missouri, where among the badlands, wood, water, and grass were found. Having had better traveling the last five days, they remained in camp August 21.

Courtesy National Archives *Photo by Illingworth*

Custer claims his grizzly. Left to right: Bloody Knife, General Custer, Private Noonan, Captain William Ludlow.

The hardships were accompanied by disciplinary problems. Colonel Tilford, who agreed to carry water kegs for companies K and H, had to turn his wagon over to the quartermaster for violation of an order by Custer, prohibiting carrying water for other companies. A teamster was spread-eagled to a wagon wheel for several hours because he had let two mules stray among the tents in camp. A long line of sick and fatigued soldiers stood outside the surgeon's tent seeking either medical attention or relief from duty. And finally, one, Sergeant Charles Sempker of Company L died of

25. Shallow graves were usually dug with haste on expeditions, and lime, often carried by the cavalry for their latrines, was scattered over the deceased as well as on the surface of the grave, as the lime helped to decompose the body, it also discouraged wild animals from digging up the remains. ("Along this line of forts, as the bodies were buried in the cemetery, the graves were covered with lime, and the ground looked as if there had been a slight snowstorm." E. B. Custer, Microfilm reel 6, No. 6402, Custer Battlefield Museum.)

26. Custer's Gold; Jackson; page 98.

chronic diarrhea and was buried August 26th by his company.

On the sixtieth day, August 30th, at 4:30 p.m., the column reached Fort Abraham Lincoln, at the end of a trail of 1,205 surveyed miles. Marching ahead were Lieutenant Wallace's scouts, behind them came mounted officers in single file with Custer. Next came the band, playing "GarryOwen," trumpeters leading the cavalry companies marching in columns of four; the wagon train, half-empty, but with some wagons filled with a natural history collection of snakes, owls, and various four-legged animals, rolled in behind exhausted rawboned mules. The infantry were the sorriest sight and last to reach the post. Clothing was spattered with mud and covered with dust. Some soldiers had wrapped their shoes with strips of gunny sack or canvas to keep them from falling off. From every dwelling on the post came forth their occupants to welcome the regiment. Soldiers waved their hats, women and children waved hankies and miniature flags, their faces streaked with tears. The chanting of Indian women began, but was drowned out by the band. As some of the officers slipped from their saddles to embrace their wives, Elizabeth Custer stepped forward to greet her husband, only to faint momentarily in his arms.

Courtesy U.S. War Department

General Custer after the Black Hills Expedition in 1874. A rose in his lapel.

Captain William Ludlow, in summarizing the information obtained on the expedition wrote, "Whatever may ultimately be determined as to the existence of large amounts of precious metal in the Black Hills, and the evidence gathered on the trip I conclude was on the whole discouraging to that supposition — the real wealth and value of the country are, beyond doubt, very great. Utterly dissimilar in character to the remaining portion of the territory in which it lies, its fertility and freshness, its variety of resource and delightful climate . . ."[27] Custer's brief summary, sent to the War Department on September 8th, touches on the Indian question and disparaged the finding of gold: "While I regard the gold discoveries as very important and of promising richness, I do not think they have been prosecuted to the extent, or that sufficient information has been obtained concerning them, to warrant an immense influx of gold hunters into that region in advance of a more thorough and deliberate examination . . ."[28]

News of the gold finds in the Black Hills brought an invasion of poverty-stricken whites. The panic of 1873 had plunged the nation into a six-year depression, and the rumors of new gold field discoveries gave the people and the economy a lift. But though the hopes of exhilarated prospectors had been aroused, they were to be disappointed. Four days after the official an-

27. Black Hills Engineer, 1929; page 260.

28. Ibid.; page 261.

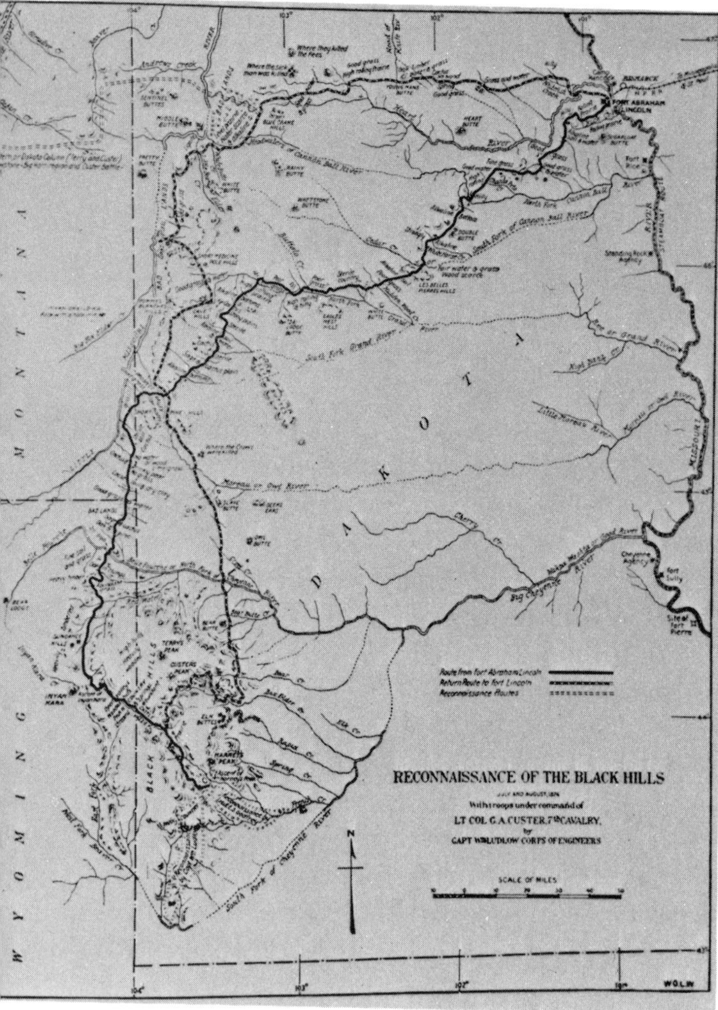

Courtesy South Dakota State Historical Society
Ludlow's map showing Custer's route to and from the Black Hills.

nouncement of the discovery of gold, General Sheridan, from his Chicago headquarters, received information concerning the "grand rush" to the Black Hills by civilians. He immediately wired General Terry, in command of the Department of Dakota, to prohibit all white persons from entering the Black Hills; with further orders to move his forces along the Missouri River and the Platte, seizing wagons and outfits of all persons attempting to enter the Indians' domain, and destroy them. Violators were to be placed under arrest and held in the nearest military post. This order was carried out in the fall of 1874 and the spring of 1875. A number of parties did succeed in reaching the diggings, but stayed for a short time because of the weather; but they came out with exaggerated stories of the richness of the placers. Those who stayed on were removed by the soldiers but were speedily acquitted by local civil courts.

The Indians were displeased with the invasion of the Black Hills, but remained peaceful. The government assured them that the public would be kept out of the territory until a treaty could be negotiated for the purchase of the Black Hills. In June, 1875, the Secretary of Interior appointed a commission to secure from the Sioux, the right of mining along with other concessions. Reservation Indians offered to sell the Black Hills for $70,000,000, rejecting the government offer of $6,000,000.[29] The non-reservation Teton bands refused to sell under any conditions, warning all white men to keep out.

Under the Treaty of 1868, three-fourths of the adult male Indians would have to consent to any instrument of sale, relinquishing title to the Blacks Hills for any sum the government would be willing to pay. No matter how hard the commission tried, they were rejected. Frustrated, the commissioners returned to Washington, leaving the issue unsettled. The Indians now believed that the hills would be taken by force, regardless of existing treaty stipulations. The government withdrew military forces guarding entrances into the Black Hills, thus opening this area to the adventurous white man who poured in from every section of the country.[30] The wild Sioux bands retreated further into the wilderness, far from the agencies, their ranks now swelling with hot-tempered young warriors. War was inevitable. Sitting Bull and Crazy Horse would soon score their greatest triumph over the white intruder.

29. History of the Dakota or Sioux Indians; by D. Robinson; page 421.

30. Ibid.; page 421.

C H A P T E R S I X

CUSTER'S MARCH TO VALHALLA

Winter and spring of 1875 found the troops performing their usual garrison duties along with endless hours of escort duty. Nefarious activity on post forced Custer to take action into his own hands and play the role of detective. He and Lieutenant Carland of the 6th Infantry, a former lawyer, had reason to believe that granary thefts on post were connected with certain characters in Bismarck. The difficulty they faced was tracing the stolen grain to the suspected parties, and what to do about it if they were successful. Custer could make no arrests outside the garrison, and any charges would have to be brought before civil authorities.

Playing the role of sleuths, the officers gathered evidence, until they uncovered a network of men implicated in the thefts. One day before the ice broke up on the river, Custer ordered the regiment to prepare to move out fully equipped and armed much to the surprise of many of his officers. Civilians in Bismarck were just as astonished when the column moved into the little town. Orders were issued to companies to search the various places pointed out by Custer, whereupon stolen grain was found bearing the government brand on each bag. Stolen grain was even found in the mayor's own warehouse, and being a prominent merchant as well as mayor, he showed a proper amount of surprise at the discovery. After a series of arrests (the mayor now collaborating with the military) the thieves were hustled back to Fort Lincoln and placed in the guardhouse. Their trial, in Fargo, Dakota Territory, continued for many months and ended with the convictions of the leading conspirators.

Early in December, 1874, Charley Reynolds had reported to Custer that an Indian at Standing Rock agency had boasted about the murders of Dr. Honsinger, the veterinarian and sutler Baliran, on the Yellowstone expedition. The Indian was named Rain-in-the-Face, a noted Sioux warrior, and he had come into the Standing, Rock agency to spend the winter, along with other Uncpapas. Custer immediately dispatched Captain George W. Yates and Lieutenant Tom Custer under sealed orders, along with a detachment of cavalry, to arrest the Indian and bring him back to Fort Lincoln. The troop left on December 12th and traveled 50 miles by night to the reservation, where Rain-in-the-Face was seized at the agency trader's store, returned to Fort Lincoln and placed in the guard house.

Kinsmen of the Sioux chief came to the garrison and pleaded for his release, but it was refused. After many hours of interrogation, Custer was successful in inducing Rain-in-the-Face to confess to the crime. The next day, a number of officers were present as witnesses, while the Sioux chief gave his account of the murders. He told of shooting Dr. Honsinger, and said the old man rode a little distance before falling from his horse. The sutler, Augustus Baliran, on seeing the Indians, had hidden in some heavy brush, but came out, signalling to them with his hands above his head. As they approached, Baliran gave them his hat as a peace offering, but they shot him, first with a gun, then pinned him to the ground with arrows. Honsinger was also shot with arrows and his brains bashed out with a stone mallet. Neither man was scalped because the doctor was bald and the sutler wore his hair short, otherwise they were badly mutilated.

Some believed that Rain-in-the-Face was nowhere near the incident, that he was far off hunting buffalo a hundred miles northeast, and that Custer had bullied him into confessing to the murders.[1] Others said that the interpreter whom Custer had selected took advantage of the opportunity to get rid of his personal enemies, and that Rain-in-the-Face did not understand what the interpreter was repeating to the white chief.

Custer could not decide what punishment would be justifiable for the crimes committed, and so he turned his attention to other matters. Rain-in-the-Face spent several months in the guardhouse until his chance came for escape. With the aid of two other prisoners, he cut a hole in the rear wall large enough to creep through and they quickly made their escape into the night.[2] There have been questions why the prisoners were not pursued by the army, and why no military action was taken against the sentry whose responsibility it was to keep a close guard on the prisoners, leading to an opinion that Rain-in-the-Face was allowed full opportunity to escape. After joining Sitting Bull's band of hostiles, the Sioux chief sent word to Fort Lincoln by way of agency Indians, that he was awaiting his revenge for his imprisonment. Legend has it that he blamed Tom Custer for his arrest and threatened to cut his heart out and eat it.

Graft and corruption were practiced by some dishonest agents of the government. On each reservation there was an Indian agent appointed by the Indian Bureau of the Department of the Interior, whose duty it was to furnish food and clothing to the Indians according to the terms stipulated in treaties. Indians in their ignorance, might sign for twenty bags of flour and receive only one. At times, a quarter portion of flour would be mixed with powdered clay, and often the flour was dark and of inferior quality. Pork rations were so poor that when the Indians received them, they threw them away in utter disgust. Cattle furnished them often were diseased, or undersized and underfed. Moth-eaten blankets and inferior clothing were issued and billed at the full value as first-class merchandise. As dishonest agents and traders grew rich with their money-making schemes, political influence in and out of the Indian Department kept investigators from finding legal evidence of fraud. Army officers, who knew the conditions, were powerless to act while they functioned under the War Department, since the Indian agents were under the Department of the Interior. The corruptive funds of this department were so great that it was impossible to abolish it even by appealing to Congress to do so through public opinion. Politicians of both parties needed election funds, and nothing other than graft money held the Indian Department together.

The summer of 1875 was without campaigns for the 7th Cavalry, dress parades and routine drills continued with the usual escort duty. The Custers spent their time reading newspapers, entertaining, and solving the daily problems of a post commander. Troopers complained of exorbitant prices charged by the sutler,[3] while in Bismarck the same item could be purchased at a cheaper price. Custer investigated and found the sutler's annual profit to be fifteen thousand dollars, three thousand of which he kept, with the remainder going to War Department grafters. When nothing seemed to induce the sutler to lower his prices, Custer instructed his officers to purchase supplies in Bismarck and resell the articles to the troopers at cost. Angered by this, the sutler wrote to Secretary of War

1. "Rain-in-the-Face and Curly, the Crow" by Thomas B. Marquis (1934)

2. A Life of Maj. Gen. G. A. Custer; Frederick Whittaker; page 536; Sheldon & Co., N.Y.

3. Robert C. Seip was civil sutler or post trader at Fort A. Lincoln.

Courtesy National Archives

Officers of the 7th U.S. Cavalry at Fort Abraham Lincoln shortly before the massacre. Front row from left to right: Second Lieutenant Bronson, 6th Infantry (sitting); Second Lieutenant G. D. Wallace, 7th Cavalry (standing); General George Armstrong Custer* (standing); Second Lieutenant B. H. Hodgson.* 7th Cavalry (standing); Elizabeth Bacon Custer, wife of General Custer (standing); Captain George W. Yates,* 7th Cavalry (sitting on step); Miss Annie Bates (sitting on step); Lieutenant Colonel W. P. Coclin, 17th Infantry (standing); Mrs. Donald McIntosh (standing; husband killed at Little Big Horn); Captain Myles Moylan, 7th Cavalry (sitting at end of row; with Reno at the Little Big Horn). Second row from left to right: Mrs. George W. Yates (first one in second row; sitting on steps; husband killed with Custer at Little Big Horn); Mrs. James Calhoun (sitting on steps; General Custer's sister; husband killed with Custer); First Lieutenant Charles A. Varnum, 7th Cavalry (sitting on steps; with Reno at the Little Big Horn; last survivor of the 7th Cavalry under Custer and as far as known he is the only one living who was in this photograph); Mrs. Myles Moylan, wife of Captain Moylan, 7th Cavalry (sitting on steps); First Lieutenant James Calhoun,* 7th Cavalry (standing); First Lieutenant Donald McIntosh.* 7th Cavalry (standing at end of row). Last row from left to right: Mrs. T. M. McDougel, wife of Captain McDougal (sitting); Captain T. M. McDougal, 7th Cavalry (with Reno at the Little Big Horn; sitting); First Lieutenant Badger, 6th Infantry; Charles Thompson (civilian; sitting; son of Captain Thompson; Colonel J. S. Poland, 17th Infantry (sitting); Captain Thomas W. Custer,* 7th Cavalry (sitting); Captain William Thompson, 7th Cavalry (in rear of Capt. Custer and standing).

*Killed with Custer at the Little Big Horn, June 25, 1876.

William W. Belknap who ordered the post commander to discontinue unauthorized purchases. Custer complied but lashed out and accused Belknap of favoritism and graft in the post-tradership racket. Col. William B. Hazen had made similar charges against the secretary of war, calling him a corrupt politician. Hazen, in reprisal for his charges, was ordered to the isolated post Fort Buford in the Northwest. Custer however, was somehow spared this embarrassment.

When Secretary Belknap stopped at Fort Abraham Lincoln in the late summer of 1875, he was snubbed by Custer. Military courtesy prescribed that Custer should have publicly welcomed Belknap; instead, the Indian fighter waited in his office for the secretary to call. When the sutler sent a basket of champagne for the reception, Custer returned it. After Belknap's visit to Fort Lincoln, the long awaited two month's leave was granted Custer. He departed with his wife and brother for a social fling in gay New York, where the theater and operatic music entranced them.

The summer of 1875 was followed by severe weather and heavy snows. Food was

Courtesy National Archives

Photograph of hunting party from Fort Abraham Lincoln, Dakota Territory 1875, at a camp on the Little Heart River. Left to right: *Lt. J. Calhoun,* 7th Cavalry; Mr. Sweet (standing), Capt. S. Baker, 6th Infantry; *Boston Custer* (in buckskin jacket); Lt. W. S. Edgerly, 7th Cavalry; Miss Watson (with fan); *Capt. M. W. Keogh,* 7th Cavalry (on Custer's right); Mrs. J. Calhoun; Mrs. George A. Custer (seated); Dr. H. O. Paulding (center, seated on ground); *George A. Custer*; Mrs. A. E. Smith; *Dr. G. E. Lord* (standing, on Custer's left); Capt. T. B. Weir (with whiskers), 7th Cavalry; *Lt. W. W. Cooke,* 7th Cavalry; Lt. R. E. Thompson, 6th Infantry, (standing on Lord's left); the Misses Wadsworth, seated; *Capt. T. W. Custer,* 7th Cavalry, *Lt. A. E. Smith,* 7th Cavalry, extreme right. Individuals that are italicized were killed during the massacre.

low at many reservations and Indian agents telegraphed for additional money to feed their charges. Congress was slow in passing the appropriations, and Indians began to starve.[4] The chiefs pleaded with the agents to let them go out and hunt buffalo in the Powder River country, as was their right under treaty. Permission was granted, and the Indians left before the heavy snows. On December 6th, 1875, the Indian Bureau issued orders that Indians not in the reservations by the end of January would be considered hostile. Runners were dispatched to locate the hunting parties and inform them that they must return immediately. In some cases the villagers answered that they could not return as they were engaged in hunting buffalo, and by the time the hides were prepared and a good supply of meat brought in to carry their families through the winter, they could hardly return within the deadline. The snows came and some of the runners themselves were not able to report back until February 11, 1876.

4. The appropriation was passed later in the spring.

When the deadline arrived, the War Department took steps to round up the non-reservation bands of Sitting Bull and Crazy Horse but it was so cold that frostbitten soldiers were unable to remain in the field, to carry out the winter campaign. General Sheridan's report stated, "General Terry also projected an expedition against Sitting Bull's band, which was then believed, from information he had received, to be located on the Little Missouri River, but afterward found to be on the Dry Fork of the Missouri, some two hundred miles further west. Before, however, the 7th Cavalry could be concentrated at Fort Abraham Lincoln, the season became so inclement — a great number of men being badly frostbitten endeavoring to reach the fort — and the snow so deep that it was thought advisable to abandon the expedition until later in the season."[5]

Courtesy U.S. Signal Corps photo (Brady Collection)
Rain in the Face — Hunkpapa Sioux.

On February 10th, 1876, the New York Herald demanded a full investigation of possible corruption within the War Department, declaring Secretary of War W. W. Belknap to be farming out traderships in the Indian country, and these appointments in turn being passed on to others who sold them to the highest bidder. Belknap had invoked an 1870 law, giving the secretary of war sole power to appoint post traderships. Orvil Grant, the President's brother, was also implicated, according to the news release and it was suggested that President Grant ask his brother how much capital he had earned starving the Indian squaws and children.

Custer had voiced loud protests with regard to irregularities in post traderships along the Missouri River, and while in New York, joined in accusing the Indian Bureau and bureaucratic politicians. Whenever opportunity arose, he made statements of things he suspected, or thought he knew to be factual forgetting that as an officer in the United States Army, he should have proof before taking on his superiors. Among Custer's many friends was James Gordon Bennett, publisher of the New York Herald, who would make the most of any comments by the Indian fighter.

Libbie was enjoying New York too much to leave it for the frontier, so Custer asked for an extension of his leave which was granted. Another spree followed, but although money was running low, Autie requested another extension giving as his reason that the snow made it impossible to return to Fort Abraham Lincoln. There were parties, dinners and theatricals and visits with old friends. Politics was always a handy topic to argue over, and Grant's administration was drawing to a close. Custer, like many others who once supported the

---

5. Army Navy Journal, Dec. 23rd, 1876, Gen. Sheridan's Report; page 309.

National Union Party, turned Democrat again, not to the surprise of his closest friends. He had reason to believe that Grant desired a third term, simply because "no other President had ever served a third term."[6] Custer also believed that General Sherman was fishing for a presidential nomination, but . . . "I think he is so unstable in his opinions that he would do like Grant did, accept from the first party that offered — with any chance of success. Sheridan would make a much stronger radical candidate than Sherman as far as controlling the soldier's vote goes, but he would be even more radical in his administration than Grant has ever been."[7] Who is to say that Custer himself had never professed ambitions toward political offices. It is believed that powerful and influential admirers saw Custer as presidential timber. A showy victory over the hostiles would make him a national hero overnight. With public acclaim and a powerful press to back him up, the Democratic convention would sit up and take notice.[8]

Autie's application for a third extension of leave was not because he and Libbie were enjoying the carefree way of New York's social life. On the contrary, their money had dwindled, but by moving across the street from the Hotel Brunswick, they were able to meet a more reasonable cost for room and board. The request for extension may have been prompted by a letter from his attorney asking him to prolong his stay in New York. It is evident that Custer was being considered to testify before a congressional committee in the Belknap scandal. The Democrats, who had won control of the House of Representatives in 1874, began rooting about, trying to dig up something to upset the Republican applecart. Heister Clymer, chairman of the Committee on Expenditures of the War Department, found some evidence linking Secretary of War William Belknap in the dishonest sales of post tradership. It seems that Custer had volunteered earlier to contribute what he thought would be evidence against Belknap's operations.

Office of S. J. Storrs,
Attorney and Counsellor,
120 Broadway

New York, January 11th, 1876

Gen. G. A. Custer

Dear Sir,

In reply to your favor of a day or two ago. I have to inform you that the suit to which you are a party of has been placed upon the calender for trial and is likely to be called up for trial at any time as the state of the calender will permit.

You are a necessary witness in the case and your absence at the trial will be necessarily fatal to your success therein.

I hope that you will be able to prolong your stay in

Courtesy National Archives

Sitting Bull — spiritual leader — did not take part in battle.

6. From a letter loaned by William A. Bond; Vernon, Texas.
7. Ibid.
8. Also see "Custer, the Statesman"; by Georg Wenzel Schneider —Wettengel; Research Review, Little Big Horn Association; Vol. IV, Fall, 1970, No. 3, page 6; a good article on Custer's political ambitions.

Courtesy U. S. Signal Corps photo (Brady Collection)

Lieutenant Colonel George Armstrong Custer, taken in 1875. His close officers called him by the nickname "Jack" — as Custer's initials "G. A. C." were stenciled on his trunks.

New York till after the trial of this cause. Please inform me of your movements so that I may see you where it becomes necessary in this case.[9]

Yours Truly,
S. J. Storrs.

When Custer's third extension for leave was denied, he and Libbie packed their luggage and boarded a train for St. Paul, where a special coach would take them to Bismarck. The trip was long, but not uneventful. West of St. Paul, the train stalled in a snow drift making it impossible to continue. After six days of imprisonment, with food and fuel running low, desperate men found a way to cut into the telegraph wire and sent a message to Fort Lincoln for assistance.[10] After 40 miles of travel, Tom Custer arrived at Crystal Springs, where the train was almost entirely buried in the snow. The Custers were rescued and hurried back to the garrison. The remainder of the crew and passengers had to wait another ten days for relief. Scarcely had they arrived at Fort Lincoln by a freezing sleigh ride, when Custer received an official dispatch ordering him to return to Washington immediately. He had anticipated such a communication, but not within such a short period of time. Custer sought council with General Terry, and acted upon his suggestion to seek another solution.

On March 16th, Custer wired Heister Clymer, leader of the congressional committee, asking if it was possible to answer questions by mail, as he was preparing to take to the field against hostile Indians early in April. A reply from Washington stated that he must appear in person to testify before the committee and any other arrangement was impossible. Custer now felt that he had brought disaster upon himself by becoming implicated in partisan political strife motivated by the Belknap scandal. His early offer to testify to the corrupt practices in the Indian agencies along with his exposé articles in the New York Herald regarding dishonest deals in army post traderships, were to be tapped by the Clymer investigating committee. Thirteen days later, Custer gave his first testimony before the Clymer committee, his statements being highly critical of Secretary of War Belknap. His allegations in the grain thefts, outrageous prices charged by post traders, and profit splitting with outsiders, were disclosed. Custer was then ordered to stand by for further questioning.

During the course of some four weeks of testimony, it seemed that Custer had little to offer the investigation committee other than hearsay. He did, however, show a hostile attitude toward the administration, and made several damaging statements implicating the President's brother, Orvil

9. Custer file; National Archives, (Rec. file).

10. First Sgt. Hugh Hynds Reminiscenes; courtesy Custer Battlefield Museum.

Grant, as heading the Indian graft ring. Custer's testimony was a direct challenge to his Commander-in-Chief's integrity and honesty, but his charges had no proof to support them. While Custer's legal advisers were guiding him over the hot coals, the investigating committee was amazed at his over-confidence. Newspapers blared forth his statements as the champion of honest government and the Democratic press billed him as a star witness. Custer fretted. He had hoped he would be permitted to return to Fort Lincoln and lead the Dakota column in what he thought would be the greatest campaign against the Sioux. He feared the command would leave before he could return.

Custer, believing that the Clymer committee had completed its soul-searching questions, and was ready to release him, received a subpoena as a witness for the prosecution at the Belknap impeachment trial. Anticipating a longer stay in Washington, Custer appealed to Sherman, general of the army, to negotiate a release for his return to Fort Lincoln. Sherman contacted the new Secretary of War Alphonso Taft, and discussed the matter in full. Taft went directly to President Grant and relayed Custer's urgent plea to be released. Grant was determined to punish Custer, and saw no reason why the Dakota column could not march without him; and Sherman stated that the Indian fighter was not the only officer in the army capable of leading the expedition.

Determined now to see President Grant and to appeal his case, Custer made tracks to the White House. In the anteroom he waited for several hours without any word from the presidential chambers. Impatient and nervous, he stormed out of the White House and headed for the war department to see General Sherman. Unfortunately, the general was in New York and wouldn't be back until evening. That afternoon, Custer again sought an appointment with the President, and again was denied permission to see him. In a last effort of communication with his Commander-in-Chief, he hastily jotted the following note:

Courtesy U.S. Signal Corps photo (Brady Collection)

General Alfred Terry, Commander of the Department of the Dakota, left Fort Abraham Lincoln on May 17, 1876, with 925 men under his command. Terry was responsible for placing Custer in charge of his cavalry.

To His Exc'y the President, May 1, 1876

Today, for the third time, I have sought an interview with the President, not to solicit a favor, except to be granted a brief hearing, but to remove from his mind certain unjust impressions concerning myself which I have reason to believe are entertained against me. I desire this opportunity simply as a matter of justice; and I regret that the President has declined to give me as opportunity to submit to him a brief statement which justice to him, as well as to me, demanded.

Resp'y submitted:

G. A. Custer
Lt. Col. 7th Cav.
Bvt. Maj. Gen. U.S.A.

Custer left Washington on May 4th, taking the night train to Chicago. When he arrived at that city and stepped from the train, he was met by one of Sheridan's staff members and informed of his arrest by order of General Sherman. Although Custer had been released from the Clymer committee, he had left Washington without seeking authorization from the war department. Grant now had the opportunity to even-up relationships with the arrogant young war hero, and he ordered him not to be allowed to engage or undertake in any part of the expedition against the Sioux. He was to remain in Chicago until he received further orders. The Chicago arrest was purposeful, the fear that Custer might escape his superiors is well-expressed in an article from the Army Navy Journal; ". . . General Custer did go in person and get temporarily excused from appearing as a witness, subject to call by telegraph, and start to join his command, when he could justly claim to go with the troops of his garrison, and therefore be out of reach of any summons, by telegraph or otherwise. In this there appeared the spirit of insubordination, and the order to stop him at Chicago became imperative."[11]

Art by E. L. Reedstrom

Custer's arrest in Chicago.

General Sheridan gave Custer an Irish tongue-lashing, which didn't seem to do much good. However, feeling somewhat sorry for his lieutenant colonel, he permitted him to send several telegrams asking for a reversal of Sherman's decision. The replies never came.

Terry was headquartered in St. Paul and had picked Colonel Hazen to accompany the column in place of Custer, but Hazen was also summoned to Washington to testify before the Clymer committee. Fearing that his detainment in Chicago would interfere with his connecting with the Dakota column, Custer disobeyed General Forsyth's arresting order, and boarded a night train for St. Paul.

The Custer luck held out, and a telegram from Sherman permitted him to carry on to Fort Lincoln, but stipulated that the President had decided he was not to go on the expedition. Custer's last resort was General Alfred Terry, whose kindness of heart would possibly find a solution. If he was going to be detained under arrest, he might

Courtesy Herb Peck, Jr.

One of Elizabeth Custer's favorite pictures of "her" General, taken in New York, 1876. Probably one of his last photos in dress uniform.

11. A.N.J.; May 27, 1876.

Courtesy Dr. Elizabeth A. Lawrence Collection
Lieutenant General Philip H. Sheridan.

"I have seen your order transmitted through the General of the Army directing that I be not permitted to accompany the expedition to move against the hostile Indians. As my entire regiment forms a part of the expedition and I am the senior officer of the regiment on duty in this department I respectfully but most earnestly request that while not allowed to go in command of the expedition I may be permitted to serve with my regiment in the field. I appeal to you as a soldier to spare me the humiliation of seeing my regiment march to meet the enemy and I not share its dangers.

(Signed) G. A. Custer"

In forwarding the above I wish to say, expressly, that I have no desire whatever to question the orders of the President or my military superiors. Whether Lieutenant Colonel Custer shall be permitted to accompany the column or not I shall go in command of it. I do not know the reasons upon which the orders given rest; but if these reasons do not forbid it, Lieutenant Colonel Custer's services would be very valuable with his regiment.

(Signed) Alfred H. Terry,
Commanding Department.

Back East, editorials blazed away at what was termed "Grant's Revenge," asserting

as well be at Fort Lincoln with his family. Arriving in St. Paul on May 6th, Custer, desperate, disappointed, and hurt, went to Terry with tears in his eyes. Choked with emotion, he couldn't control himself and broke down and wept. Terry was deeply moved by the sight of his old comrade begging his help. How could he possibly refuse him?

With the aid of Terry, Custer penned a telegram with most humble words, forwarding it through military channels with an indorsement added by his department commander.

Headquarters Department of Dakota,
St. Paul, Minne., May 6, 1876.

The Adjutant General,
Division of the Missouri, Chicago.
I forward the following:
"To His Excellency, The President:
(Through Military Channels.)

Courtesy Dr. Elizabeth A. Lawrence Collection
Brigadier General Alfred H. Terry was ordered by Sheridan to organize the Expedition to the Black Hills.

that Custer was persecuted for his decent opinions and honest testimony before the Clymer committee. Grant was branded as an irresponsible tyrant, for wreaking such vengeance against the Cavalier of the Plains. Angered Democrats threw up a shaking fist against Grant's continued abuse of his official power.

In Chicago, Sheridan received the dual dispatch, and forwarded it through the respective channels with an additional indorsement of his own.

Chicago, Ill., May 7, 1876

Brig. General E. D. Townsend,
Washington, D. C.

The following dispatch from General Terry is respectfully forwarded. I am sorry Lieut. Colonel Custer did not manifest as much interest in staying at his post to organize and get ready his regiment and the expedition as he now does to accompany it. On a previous occasion in eighteen sixty-eight I asked executive clemency for Colonel Custer to enable him to accompany his regiment against the Indians, and I sincerely hope that if granted this time it may have sufficient effect to prevent him from again attempting to throw discredit on his profession and his brother officers.

(Signed) P. H. Sheridan, Lieutenant General.

Sherman's telegraphic message was received on the morning of the 8th, and passed on to Custer, who was anxiously awaiting the reply. He was overjoyed when he read the following communication;

Headquarters of the Army,
Washington, May 8th, 1876.

To General A. H. Terry, St. Paul, Minn.:

General Sheridan's enclosing yours of yesterday touching General Custer's urgent request to go under your command with his regiment has been submitted to the President, who sent me word that if you want General Custer along he withdraws his objections. Advise Custer to be prudent, not to take along any newspaper men, who always make mischief, and to abstain from personalities in the future . . .

(Signed) W. T. Sherman,
General.

After receiving the telegram, Custer dashed the few blocks to his hotel to pack his bags for a hasty journey to Fort Lincoln with Terry. On his way to the hotel, he accidentally bumped into Captain William Ludlow of the Engineer Corps, presently on Terry's staff, but under orders to change stations. Both men greeted each other warmly and conversed for a time, Custer informing Ludlow that he had just recently been restored to duty and was making ready to join his command at Fort Lincoln once more. In Custer's excitement, he blurted out that once the command was underway, he would "cut loose and swing clear of Terry" making his operations independent of Terry's, as he alone saw fit to do. Ludlow did not take this favorably and he related Custer's remarks to several other officers on Terry's staff.[12] These officers thought that Terry should have full knowledge of Custer's intentions so that he would know how to deal with the situation. Terry did not get wind of Custer's remarks until he returned to St. Paul late in September of that year. Was this the appreciation one officer deserved from another? Had Terry been informed that same day of Custer's remarks, a whole chain of historical events might never have taken place. However, since it did not occur, the golden-haired Cavalier of the Plains continued to keep his date with destiny at the Little Big Horn.

Preparations having been completed for the summer's campaign against the growing force of Sitting Bull's hostiles and the continuous flow of reservation Indians joining them, the 7th Cavalry had been taken out of its barracks at Fort Abraham Lincoln to camp a short distance away from the garrison. Major Marcus Reno, commanding the 7th during Custer's absence, had divided the regiment into four battalions, captains commanding them. When Custer returned from Washington, he was sensitive to changes made without his concurrence and changed the order,

12. *Custer Tragedy*, by Fred Dustin; also *Custer's Luck*, by E. I. Stewart.

dividing the regiment into two wings, Reno commanding the right wing and Benteen the left.[13] This, of course, was resented by Reno. It would look as if he was incompetent of any major decisions without complying with other officers, and he resented Custer's actions.

While Custer was preparing the 7th for the expedition, other troops had been organized and placed under canvas, three miles below Fort Lincoln, on Cannon Ball Creek. When orders came through to be ready to move on the morning of May 17, the order of march was taken up outside the post, with the battery in advance, supported by the infantry and followed by the wagon train with the cavalry acting as advance guard and rear guard flankers.[14]

On the 17th of May, 1876, the expedition broke camp in an air of confidence, pomp, and regalia. "GaryOwen" the 7th Cavalry's battle tune broke the early morning silence as columns of platoons marched around the parade ground of Fort Lincoln. By their formidable appearance it seemed that they would be able to cope with any enemy which they might encounter. Despite this, only a few spectators and members of the officers' families came out to witness the pageantry, but many tear-filled eyes looked from the windows.

Custer promised Libbie and sister Margaret that they could accompany the column by horseback as far as the Little Heart River where a first campsite would be established. Libbie, in her quaint little riding habit simulating a tight form-fitting shell jacket with a row of brass sleeve buttons in front, rode next to her husband on Dandy.[15] After the regiment passed in review before their commanding officer, the Custers galloped off to take their place before the column. From time to time, Autie would glance back to admire his men, and could not refrain from calling Libbie's attention to their grand appearance.

During the sunrise it was discovered a mist had enveloped everything. As the column marched off across the prairie, there occurred one of the rarest phenomena of the plains. The mist slowly began to lift and the sun shone through with its rays creating the colors of a rainbow. The column of troops moving over the ground, was mirrored as if in water in the sky above them.[16] A scene of wonder and beauty appeared as the mirage, taking up half the length of the cavalry, gave Libbie a premonition of disaster. This premonition was to stay with her, no matter how hard she tried to forget it, until the fatal news was brought to her.

At 2 p.m. the main body of the command reached the first crossing of the Little Heart River, having marched 13½ miles directly west from Fort Lincoln. The first camp being pitched at this point.[17] Libbie stayed that night with her husband, the last they were ever to know together. She could not help remembering his buoyant spirits over being in the field once again. The thought of departing in the morning to return to Fort Lincoln, again brought the premonition of disaster. That evening, the paymaster made his disbursements to the soldiers so that debts could be settled.

After reveille and breakfast the morning of May 18 Libbie and Margaret were to return to Fort Lincoln with the paymaster. As the troops were making ready for the day's march, Libbie said her goodbyes to Autie, showing no signs of apprehension. John Burkman, Custer's orderly, helped the women to their mounts, Libbie saying to him playfully, "Goodby, John. You'll look after the general, won't you?" Smiling at her

13. E. B. Custer, microfilm Reel 11, item 3089; Custer Battlefield Museum.

14. Narrative by Hugh Hynds, 1st Sgt. of Gatling Battery, Courtesy Custer Battlefield Museum.

15. Letter from Col. Brice C. W. Custer; Monterey, California; to author April 19, 1968.

16. E. B. Custer; Boots & Saddles.

17. Gen. Terry's Field Diary.

husband, she rode off. Burkman remembered that Custer hadn't returned her smile. Being a man of strong, simple emotions, apt to take himself seriously, and deeply devoted to his wife, Custer said to Burkman in a low tone, "A good soldier has two mistresses. While he's loyal to one, the other must suffer."[18]

The expedition consisted of the 7th Cavalry, commanded by Lt. Col. George A. Custer, 28 officers and 747 men; two companies of the 17th Infantry, and one company of the 6th Infantry, comprising eight officers and 135 men; one platoon of Gatling guns, two officers and 32 men in charge (from the 20th Infantry); and 45 enlisted Arikara or "Ree" Indian scouts. The wagon train had 114 six-mule teams, 37 two-horse teams, and 70 other vehicles, including ambulances, with 85 pack mules, employing 179 civilian drivers. Commanding the expeditionary forces was Brigadier-General Alfred H. Terry, department commander.

The marching formation of the 7th Cavalry was divided into two columns, designated right and left wings, commanded by Reno and Benteen. Each wing was subdivided into two battalions of three troops each. One battalion was advanced guard, one was rear-guard, and one marched on each flank of the train and the camping places at the end of the day's march. Two troops of the advance guard reported at headquarters for pioneer or fatigue duty to build bridges and creek crossings. The rear-guard remained behind everything. When it came to a wagon stalled in the mire, it helped to put the wagon forward. The battalions on the flanks were to keep within 500 yards of the trail and not to get more than a half-mile in advance or rear of the train. To avoid dismounting any more often than necessary, one troop marched until about a half-mile in advance of the train; it then dismounted, the horses unbitted and allowed to graze until the train had passed and was about a half-mile in advance. At that time it took up the march again. Each of the two other troops would conduct their march in the same manner so that two troops would be alongside the train at all times. If the country was much broken, a half-dozen flankers were thrown out to guard against surprise. The flankers regulated their march to keep abreast of their troop. The pack animals and beef herd were driven alongside the train by the packers and herders.

The following day-by-day itinerary has been gathered from three sources, the Field Diary of Lieutenant Edward Settle Godfrey,[19] Mark Kellog's diary,[20] and General Alfred H. Terry's journal.[21] As most of the entries are brief, by weaving them together we can assimilate a better picture of daily events, with added notes on the column's progress.

The advance of the regiment left camp at 5 a.m., the train crossing the Little Heart River at 8:30 a.m. The main body of the command moved out at 9 a.m., a halt being made at 10:15, and a previously-selected campsite for the night was reached at 2 p.m., the first day's march covering 10.8 miles.[22]

May 19th, reveille sounded at 3 a.m. The men breakfasted and were on the march at 5 a.m. Three-quarters of a mile out, they came upon a ravine made impassable by high water. There was nothing else to do but return to camp and go around the ravine at a shallow ford. After this was done, a march of only three-quarters of a mile was made passing through a prairie dog village. At this point, a halt was ordered to close up

18. Old Neutriment; by Glendolin D. Wagner — Sol Lewis — N.Y. 1973 — (page 124).

19. Lt. E. S. Godfrey, Field Diary of; Publ. by Champoeg Press, 1957, 1000 copies.

20. Mark Kellogg's Diary, The Westerners Brand Book, 1945-46, Chicago Corral.

21. Gen. Alfred H. Terry, Publ. by Old Army Press, Ft. Collins, Colo., Intro by Mike Koury.

22. Gen. Terry's Field Diary.

the wagon train. Heavy rains the night before made travel heavy for forage and camp teams. Guide Charlie Reynolds, with a well-placed shot, bagged an antelope. Custer pioneered ahead with scouts and two companies all day. The day had begun very cloudy, clearing later in the morning, but at noon a violent thunderstorm with hail began and lasted into the afternoon. Scouts reached the column with mail and news that a Black Hills party had been massacred. Wood scarce, grazing very light. The last team came in at dark. A total of 13¾ miles had been covered during the day.[23]

Because of the hard going of the previous day, the command was late getting started May 20th. Reveille sounded at 5 a.m., and camp broke at 8 a.m. Artillery team stampeded and ran a mile. Went into camp on the west side of the Little Muddy about noon. A bridge had to be built, which took the rest of the day and wasn't finished by dark. Slight showers through afternoon with a westerly wind. Marched 9½ miles.[24]

May 21st, bridge completed at 6:30 a.m., the march being resumed with the customary halts. Weather misty, heavy dark clouds overhead threatening rain, but passing by noon. Indian scouts bring in seven antelope. Terry and Custer out in front most of day. Roads better. One mule shot, diseased with glanders. Another, played out and was left behind. Plenty water, no wood. Three men invalids riding in ambulances, one accidentally shot in heel. Unusual names of various high buttes, Wolf's Den, Rattlesnake Den, Cherry Ridge, Maiden's Breasts. Camp reached at 3:30 p.m., distance covered 13½ miles. The command tired from its bridge-building.[25]

Courtesy Custer Battlefield Museum
Major Marcus Reno was given orders to cross the Little Big Horn with Companies A, G and M, of the 7th Cavalry.

Courtesy Custer Battlefield Museum
The Steamer "Far West". The 950 mile trip with wounded aboard took Captain Grant Marsh 54 hours, a record breaking time, never equaled since.

23. Terry Diary and Mark Kellogg's journal.

24. Ibid.

25. Ibid.

May 22nd, unlike the two previous days. Reveille at 3 a.m., camp broke up at 6 a.m. Weather cool and clear. Roads harder and drier. Little scouting done this day. Fourteen antelope brought in, Reynolds bags three. Struck Custer's Black Hills return trail in 1874. One wagon upset injuring driver seriously. The command covered 15⅓ miles before going into camp. Any traveling in this part of the country was no pleasure jaunt. But nothing seems to faze Custer; he thrives on hardship, and thinks everyone else should, too.[26]

May 23rd, camp broke at 5 a.m. Weather cool and clear with southerly winds. Plenty of wood was found for cook-fires, cold clear spring water for drinking, and good grass for the animals. The Great American Desert did have its occasional oasis. Everyone made the most of it. While chasing elk ahead of advance, Custer came across a fresh camp fire left by hostiles. Marched eight miles and went into camp at Young Men's Buttes. The reason for such a short march was to give the column a chance to rest, as a longer march was expected the next day. Custer constantly visits with his Indian scouts, seems much at home with them. Indians were seen at dusk about three miles away, moving on top of Coteau.[27]

May 24th, broke camp at usual hour. Weather cool and clear. Good marching. Custer and brother Tom miles away on right flank hunting most of the day, killing a lynx and elk. Distance of this day's march was increased, 19 miles being covered. Unless in hot pursuit of an enemy or following a fresh trail, cavalry marches were made in easy stages both in length and duration. Reached Big Heart at 3 p.m. Plenty of wood and grass excellent. Stream clear and cold. Men fished and bathed. Rations were first issued all around.[28]

26. Terry and Kellogg's diary.

27. Ibid.

28. Ibid.

Courtesy U.S. Signal Corps photo (Brady Collection)

General John Gibbon led his cavalry from Fort Shaw, Montana, with a force of infantry, moving east down the Yellowstone River. His was one of the three pronged movements against the Indians.

Art by E. L. Reedstrom

A .50 caliber Gatling gun.

Courtesy Chicago Historical Society

General Ulysses Grant's hat. Straw hats, like the one displayed here, were permitted to be worn in the field. Navy straw hats were purchased from sutlers at 25 cents to 50 cents each.

May 25th, column got under way at 5 a.m., marched over valley country with easy slopes for the most part. Weather beautiful, plenty grass, water, wood. Four men on sick report. Two government mules played out, had to be left behind. Millions of tiny locusts found in grass. Nineteen miles were again covered. Another bridge under construction.[29]

May 26th was uneventful. Camp broke at 5:30 a.m. Weather hot and dry, first day of real heat experienced. Good grass and water, but no wood. Three days without any signs of Indians. Went into camp at 2:30 p.m., marched 12 miles. Custer plans and picks all campsites. Mail arrives at 3 a.m. Considerable cactus found in the area, Custer's dogs having a hard time at it. Sometimes they ride in the ambulance to avoid cactus. Gentle rain this night.[30]

May 27th, column on march by 5 a.m. Weather warm and clear. After 10 miles of marching, the Bad Lands of the Little Missouri were sighted. Grass excellent, but water beginning to show signs of alkali. Total distance marched was 17¾ miles, going into camp at the head of Davis Creek. Everyone trying to spot General Stanley's old trail, going out of their way to locate it and wasting time. Band played while marching, and in the evening after supper. Custer familiar with the area from his '74 trip from the Black Hills.[31]

29. Terry and Kellogg's diary.
30. Ibid.
31. Ibid.

Courtesy Custer Battlefield Museum

Captain Thomas Ward Custer was 31 years old when he met his fate at the Little Big Horn. His body was mutilated beyond recognition.

Courtesy Custer Battlefield Museum

Lieutenant W. W. Cooke, a Canadian, was with Custer to the end. On a scrap of paper he scribbled out his commanders last orders to bring up the ammunition packs.

May 28th, the first crossing of Davis Creek was reached at 5:45 a.m., this was one of those western streams with as many turns as a corkscrew, necessitating being crossed 10 times within eight miles. Sides were high and the bed miry. Marched 7¾ miles, pioneers ahead. Plenty wood, but water alkaline.[32]

May 29th, more bridge-building, rattlesnakes a hazard, one man bitten. No signs of Indians.[33]

May 30th, the main body of the command remained in camp. Only Custer turned out at 5 a.m. to scout for Indians or signs of them, finding neither after a scout of some 21 to 25 miles, returning to camp at 6 p.m. Men fished in the Little Missouri, catching a considerable amount. Hunting was not allowed. This evening it rained heavily, lightning lit up the night with lurid flashes.[34]

May 31st, broke camp at 8 a.m., skies dark, misty, threatening rain. Later heavy clouds lifted and weather turned more pleasant. Custer left the command early in the morning, without authority from General Terry. Apparently, Terry only complained about the matter in his field diary, but he also noted in a previous entry of this date that Custer had been "playing Wagon Master". It is evident from these notations the expedition's commander was becoming irritated with his chief subordinate. However, Custer wasn't being deliberately disobedient, he was simply used to having pretty much of a free hand. Terry should have told him in no uncertain terms this would not do. Custer always cheerfully obeyed a direct order. No order, or an ambiguous one was something else. Terry had chief command, but he simply did not exercise it with Custer or anyone of his subordinates. This was to be one of the fatal flaws in the whole campaign. Crossing of

Courtesy Custer Battlefield Museum

Boston "Bos" Custer the last man to join his General's doom. Only 25 years old he had served as a civilian forager with the 7th Cavalry.

the Little Missouri came off without difficulties. The trail over broken country, with one hill after another, was torture for mules and wagons. Marched 12⁹⁄₁₀ miles, camping at 2 p.m. in a valley. Wood and water available. Reynolds and Kellogg shot three Rocky Mountain sheep, and brought them back to camp dressed out. Rained heavy at 7 p.m.[35]

It commenced to snow on midnight of May 31st, continuing the next day, June 1st, until almost three inches had fallen. Since he felt under such conditions the command could not make more than 10 miles that day, Terry decided to remain in camp. Many played cards to pass the time, others rested, camp duties were endless. Still more snow the following day, June 2nd. Warning that marching in such bad weather might result

32. Terry and Kellogg Diary.

33. Ibid.

34. Ibid.

35. Terry and Kellogg Diary.

in much illness, such as diarrhea and colds, the expedition's chief medical officer, Dr. Williams, advised Terry to remain in camp. Terry agreed, delaying the march until next morning. Snowing heavy, the weather very cold. Wagons hauled over crossing and up hill in preparation for an early start in the morning.[36]

June 3rd, camp broke at 5 a.m., weather cold and clear with northwest wind. Met two white men and one Indian scout at head of column with dispatches from Gibbon's column on Rosebud, Gibbon on half rations. Same scouts were sent back to Gibbon with dispatches. Marched 25 miles and camped on Beaver Creek. Upon reaching Beaver Creek in the afternoon, it was found necessary to build another bridge, Stanley's old bridge being partly washed away.[37]

June 4th, column moved out at 5 a.m., weather clear and cool. Plenty of fresh water cool and clear, wood in abundance. Terry tired out and rode in an ambulance, four miles from camp. Passed through another prairie dog village, caution being taken so that horses would not step into any burrows. Most of day was spent in bridge-building. First discovery of Indian signs, three wickiups with the leaves still green. Two mules died during this night.[38]

June 5th, camp broke at the usual time. Descended into the Bad Lands. Another creek requiring another bridge. But the march was resumed "over very fine rolling country with luxuriant grass." Still, some road-making had to be done; More antelope were killed. First signs of buffalo. A distance of 20.5 miles had been covered. Grass and water fair, no wood. Sagebrush was used for fuel.[39]

June 6th, under way at 4:30 a.m. Weather cool, clear and breezy. The command's guides went astray, leading the column to the South Fork of O'Fallon's Creek instead of to the main stream. This necessitated back tracking plus another bridge. First buffalo killed today. Pvt. McWilliams from Troop H, accidentally shot himself with his revolver, bullet entering calf of leg. He rides in an ambulance. Distance marched 16 miles.[40]

June 7th, column under way at 4:45 a.m., weather misty, clouds heavy and threatening rain. Pioneers spent most of the day in road cutting. Several mules and a few horses dropped out of teams, some wagons damaged. Camp pitched on a branch of Powder River, scouts being sent to its mouth at 10 p.m. Orders went out, no shooting or hunting. Excellent camp, good water, ample wood and sufficient grass. Men tired, stock completely so.[41]

36. Ibid.
37. Terry and Kellogg Diary.
38. Ibid.
39. Ibid.
40. Terry and Kellogg Diary.
41. Ibid.

Courtesy Custer Battlefield Museum

Captain Frederick W. Benteen, 7th U.S. Cavalry, received Custer's last message, "Benteen — come on — Big Village — be quick — bring packs. W. W. Cooke. P.S. Bring pacs." Benteen had command of Companies D, H, and K.

June 8th, Terry decided it was time to meet with General Gibbon's Montana column which had been marching eastward to join the Dakota column. The steamer *Far West,* which had been more or less accompanying the expedition where deep rivers made it possible, reached the mouth of the Powder. At noon, camp broke and Keogh's and Moylan's companies, along with Terry, went in advance on the march to the mouth of the Powder River. Much time was lost by the main command trying to find a ford practicable for the wagon train. Scouts sent by Terry the night before to the Powder's mouth, returned with mail from the steamer *Far West*. Gibbon's scouts, who met the forward column several days earlier, were driven back by hostiles while trying to make contact with that command. They finally had to retire to a stockade for protection. Hostiles were believed near the mouth of the Powder, or within the area of the Tongue River. Preparations are being made for an eight-day cavalry scout.[42]

Courtesy Custer Battlefield Museum

White Swan — one of Custer's scouts.

June 9th, weather disagreeable and raining, laid over in camp. Scouts in from steamer brought news that Terry had gone up Yellowstone river 30 miles on *Far West* to meet Gibbon, marching down Yellowstone river valley. Terry returned late and preparations made for a scout, but nobody knows which companies or how many go out. Orders are for two days rations and forage on horses. One hundred rounds of carbine ammunition on person, six days ration and forage on pack mules.[43]

The next day, June 10th, Terry ordered Major Reno with six companies, B, C, E, F, I, and L, to scout up the Powder to its forks, thence to the head of Mizpah Creek, down to its mouth, then by Pumpkin Creek to the Tongue River. Reno left at 5 p.m. No doubt Custer enviously watched his departure, as he had hoped to be sent instead. In any case, Custer was sure, with good reason, Reno would botch it. The 7th's junior Major was a good officer only when there was someone else along to tell him what to do and how to do it. Both the officers and men of the command wondered at Terry's decision to send Reno instead of Custer, but Terry offered no explanation. Terry noted in his field diary at this time: "Also sent Gibson to find pass to plateau. Gibson did nothing."[44]

June 11th, Gibson having not returned, Terry decided to move out. Camp broke late because of the rain, canvases had to be dried out before storing. Sending Custer in advance with one company, Terry followed with the main body. There ensued much road-making until the plateau's pass was found. A march was then made on the plateau for three-quarters of a mile until the head of a ravine was reached where a halt

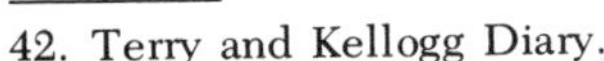

42. Terry and Kellogg Diary.
43. Ibid.

44. Terry's diary. In both diaries of Godfrey and Kellogg, it is mentioned that Reno had taken with him 12 days rations and forage.

Courtesy Tom Heski *Photo by Barry*
One of Custer's Crow scouts. (Name unknown)

was made. Roads were heavy and hills difficult for pack mules to climb. Pack train lagged some three miles behind. Descending to the bottom lands of the Powder, another bridge had to be erected. Then back onto the plateau, more road-making, camp finally being made on the Yellowstone. Twenty-four miles traveled.[45]

The *Far West* having arrived at that point, June 12th, the day was spent in unloading her stores. She was then sent back down the river for more supplies and to carry the command's mail. June 13th was spent awaiting her return. June 14th Terry issued Custer orders to take six companies of the 7th the next morning for the Tongue River. June 15th, Custer moved out for the Tongue at 7 a.m., Terry with his staff and a company of infantry following on the *Far West*. Fifteen miles from the Powder the steamer's machinery broke down. It was repaired by the next day, June 16th, Terry joined Custer at the Custer camp.[46]

The next three days, June 17th to 19th were spent awaiting news from Reno's scout. The afternoon of the 19th, a courier brought Terry dispatches from Reno to the effect that he had been to the mouth of the Rosebud, where he had no business being, according to the expedition commander's orders. He had found a considerably large Indian trail about nine days old leading to the valley of the Little Big Horn, but forebore, however, to follow it up. Immediately upon receipt of this dispatch, Terry sent his brother-in-law Captain Hughes, who was

45. Terry's diary and Godfrey's journal.

46. Terry's diary.

Courtesy Custer Battlefield Museum
Curley, one of Custer's Crow scouts — claimed he watched Custer's men massacred by the Sioux through field glasses.

Courtesy Tom Heski

Curley was told by Mitch Bouyer to leave the command and go to Terry. "That man (Custer) will stop at nothing . . . we have no chance at all."

on his staff, to meet the major. The expedition commander plaintively noted in his field diary: "Reno gave him no reason for his disobedience of Orders."[47]

It was now known that there were no Indians on the Tongue or Powder rivers, and the net had narrowed to the Rosebud, Little Horn, and Big Horn rivers. June 20th, Terry ordered Custer to cross the Tongue and join Reno with the rest of the 7th. He was then to receive supplies from the *Far West* and march on to the Rosebud with the whole 7th. Terry, following Custer, reached Reno's camp at 12:30 p.m., then went on to Gibbon's the next day, June 21st.[48]

General Gibbon was found in camp at the mouth of the Rosebud, awaiting developments. The evening of June 21st, Terry called a conference of his principal officers aboard the *Far West*. Gibbon, Custer, Major Brisbin, commanding Gibbon's cavalry, together with some of Terry's staff attended. They knew General Crook was in the field against these same hostiles, but they did not know just where his command was operating. Obviously, his movements could not be coordinated with theirs; in fact, they could not even coordinate their own, except in the most general way. In sending three columns against large numbers of hostiles it was always hoped that the columns would converge on them, but at least prevent them from escaping. It was highly unlikely that Crook's Wyoming column would be able to assist the Montana and Dakota columns. It was not certain the latter two would be able to assist one another. There can be no question that Terry was very doubtful of this, regardless of what he was to say later. A few hours before the conference on the *Far West* took place, he ended a dispatch to

Courtesy Custer Battlefield Museum

White Man Runs Him, scout with Custer.

47. Terry's diary.

48. Ibid.

Sheridan with the words: "I only hope that one of the two columns will find the Indians. I go personally with Gibbon."[49] The key words are: "I only hope . . ."

It was believed that the Indians were at the head of the Rosebud, or on the Little Big Horn, a divide of only 15 or 20 miles of ridges separating the two streams. Terry decided that Custer's column would strike the blow. Gibbon, upon hearing this, was disappointed, but not surprised. There was great rivalry between the columns, and each wanted desperately to be in at the death. General Gibbon's cavalry had been in the field since February 22nd, herding and watching these Indians, while the infantry had been in the field since early last March. They had come to regard the Yellowstone Indians as their peculiar property, and had worked and waited five months until the Indians could be corraled and concentrated, with Crook and Terry in position to prevent their escape.

However, Terry's reasons for according the honor of the attack to Custer were good ones. Custer had all cavalry and could pursue the Indians if they attempted to escape, while Gibbon's column was half infantry, and in rapid marching in approaching the village, as well as in pursuing the Indians after the fight, Gibbon's cavalry and infantry probably would become separated and the strength of the column weakened. Custer's column was numerically stronger than Gibbon's, and Terry decided that the strongest column would strike the Indians. A report from the commissioner of Indian Affairs in regard to the number of hostiles absent from the agencies, estimated a figure of not more than 1,500 warriors.[50] Custer had reason to believe that this figure was not correct, and stated that they would probably face three times that number.

Courtesy Custer Battlefield Museum
Hairy Moccasin — one of Custer's scouts.

The conference on the *Far West* lasted from three in the afternoon till near sundown. Custer emerged apparently depressed, no one knew why, but it was noticed by some of his officers. Terry and Gibbon accompanied Custer to his tent, where a few moments were spent in conversation. Terry said he would give Custer written orders in the morning, being exhausted from the long hard ride he would also direct the campaign from the steamer *Far West*, which would ferry Gibbon's column to the south side of the Yellowstone and navigate as far as the Big Horn would allow.

Officer's call brought 7th Cavalry subordinates to Custer's tent. Orders were given

---

49. Edgar I. Stewart, Custer's Luck, page 239.

50. Legend Into History, Charles Kuhlman; Stackpole Company, 1951; page 32.

Also see The New York Times, April 13, 1874; page 1, col. 4; "A show of counting the Indians has been made here — that is, the agent called in the head-men and took their word for the number they had . . ."

Courtesy Custer Battlefield Museum

Harry Armstrong Reed. Nicknamed "Autie" after his uncle, G. A. Custer, at the age of 18 followed his three uncles to their end.

to prepare the pack mules[51] in the morning with 15 days rations of hardtack, coffee, and sugar, and 12 days rations of bacon. Twelve strongest pack animals were to carry 24,000 rounds of reserve ammunition, and it was understood that no badly used-up animals were to be sent with the expedition. Each man was to be issued 100 rounds of carbine and 24 rounds of pistol ammunition, to be carried on his person or in his saddle bag. Sabers were ordered packed and stored on the steamer *Far West* until they returned. For every horse, 12 pounds of oats were to be carried by each trooper, with care to ration it after lengthy marches. Custer suggested that additional forage might come in handy, but troop commanders foresaw the difficulties of extra forage being packed, and cautioned that it was certain the mules would break down sometime during the march if this was allowed. "Well, gentlemen," Custer replied in an excited manner, ". . . you may carry what supplies you please; you will be held responsible for your companies. The extra forage was only a suggestion, but this fact bear in mind: We will follow the trail for 15 days unless we catch them before that time expires, no matter how far it takes us from our base of supplies. We may not see the supply steamer again."[52] Custer continued, "You had better carry along an extra supply of salt; we may have to live on horse meat before we get through." As Custer retired to his tent, the wing and battalion commanders broke up and scattered in groups returning to their campsites.

After the officers informed their men that they were to move out the next day, letters home were hastily penciled, troop commanders made out their wills, and others gave verbal instructions for personal effects and mementos to be distributed to families back east. Many seemed to have an ominous presentment of disaster. While others fancied a night-long card game accompanied with a cup full of whiskey, which Terry gave permission to tap from the kegs. Custer returned to the *Far West* later that evening and was accosted by Major James S. Brisbin, Gibbon's second in command. Brisbin offered Custer four troops of the 2nd Cavalry to join the 7th, but Custer shook his head, "The 7th can handle anything it meets." An earlier plea made by Lieutenant Low to take all or part of his Gatling battery also was refused, on the ground that the cumbersome guns might impede the 7th's march.[53]

Gibbon's men grumbled about the favoritism the 7th was getting. Even Mitch Bouyer, the half-blood Sioux Indian interpreter, was assigned to Custer, leaving

51. There were 12 mules assigned to each troop. See Glory Hunter, Van De Water, page 317.

52. Custer's Last Battle; Gen. E. S. Godfrey, Century Magazine; Jan. 1892.

53. Legend into History; Charles Kuhlman; Stackpole Company, 1951, page 28.

Gibbon without a guide. The 7th seemed to be getting every assistance from Terry to make a successful pursuit.

The sutler, on board the steamer, had been kept busy selling last minute items to officers and troopers, including snuff, tobacco, sperm candles, small print flannel shirts, and straw hats* for the heat of the day. Little has been written about these straw hats and they are not described, but there is mention of soldiers purchasing straw hats from the sutler on board the *Far West* for 25 or 50 cents each.[54] It is probable that several types were sold by the sutler, a broad-brimmed civilian field hat and another with a small brim and low crown. The smaller straw hat was authorized for navy personnel for summer or tropical use and may have been purchased by the sutler from government surplus stores. The brim of the hat was three and one-half inches, and the body was six inches high, in shades of off-white or manila.[55] Photographs show that it was not uncommon to see a navy straw hat worn by a cavalryman.

All morning of June 22nd was spent preparing the 7th Cavalry for the 15-day planned expedition. Several hours before the regiment marched out, Custer received Terry's written orders. The instructions were implicit and fixed the location of the hostiles. It is quoted in its entirety:

CAMP AT MOUTH OF ROSEBUD RIVER, MONTANA TERRITORY, June 22d, 1876. LIEUTENANT-COLONEL CUSTER, 7TH CAVALRY. COLONEL: The Brigadier-General Commanding directs that, as soon as your regiment can be made ready for the march, you will proceed up the Rosebud in pursuit of the Indians whose trail was discovered by Major Reno a few days since. It is, of course, impossible to give you any definite instructions in regard to this movement, and were it not impossible to do so the Department Commander places too much confidence in your zeal, energy, and ability to wish to impose upon you precise orders which might hamper your action when nearly in contact with the enemy. He will, however, indicate to you his own views of what your action should be, and he desires that you should conform to them unless you shall see sufficient reason for departing from them. He thinks that you should proceed up the Rosebud until you ascertain definitely the direction in which the trail above spoken leads. Should it be found (as it appears almost certain that it will be found) to turn towards the Little Horn, he thinks that you should still proceed southward, perhaps as far as the headwaters of the Tongue, and then turn towards the Little Horn, feeling constantly, however, to your left, so as to preclude the possibility of the escape of the Indians to the south or southeast by passing around your left flank. The column of Colonel Gibbon is now in motion for the mouth of the Big Horn. As soon as it reaches that point it will cross the Yellowstone and move up at least as far as the forks of the Big and Little Horns. Of course its future movements must be controlled by circumstances as they arise, but it is hoped that the Indians, if upon the Little Horn, may be so nearly inclosed by the two columns that their escape will be impossible.

The Department Commander desires that on your way up the Rosebud you should thoroughly examine the upper part of Tullock's Creek, and that you should endeavor to send a scout through to Colonel Gibbon's column, with information of the result of your examination. The lower part of this creek will be examined by a detachment from Colonel Gibbon's command. The supply steamer will be pushed up the Big Horn as far as the forks if the river is found to be navigable for that distance, and

---

*Author's Note: Small and wide brim straw hats, many were from naval surplus with small brims. (Chicago Historical Society)

54. Reno Court of Inquiry; The Old Army Press — 1972 — page 411.

55. The Uniforms of the United States Navy; James C. Tily, Thomas Yoseloff, 1964.

the Department Commander who will accompany the column of Colonel Gibbon, desires you to report to him there not later than the expiration of the time for which your troops are rationed, unless in the mean time you receive further orders. Very respectfully, your obedient servant, E. W. SMITH, Captain 18th Infantry, Acting Assistant Adjutant-General.[56]

Terry's "Letter of Instructions," as some have termed it, prescribed what he expected Custer to find and what he should do in the most general way. Much ado about nothing has been made of it by Custerphobes. The young Indian fighter certainly used his own judgment, which his commander had authorized in his order. Terry was not an experienced Indian fighter, Custer was.[57]

Confident of a successful expedition, Custer jotted a few lines in a letter to Libbie, emphasizing Terry's highly praised words, "the Department Commander places too much confidence in your zeal, energy and ability . . . " This letter was to be Custer's last to his wife, she would cherish it the rest of her life.

At noon, on the 22nd of June, 1876, "forward" was sounded and the regiment marched out of camp in column of fours, pack mules heavily burdened, following each troop. Generals Terry, Gibbon, and Custer reviewed the line of marching men and animals, returning salutes to each passing officer, Terry having a pleasant word for each of the troop commanders. The sky was gray, a raw northwest wind tormented the swallow-tailed banner, red and blue, with white crossed sabers, Custer's personal standard since the Civil War. As the column marched by, rank and file gave the appearance of veterans, although many had little battle experience. The sun had tanned their faces, and an outcrop of new beards evidenced a month's journey in the field.

Custer, in a fringed buckskin suit, sported two English self-cocking white-handled pistols with a ring in the butt for a lanyard, a hunting knife in a beaded, fringed scabbard, and a canvas cartridge belt supporting these tools of war. Snugly fitted into a Spencer carbine scabbard was a Remington sporting rifle, octagon barrel, and calibrated for the 50-70 center-fire cartridge. He wore a light gray hat, broad-brimmed and low-crowned to protect his sensitive face from the sun, but no matter how hard he tried to protect himself from the heat of the day, his boyish freckles would appear to his embarrassment. Captains Tom Custer, Calhoun, and Keogh, along with Adjutant Cooke and Bos Custer, dressed in fringed buckskin jackets, a fashion adopted by plainsmen since the opening of the west. When buckskins were not readily available, heavy cloth or canvas substituted, with added imitation fringe on sleeves and trouser legs. Like many other officers in the command, Major Reno wore an army blouse topped off with a rough-looking straw hat. Benteen also stayed away from buckskins, considering that they were too hot during the day, and when soaked by rain, they weighed heavily on a person.

As the end of the column neared, Terry and Gibbon passed compliments to Custer. Shaking hands with the two commanders, he spurred his horse and headed to the forward point. Gibbon called after him in jest, "Now, Custer! Don't be greedy! Wait for us!"[58] The buckskinned lieutenant colonel turns in his saddle and called back ambiguously, "No, . . . I won't."[59]

Lieutenant George D. Wallace, who kept the official itinerary of the 7th's march June 22nd through June 25th, wrote in his report to the chief engineer, department of

56. Custer's Luck; Edgar I. Stewart, page 239.

57. Report of the Chief of Engineers to the Secretary of War, 1876, Vol. II, Part III, Appendix 00; page 700.

58. Glory Hunter; Van De Water, page 324.

59. Ibid.

Dakota: "June 22 — At 12 noon the Regiment under Lieut. Col. George A. Custer, left camp on the Yellowstone and moved up that stream two miles to the mouth of the Rosebud, crossing the latter near its mouth. The Rosebud was there from thirty to forty feet wide and about three feet deep; clear running, slightly alkaline water and gravelly bottom. On account of delays to the pack train, the command marched only about twelve miles, camping at the base of a steep bluff on the left bank of the river; plenty of wood, grass and water."[60]

That evening, trumpeter John Martini, was sent by Custer to notify all officers of the regiment that he wished to see them at his headquarters upstream. After all the officers had gathered together, Custer revealed his plans and also warned them that the Indians would escape if they knew the presence of the command. Caution must be maintained. All commands would be given vocally and not by trumpet, there must be no shooting, and no other unnecessary noise. Then Custer asked for any suggestions from his officers. He also made it quite clear that strictest compliance with any orders from anyone senior to him would be faithfully carried out without discontent. Benteen covers the incident, in an unfinished, undated manuscript:

". . . after arrival of the last officer, General Custer commenced his talk; which was to the effect, that it had come to his knowledge that his official actions had been criticised by some of the officers of the regiment at headquarters of the Department, and, that while he was willing to accept recommendations from the junior second lieutenant of the regiment, he wished the same to come in a proper manner; calling our attention to the paragraph of Army Regulations referring to the criticism of actions of commanding officers; and said he would take the necessary steps to punish, should there be reoccurence of the offense.

I said to General Custer, it seems to me you are lashing the shoulders of *all*, to get at some; now, as we are all present, would it not do to specify the officers whom you accuse? He said, Colonel Benteen, I am not here to be catechised by you, but for your own information, will state that none of my remarks have been directed towards you; then, after giving a few excellent general orders as to what should be done by each troop of the regiment in case of an attack on our bivouac at any time, the meeting of the officers was over, and each adjourned to his palatial 'pup tent.'[61]

"June 23rd — Orders given last night to discontinue trumpet signals, stable guards to wake their respective companies at 3 a.m. and the command would move at 5. General Custer stated that for the first few days short marches would be made, and then increased. All were ready at the appointed time; moving out, we crossed to the right bank of the Rosebud.

"A very broken bluff obliged us to follow the valley for some distance, crossing the stream five times in three miles, thence up the right side for about 10 miles, where we halted to allow the pack train to close up. Soon after starting, we recrossed to the left bank; and, following that for 15 miles, camped on the right bank at 4:30 p.m., making over 30 miles. The last of the pack train did not arrive until near sunset.

"About five miles out today we came to the trail made by Major Reno several days ago, and a few miles farther on saw the first traces of Indians. All the signs were old, but everything indicated large numbers . . ."[62]

Several Indian camping places were found at this time and the command was halted at each one so the scouts could de-

60. Annual Report of the Chief of Engineers (1876) — Report of the Secretary of War — 1877.

61. From the collection of manuscript division, Library of Congress; W. J. Ghent collection, Box 2, correspondent file.

62. Annual Report of the Chief of Engineers (1876) to the Secretary of War (printed 1877).

Courtesy Custer Battlefield Museum

The Seventh's Regimental Standard of 1876. This flag was carried by the regiment to the Little Big Horn, but was encased and placed with the pack train. It was not unfurled during the battle. From the Revised U.S. Army Regulations, 1863 Standards and Guidons of Mounted Regiments; Paragraph 1468: Each regiment will have a silken standard, and each company a silken guidon. The standard to bear the arms of the United States, embroidered in silk, on a blue ground, with the number and name of the regiment, in a scroll underneath the eagle. The flag of the standard to be two feet five inches wide, and two feet three inches on the lance, and to be edged with yellow silk fringe.

termine how long before the Indians had camped there and roughly how many the 7th might encounter. The scout's estimates were high, much higher than Custer's and those of most of his officers. The officers, of course, still based their estimates on the numbers the agents had given on how many of their charges had jumped the reservations. There is no question that the agents' figures were too low, whether through ignorance or deceit. But, it has always been debated just how many warriors there were at Little Big Horn.

Continuing the Wallace report: "June

24th — Started 5 a.m.; in about an hour the Crow scouts came in and reported fresh signs of Indians, but not in great numbers. After a short consultation, Gen. Custer with an escort of two companies moved out in advance, and the remainder of the command at a distance of about ½ mile. We followed the right bank of the Rosebud, crossing the first two running tributaries seen.

"At 1 p.m. the column was halted, scouts sent ahead and coffee made; about 4 the scouts returned with reports of a fresh camp at the forks of the Rosebud. It was now generally believed that the Indians were not more than 30 miles away. At 5 p.m. the command moved out, crossed to the left bank of the Rosebud and passed through what had been several large camps; the trail was then fresh, and the whole valley scratched up by trailing lodge poles.

"Camped, 7:45 p.m. on the right bank of the Rosebud, after a day's march of about 28 miles; weather clear and warm . . . Scouts sent ahead to ascertain which branch of the stream the Indians had followed, returned about 9 p.m., reporting that they had crossed the divide to the Little Big Horn River. General Custer then decided to continue on that night to conceal the movement, locate the Indian village the next day and attack at daylight the following morning. Orders were accordingly given to resume the march at midnight."

It should be clear by now from this official report of Wallace, (who was no great admirer of his commander), that Custer had not been pushing the 7th to exhaustion, all Custerphobes to the contrary notwithstanding. His plan was a good one and might well have fully succeeded. Unfortunately, as we shall see, he was unable to carry it out.

His intention to wait until June 26th before attacking had nothing whatsoever to do with Terry and Gibbon. He had no reason to expect their arrival in the valley of the Little Big Horn on June 26th or any other specific date. (In fact, they did not arrive

Courtesy Custer Battlefield Museum

In 1861, cavalry guidons were swallow tailed, dividing at the fork the top was red, below white. The letter of the company in red on the white field, on the red was U.S. in white. Later in 1863, regulations gave both cavalry and artillery the swallow-tail guidon in the Stars and Stripes. This provision was withdrawn in 1865, however, some regiments continued to use them regardless of regulations. Custer's famed Seventh carried at least one of these guidons to the Little Big Horn, pictured here is the Stars and Stripes guidon captured some two and a half months later from Indians in the Slim Buttes fight. Size: From lance to end of swallow-tail, 3′5″; from lance to middle of fork, 15″; height of flag, 2′3″. Blue field, 14″ x 14″; width of bars, 2¼″. 35 stars, each star 1⅓″ diameter from point to point.

Courtesy U.S. Signal Corps photo (Brady Collection)

In this Indian beaded bag was found Custer's Stars and Bars swallow tail guidon. The pouch and guidon were taken from Indians at Slim Buttes.

there until June 27th). Indeed, if Custer had followed Terry's suggestion as to the course he should take, the 7th would have been nowhere near the valley of the Little Big Horn on June 27th.[63] There then could have been not a CUSTER'S LAST STAND but a TERRY-GIBBON LAST STAND!

To return to Wallace again: "June 25th — Unable to start until near 1 a.m., and owing to delays with the pack train, had gone only about eight miles by early daylight, when the column was halted and the men prepared coffee. While waiting there a scout came from Lieutenant Charles A. Varnum, who had been sent ahead the night before; in a note, Varnum stated to Custer that he could see the smoke of a village on the Little Big Horn about 20 miles away. The returning scout pointed out the butte, then about eight miles distant, from which it was visible.

"Nearing the butte on our march, Lieutenant Varnum joined us, reporting that the Indians had discovered the command, and couriers had been seen going in the direction of their village. General Custer then assembled the officers, told them what he had learned, and said that he would go ahead to attack as soon as possible. The route led through a section of low hills, poor soil and short grass, up the left branch of the Rosebud, then to and up a dry ravine to the crest of the divide between the Rosebud and the Little Big Horn.

"At noon we recrossed the divide from which the valley of the Little Big Horn could be seen; and from 15 to 20 miles to the northwest, a light blue cloud — showing to practised eyes that the Indian village was

63. Dr. Charles Kuhlman, "Did Custer Disobey Orders at the Battle of the Little Big Horn?" Stackpole Co., 1957.

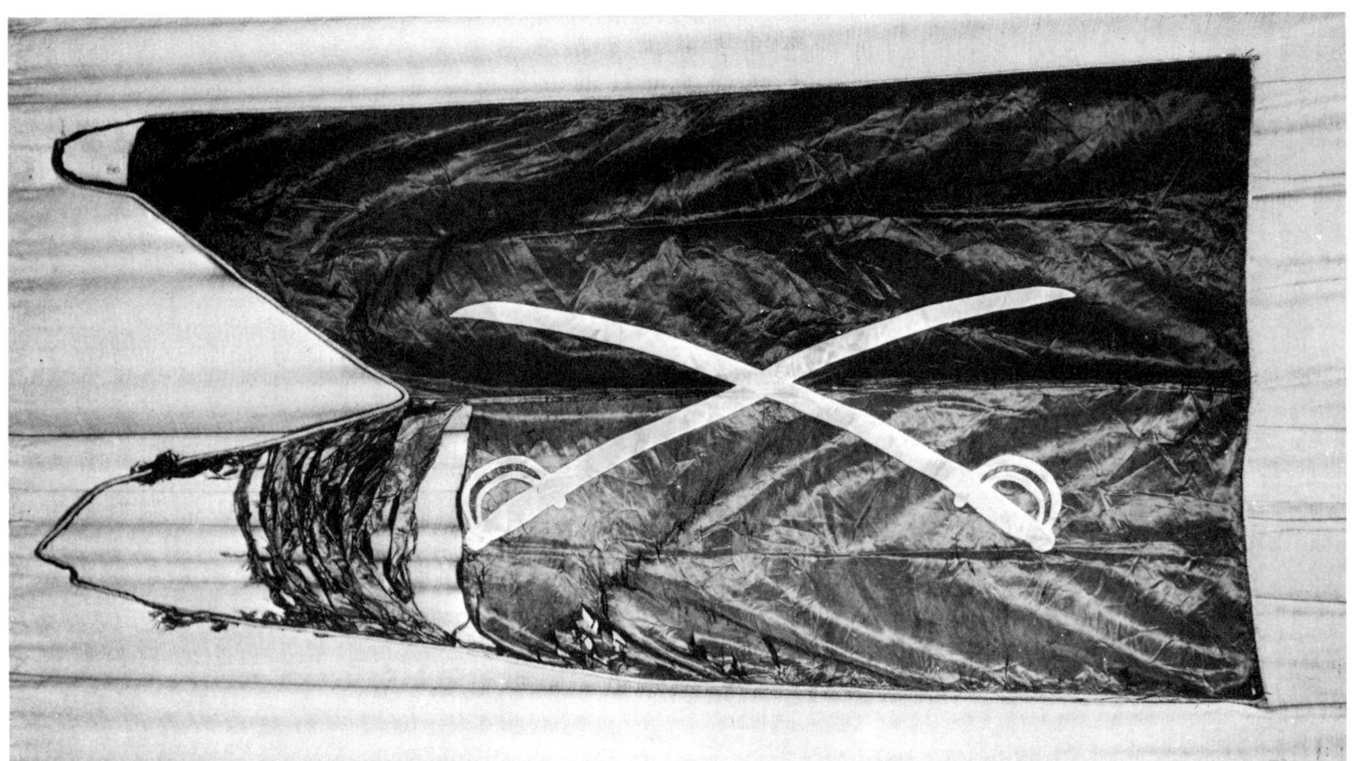

Courtesy Dr. Lawrence Frost

The personal Headquarters Flag of General Custer is 36 inches high, 5½ feet long, the center of the swallow tail cutting back about 22 inches. The crossed white sabers with points up are the length of an issue saber of the Civil War period and are on both sides (stitched on). The top half of the flag is red silk and the bottom is blue. The whole is bound in a ¼ inch woven silk cord. There are two ties each at the top and bottom corners. This flag was carried during the Civil War but is the same as the one Custer carried to the Little Big Horn. As a general officer (brevet), Custer retained the right to carry a personal flag. (See "The Custer Story". by Marguerite Merington.) pg. 147

Courtesy U.S. Signal Corps photo (Brady Collection)

Gall, a Sioux-Hunkpapa chief, led the main attack against Custer, after hitting Reno's line first.

Courtesy Tom Heski *photo by Barry*

Rain-in-the-Face, Hunkpapa Sioux chieftan, who boasted of cutting the heart out of Tom Custer and eating a portion of it.

near. A small stream which started from a point near where we had passed over the crest flowed in the direction of the smoke. From there to the Little Big Horn the country is broken and the valley narrow, with some timber along the little stream we followed down.

"After assigning the battalions, General Custer continued down the right bank of this creek and Major Reno the left; when within three miles of the Little Big Horn, Reno was ordered to cross to the right bank, and the two columns marched for some distance together. Following orders to go ahead, Reno then recrossed the stream, moved down it and across the Little Big Horn; halting his column, he formed line and continued down the valley of the Little Big Horn, beginning the battle of June 25th, 1876."

The scout's report that the hostiles knew of the command's presence had been erroneous, however honestly believed. (Some of the Indians had seen the command, but they failed to warn the village.) So Custer was forced to attack prematurely, playing wholly by ear, not by sight or any preconcerted plan. Naturally, Wallace's official report is a condensed version of events, his main duty being to retell the 7th's actions.

On the morning of June 25th, Custer didn't know where in the valley of the Little Big Horn the hostiles were encamped or even if there really was such an encampment. True, his scouts had said they had seen the smoke from its campfires and even a vast pony herd. Custer himself had seen nothing, even after he had joined them on the height called the Crows Nest, which gave a good view of the Little Big Horn's valley, straining his eyes through his field-glasses. He knew his scouts to be competent, but they could be mistaken.

After returning to his command from the Crows Nest, Custer decided to send Captain Benteen with three companies on a scout to the left of the 7th's line of march to find the Little Big Horn's valley, and to see if there actually were any hostiles in it; this was about noon. The rest of the command he kept with himself until it was reported to him that Indians had been seen "running like devils" in the Little Big Horn's valley. Custer then detached Major Reno with three companies to chase them, telling the major he would "be supported by the whole outfit," or words to that effect.

He still had not seen anything himself. "The Fog of War" was thick about him. In any case, while Reno said later he expected his commander to support him from the rear, Custer decided to march his five companies along the bluffs of the Little Big Horn, find a practicable ford and attack the hostile encampment, wherever it might be, from the flank, which had been his usual tactic throughout the Civil War. Reno should have known this was Custer's favorite maneuver, since he "had known him throughout the war."

In any case, Reno, inexperienced in Indian fighting, incompetent as he was unless directly overseen by a superior officer, and seeing more hostiles than he had ever seen in his life, all apparently hankering after his scalp, and not seeing Custer coming up behind him in support, disobeyed orders, stopped his charge, made an abortive stand in some timber, finally fleeing *sauve qui peut** to the top of the bluffs. Here he was shortly joined by Benteen, who also disobeyed orders, having received a written communication from Custer through the regimental adjutant to join him at once with the ammunition packs. The pack train, of course, guarded by one company, was several miles back on the regiment's main trail. Benteen did nothing to join Custer with the ammunition packs even after the pack train finally came up, until Captain Weir forced Benteen's and Reno's hand by moving out in the direction Custer had gone without

*From the French meaning — "Save himself who can."

Courtesy U.S. Signal Corps photo (Brady Collection)

Sitting Bull was the great spiritual leader of the Sioux Indians. At the sun dance, early in June 1876, he saw a vision of many soldiers coming up-side down into camp. In camp beside the Little Big Horn River, Sitting Bull again made medicine for strength and victory on the eve of Custer's Battle. Warriors believed his medicine was strong.

Courtesy Custer Battlefield Museum *Photo by Barry*

Low Dog — Ogallala Sioux Chief.

Courtesy U.S. Signal Corps photo (Brady Collection)

Crow King — Sioux warrior Hunkpapa. Counted many coup that day.

Courtesy U.S. Signal Corps photo (Brady Collection)

Dull Knife — Cheyenne; it was a good day to die.

Courtesy U.S. Signal Corps photo (Brady Collection)

Little Big Man — Sioux — Ogalalas.

orders to do so. Firing from that direction had been heard more or less plainly by everyone in the command with Benteen and Reno, except themselves. Eventually, Custer and his five companies were wiped out to the last man, Reno and Benteen being effectively corralled by the hostiles on the bluffs until the final arrival of Terry and Gibbon on June 27th.

So, Libbie Custer's premonition of disaster had come true. Still, disaster though it was, it immortalized George Armstrong Custer and his 7th Cavalry as nothing else could have done. Yet, just as the rose has its

Courtesy of Herb Peck, Jr.

Sioux warriors, young and old.

Courtesy Herb Peck, Jr.

Sitting Bull. His autograph generally followed these prints.

thorn, the Little Big Horn has its sting. Custer's brilliant Civil War record is largely forgotten along with his almost equally brilliant nine years of service on the Great Plains prior to the Little Big Horn. The 7th Cavalry's splendid service to its country did not end on the banks of the Little Big Horn. It continued to gather laurels in nearly all of America's wars since. But it is chiefly remembered for the one battle it lost. *Sic transit gloria mundi!*

Instead of speculation concerning the annihilation of Custer's five companies of the 7th Cavalry, C, E, F, I, and L, and the rescue of the remaining seven companies by the timely arrival of General Terry, this author includes several communications and reports by the principal surviving officers of the Little Big Horn engagement. From these reports we can reconstruct a closer picture of the events. In many volumes on the battle, it has been found that official documents are quoted by extracts, leaving out the important context sought after by researchers. With these eyewitness reports there is no possible way we can stray from the truth, unless the particular officer had personal reasons to distort his story. Historians have questioned the credibility of some officers, as to the events leading up to the battle, but nothing officially is known concerning the actions of Custer's five companies and their staggering death toll. There has been a good deal of controversy over the years about this engagement, relying heavily on what the Indians have related, and the credibility of their testimony. And so some writers have pictured Custer as a blundering idiot who led his men down the path of death, while others envisioned him as doing no wrong, placed the blame on the shoulders of the regiment's second in command, Major Marcus A. Reno.

Following is General Alfred H. Terry's

first report of the battle, which was carried to Fort Ellis, Montana, by the civilian scout "Muggins" Taylor, and telegraphed there to the adjutant general in Chicago, Illinois:

Headquarters Department of Dakota
Camp on Little Big Horn River, Montana
June 27, 1876

To the Adjutant General of the
Military Division of the Missouri,
Chicago, Illinois, via Fort Ellis.

It is my painful duty to report that day before yesterday, the 25th instant, a great disaster overtook General Custer and the troops under his command. At 12 o'clock of the 22nd instant he started with his whole regiment and a strong detachment of scouts and guides from the mouth of the Rosebud. Proceeding up that river about twenty miles he struck a very heavy Indian trail, which had previously been discovered, and pursuing it, found that it led, as it was supposed it would lead, to the Little Big Horn River. Here he found a village of almost unlimited extent, and at once attacked it with that portion of his command which was immediately at hand. Major Reno, with three companies (A, G, and M) of the regiment, was sent into the valley of the stream at the point where the trail struck it. General Custer, with five companies, (C, E, F, I, and L,) attempted to enter about three miles lower down. Reno forded the river, charged down its left bank, and fought on foot until finally, completely overwhelmed by numbers, he was compelled to mount and recross the river, and seek a refuge on the high bluffs which overlook its right bank. Just as he recrossed, Captain Benteen, who, with three companies, (D, H, and K,) was some two miles to the left of Reno when the action commenced, but who had been ordered by General Custer to return, came to the river, and rightly concluding that it was useless for his force to renew the fight in the valley, he joined Reno on the bluffs. Captain McDougall, with his company, (B,) was, at first, some distance in the rear with a train of pack-mules; he also came up to Reno. Soon this united force was nearly surrounded by Indians, many of whom, armed with rifles, occupied positions which commanded the ground held by the cavalry — ground

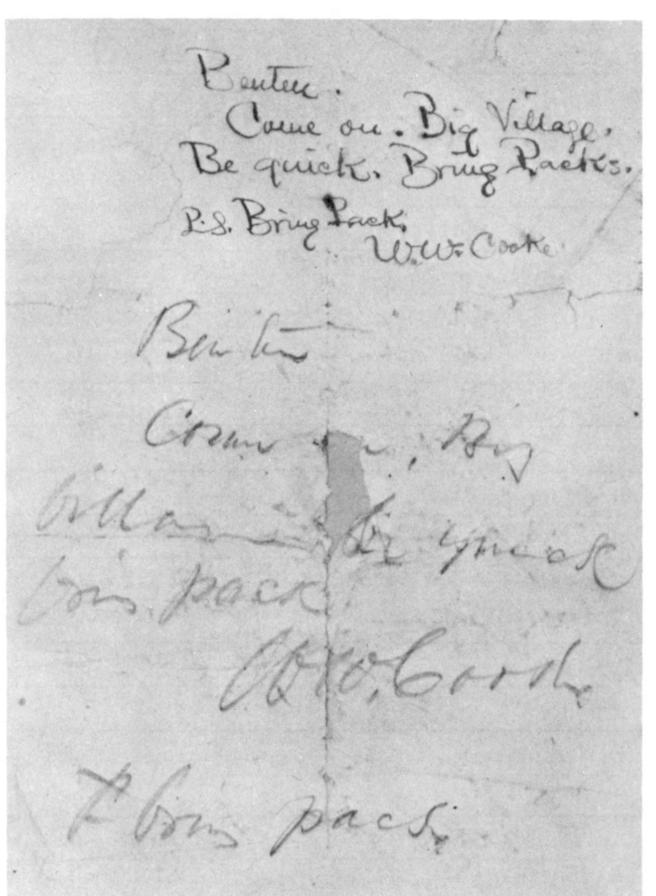

Benteen.
Come on. Big Village.
Be quick. Bring Packs.
P.S. Bring Packs.
W.W. Cooke

Courtesy West Point Museum Collections

A desperate message for ammunition, hurriedly scribbled by Custer's adjutant W. W. Cooke to Captain F. W. Benteen. The message was carried back to the pack train by trumpeter John Martini who was the last trooper to see General Custer alive. *Benteen: Come on. Big Village. Be quick. Bring packs. W. W. Cooke. P.S. Bring packs.*

Art by E. L. Reedstrom

Martini bringing Custer's last message. Benteen receives it and hears from the trumpeter that the Indians are "skedadelling."

from which there was no escape. Rifle-pits were dug, and the fight was maintained, though with heavy loss, from about half past 2 o'clock of the 25th till 6 o'clock of the 26th, when the Indians withdrew from the valley, taking with them their village. Of the movements of General Custer and the five companies under his immediate command, scarcely anything is known from those who witnessed them, for no officer or soldier who accompanied him has yet been found alive. His trail from the point where Reno crossed the stream passes along and in the rear of the crest of the bluffs on the right bank for nearly or quite three miles; then it comes down to the bank of the river, but at once diverges from it as if he had unsuccessfully attempted to cross; then turns upon itself, almost completing a circle, and closes. It is marked by the remains of his officers and men, and the bodies of his horses, some of them strewn along the path; others heaped where halts appear to have been made. There is abundant evidence that a gallant resistance was offered by the troops, but they were beset on all sides by overpowering numbers.

The officers known to be killed are General Custer, Captains Keogh, Yates, and Custer, Lieutenants Cooke, Smith, McIntosh, Calhoun, Porter, Hodgson, Sturgis, and Reilly of the cavalry; Lieutenant Crittenden, of the Twentieth Infantry, and Acting Assistant Surgeon De Wolf, Lieutenant Harrington, of the cavalry, and Assistant Surgeon Lord are missing. Captain Benteen and Lieutenant Varnum, of the cavalry, are slightly wounded. Mr. B. Custer, a brother, and Mr. Reed, a nephew of General Custer, were with him and were killed. No other officers than those whom I have named are among the killed, wounded, and missing. It is impossible yet to obtain a reliable list of the enlisted men who were killed and wounded, but the number of killed, including officers, must reach two hundred and fifty; the number of wounded is fifty-one.

Courtesy Custer Battlefield Museum

Trumpeter John Martini was the last to see Custer alive. He carried the famous "last message" to Captain Benteen, written by Lieutenant W. W. Cooke.

At the mouth of the Rosebud I informed General Custer that I should take the supply-steamer Far West up the Yellowstone, to ferry General Gibbon's column over the river; that I should personally accompany that column, and that it would in all probability reach the mouth of the Little Big Horn on the 26th Instant. The steamer reached General Gibbon's troops, near the mouth of the Big Horn, early in the morning of the 24th, and at 4 o'clock in the afternoon all his men and animals were across the Yellowstone. At 5 o'clock the column, consisting of five companies of the Seventh Infantry, four companies Second Cavalry, and a battery of Gatling guns, marched out to and across Tullock's Creek. Starting soon after 5 o'clock in the morning of the 25th, the infantry made a march of twenty-two miles over the most difficult country which I have ever seen. In order that scouts might be sent into the valley of the Little Big Horn, the cavalry, with the battery, were then pushed on thirteen or fourteen miles further, reaching camp at midnight. The scouts were sent out at 4:30 on the morning of the 26th. They discovered three Indians, who were at first supposed to be Sioux, but, when overtaken, proved to be Crows, who had been with General Custer. They brought the first intelligence of the battle. Their story was not credited. It was supposed that some fighting, perhaps severe fighting, had taken place, but it was not believed that disaster could have overtaken so large a force as twelve companies of cavalry. The infantry which had broken camp very early, soon came up, and the whole column entered and moved up the valley of the Little Big Horn. During the afternoon efforts were made to send scouts through to what was supposed to be General Custer's position, and to obtain information of the condition of affairs, but those who were sent out were driven back by parties of Indians, who, in increasing numbers, were seen hovering in General Gibbon's front. At 8.40 in the evening the infantry had marched twenty-nine or thirty miles. The men were very weary. Daylight was failing. The column was therefore halted for the night at a point about eleven miles in a straight line above the mouth of the stream. In the morning the march was resumed, and after marching nine miles Major Reno's intrenched position was reached. The withdrawal of the Indians from around Reno's command and from the valley was undoubtedly caused by the appearance of General Gibbon's troops. Major Reno and Captain Benteen, both of whom are officers of great experience, accustomed to see large masses of mounted men, estimate the number of Indians engaged at not less than twenty-five hundred; other officers think the number was greater than this. The village in the valley was about three miles in length, and about a mile in width. Besides the lodges proper, a great number of temporary brushwood shelter was found in it, indicating that more men besides its proper inhabitants had gathered together there. Major Reno is very confident that there were a number of white men fighting with the Indians. It is believed that the loss of the Indians was larger. I have as yet received no official reports in regard to the battle, but what is stated here is gathered from the officers who were on the ground there and from those who have been over it since.[64]

Alfred H. Terry
Brigadier General

On July 5th, Major Marcus Reno, senior surviving officer of the 7th Cavalry, sent his report addressed to Terry's adjutant general:

64. The report of the Secretary of War for 1876; Volume I.

Headquarters 7th U. S. Cavalry
Camp on the Yellowstone River
July 5th, 1876
Captain E. W. Smith
A. D. C. and A. A. A. G.

The command of the regiment having devolved upon me, as the senior surviving officer, from the battles of June 25 and 26, between the 7th Cavalry and Sitting Bull's band of hostile Sioux, on the Little Big Horn River, I have the honor to submit the following report of its operations from the time of leaving the main column until the command was united in the vicinity of the Indian village:

The regiment left the camp at the mouth of Rosebud River, after passing in review before the department commander, under command of Brevet Major-General G. A. Custer, Lieutenant-Colonel, on the afternoon of the 22nd of June, and marched up the Rosebud twelve miles and encamped; 23d, marched up the Rosebud, passing many old Indian camps, and following a very large lodge-pole trail, but not fresh, making thirty-three miles; 24th, the march was continued up the Rosebud, the trail and signs freshening with every mile, until we had made twenty-eight miles, and we then encamped and waited for information from the scouts. At 9.25 p.m., Custer called the officers together and informed us that, beyond a doubt, the village was in the valley of the Little Big Horn, and that to reach it, it was neces-

Courtesy Dr. Larry Frost *Art by E. L. Reedstrom*

"Tom Custer and his brother George — at the final hour."

sary to cross the divide between Rosebud and Little Big Horn, and it would be impossible to do so in the day-time without discovering our march to the Indians; that we would prepare to move at 11 p.m. This was done, the line of march turning from the Rosebud to the right, up one of its branches, which headed near the summit of the divide. About 2 a.m. of the 25th the scouts told him that he could not cross the divide before daylight. We then made coffee and rested for three hours, at the expiration of which time the march was resumed, the divide crossed, and about 8 a.m. the command was in the valley of one of the branches of the Little Big Horn. By this time Indians had been seen, and it was certain that we could not surprise them, and it was determined to move at once to the attack. Previous to this no division of the regiment had been made since the order was issued, in the Yellowstone, annulling wing and battalion organization, but Custer informed me he would assign commands on the march.

I was ordered by Lieutenant W. W. Cooke, adjutant, to assume command of Companies M, A, and G; Captain Benteen of Companies H, D, and K; Custer retaining C, E, F, I, and L under his immediate command, and Company B, Captain McDougall, in rear of the pack-train. I assumed command of the companies assigned to me, and without any definite orders moved forward with the rest of the column, and well to its left. I saw Benteen moving further to the left, and as they passed he told me he had orders to move well to the left, and sweep everything before him. I did not see him again until about 2.30 p.m. The command moved down the creek toward the Little Big Horn Valley; Custer, with five companies, on the right bank; myself and three companies on the left bank, and Benteen further to the left and out of sight.

Courtesy Custer Battlefield Museum

Captain Myles W. Keogh and Company I, perished on the eastern slope of the Battle Ridge. He was identified by a crucifix about his neck. His horse "Comanche" was the only living thing that survived the battle.

As we approached a deserted village, and in which was standing one tepee, about 11 a.m. Custer motioned me to cross to him, which I did, and moved nearer to his column, until about 12.30 a.m., when Lieutenant Cooke, adjutant, came to me, and said the village was only two miles ahead, and running away, "to move forward at as rapid gait as I thought prudent, and to charge afterward, and that the whole outfit would support me." I think those were his exact words. I at once took a fast trot and moved down about two miles, when I came to a ford of the river. I crossed immediately and halted about ten minutes, or less, to gather the battalion, sending word to Custer that I had everything in front of me, and that they were strong. I deployed, and with the Ree scouts on my left charged down the valley, driving the Indians with great ease for about two and a half miles. I, however, soon saw that I was being drawn into some trap, as they certainly would fight harder, and especially as we were nearing their village, which was still standing; besides, I could not see Custer or any other support, and at the same time the very earth seemed to grow Indians, and they were running toward me in swarms, and from all directions.

I saw I must defend myself and give up the attack, mounted. This I did; taking possession of a point of woods, and which furnished, near its edge, a shelter for the horses, I dismounted and fought them on foot, making headway through the wood. I soon found myself in the near vicinity of the village; saw that I was fighting odds of at least five to one, and that my only hope was to get out of the wood, where I would soon have been surrounded, and gain some high ground. I accomplished this by mounting and charging the Indians between me and the bluffs on the opposite side of the river. In this charge, First Lieut. Donald McIntosh, Second Lieut. Benjamin H. Hodgson, Seventh Cavalry, and Acting Assistant Surgeon J. M. DeWolf were killed. I succeeded in reaching the top of the bluffs, with a loss of the three officers and twenty-nine enlisted men killed and seven wounded. Almost at the same time I reached the top, mounted men were seen to be coming toward us, and it proved to be Colonel Benteen's battalion, Companies H, D, and K. We joined forces, and in a short time the pack-train came up. As senior, my command was then Companies A, B, D, G. H, K, and

M, about 380 men, and the following officers: Captains Benteen, Weir, French, and McDougall; First Lieutenants Godfrey, Mathey and Gibson; Second Lieutenants Edgerly, Wallace, Varnum, and Hare, and Acting Assistant Surgeon Porter.

First Lieutenant De Rudio was in the dismounted fight in the woods, but, having some trouble with his horse, did not join the command in the charge out, and, hiding himself in the woods, joined the command after nightfall of the 26th.

Still hearing nothing from Custer, and with this re-enforcement, I moved down the river in the direction of the village, keeping on the bluffs. We had heard firing in that direction and knew it could only be Custer. I moved to the summit of the highest bluff, but seeing and hearing nothing, sent Captain Weir, with his company, to open communication with the other command. He soon sent back word by Lieutenant Hare that he could go no further, and that the Indians were getting around him. At this time he was keeping up a heavy fire from the skirmish-line. I at once turned everything back to the first position I had taken on the bluffs, and which seemed to me the best. I dismounted the men, had the horses and the mules of the pack-train driven together in a depression, put the men on the crests of the hills making the depression, and had hardly done so when I was furiously attacked. This was about 6 p.m. We held our ground, with the loss of eighteen enlisted men killed and forty-six wounded, until the attack ceased, about 9 p.m. As I knew by this time their overwhelming numbers, and had given up any hope of support from the portion of the regiment with Custer, I had the men dig rifle-pits, barricaded with dead horses and mules and boxes of hard bread the opening of the depression toward the Indians in which the ani-

Courtesy Custer Battlefield Museum

Lieutenant James E. Porter, Company I, was reported missing with the Custer Battalion, but presumed killed. His remains were never identified.

Courtesy National Archives

(Right) — Brigadier General E. S. Godfrey, (retired) and White Man Runs Him pose in 1926 at the battlesite to propose a monument to the 7th Regimental Cavalry. Indians who were old enough to help dedicate the monument participated. In the ceremonies Godfrey wiped tears from his eyes, as he was emotionally moved. Godfrey, while commanding Company "K" held the rank of 1st Lieutenant.

Courtesy North Dakota State Historical Society

Mark Kellogg's shirt, found at the battlefield, 1876, along with several other items belonging to him. (Housed at the North Dakota State Historical Society.)

mals were herded, and made every exertion to be ready for what I saw would be a terrific assault the next day. All this night the men were busy, and the Indians holding a scalp-dance underneath us, in the bottom, and in our hearing. On the morning of the 26th, I felt confident that I could hold my own, and was ready as far as I could be, when at daylight, about 2.30 a.m., I heard the crack of two rifles. This was the signal for the beginning of a fire that I have never seen equaled. Every rifle was handled by an expert and skilled marksman, and with a range that exceeded our carbine, and it was simply impossible to show any part of the body before it was struck.

We could see, as the daylight brightened, countless hordes of them passing up the valley, from out the village, and scampering over the high points toward the places designated for them by their chiefs, and which entirely surrounded our position. They had sufficient numbers to completely encircle us, and men were struck on opposite sides of the lines from where the shots were fired. I think we were fighting all the Sioux Nation, and also all the desperadoes, renegades, half-breeds, and squaw-men between the Missouri and the Arkansas east of the Rocky Mountains, and they must have numbered at least 2,500 warriors. The fire did not slacken until about 9.30 a.m., and then we discovered that they were making a last desperate attempt, and which was directed against the lines held by Companies H and M. In this attack they charged close enough to use their bows and arrows, and one man lying dead within our lines was touched by the "coup-stick" of one of the foremost Indians. When I say the stick was only about ten or twelve feet long, some idea of the desperate and reckless fighting of these people may be understood. This charge of theirs was gallantly repulsed by the men on that line led, by Colonel Benteen. They also came close enough to send their arrows into the line held by Companies D and K, but were driven away by a like charge of the line, which I accompanied.

We now had many wounded, and the question of water was vital, as from 6 p.m. of the previous evening until now, 10 a.m., about 16 hours, we had been without any. A skirmish-line was formed under Colonel Benteen to protect the descent of volunteers down the hill in front of his position to reach the water. We succeeded in getting some canteens, although many of the men were hit in doing so. The fury of the attack was now over, and, to my astonishment, the Indians were seen going in parties toward the village. But two solutions occurred to us for the movement — that they were going for something to eat and more ammunition, (as they had been throwing arrows,) or that Custer was coming. We took advantage of this lull to fill all vessels with water, and soon had it by the camp-kettleful; but they continued to withdraw, and all firing ceased, save occasional shots from sharpshooters, sent to annoy us about the water.

Courtesy National Archives

"The Northern Pacific, to protect whose right of way my husband and his men had died, provided us with transport, not the government. Nothing beyond the cold official report came from the War Department. President Grant took no official notice of the tragedy." Elizabeth Bacon Custer, under her black crepe bonnet smiles weakly for a photographer. *Circa 1877*

Courtesy Library of Congress

Elizabeth Custer and the General's only sister, Margaret Custer. Photo taken 1879.

About 2 p.m. the grass in the bottom was set on fire and followed up by Indians who encouraged its burning, and it was evident to me that it was done for a purpose, and which purpose I discovered later on to be the creation of a dense cloud of smoke, behind which they were packing and preparing to move their tepees. It was between 6 and 7 p.m. that the village came out from behind the clouds of smoke and dust. We had a close and good view of them as they filed away in the direction of Big Horn Mountains, moving in almost perfect military order. The length of the column was fully equal to that of a large division of the cavalry corps of the Army of the Potomac, as I have seen it on its march.

We now thought of Custer, of whom nothing had been seen and nothing heard since the firing in his direction about 6 p.m. on the eve of the 25th, and we concluded that the Indians had gotten between him and us and driven him toward the boat at the mouth of Little Big Horn River; the awful fate that did befall him never occurring to any of us as within the limits of possibilities. During the night I changed my position in order to secure an unlimited supply of water, and was prepared for their return, feeling sure they would do so, as they were in such numbers; but early on the morning of the 27th, and while we were on the qui vive for Indians, I saw with my glass a dust some distance down the valley. There was no certainty for some time what they were, but finally I satisfied myself they were cavalry, and, if so, could only be Custer, as it was ahead of the time that I understood that General Terry could be expected. Before this time, however, I had written a communication to General Terry, and three volunteers were to try to reach him. (I had no confidence in the Indians with me, and could not get them to do anything.) If this dust were Indians, it was possible they would not expect any one to leave. The men started and were told to go as near as was safe to determine if the approaching column was of white men, and to return at once in case they found it so, but if they were Indians to push on to General Terry. In a short time we saw them returning over the high bluff already alluded to. They were attended by a scout, who had a note from Terry to Custer saying: "Crow scout had come to camp saying he had been whipped, but that it was not believed." I think it was about 10.30 a.m. that General Terry rode into my lines, and the fate of Custer and his brave men was soon determined by Captain Benteen proceeding with his company to his battle-ground, and where were recognized the following officers, who were surrounded by the dead bodies of many of their men: General G. A. Custer; Col. W. W. Cooke, adjutant: Capts. M. W. Keogh, G. W. Yates, and T. W. Custer; First Lieuts. A. E. Smith, James Calhoun; Second Lieuts. W. V. Reilly, of the Seventh Cavalry, and J. J. Crittenden, Twentieth Infantry, temporarily attached to this regiment. The bodies of First Lieut. J. E. Porter and Second Lieuts. H. M. Harrington and J. G. Sturgis, Seventh Cavalry, and Asst. Surg. G. W. Lord, U.S.A., were not recognized, but there is every reasonable probability they were killed.

The wounded in my lines were, during the afternoon and evening of the 27th, moved to the camp of General Terry, and at 5 a.m. of the 28th I proceeded with the regiment to the battle-ground of Custer and buried 204 bodies, including the following-named citizens: Mr. Boston Custer, Mr. Reed, (a young nephew of General Custer,) and Mr. Kellogg, a correspondent for the New York Herald.

The following-named citizens and Indians who were with my command were also killed: Charles Reynolds, guide and hunter; Isiah, (Isaiah Dorman, colored interpreter); "Bloodly Knife," (who fell immediately by my side,) "Bob-tailed Bull," and "Stab," of the Indian scouts.

After following over his trail it was evident to me that Custer intended to support me by moving farther down the stream and attacking the village in flank; that he found the distance greater to the ford than he anticipated; that he did charge, but his march had taken so long, although his trail shows he moved rapidly, that they were ready for him; that Companies C and I, and perhaps part of Company E, crossed to the village, or attempted it at the charge, and were met by a staggering fire, and that they fell back to secure a position from which to defend themselves, but were followed too closely by the Indians to permit him to form any kind of a line. I think had the regiment gone in as a body, and from the woods in which I fought advanced on the village, that its direction was certain, but General Custer was fully confident they were running or he would not have turned from me.

I think (after the great number of Indians there were in the village) that the following reasons obtain for the misfortune: His rapid marching for two days and one night before the fight; attacking in the daytime at 12 m., and when they were on the qui vive, instead of early in the morning; and lastly, his unfortunate division of the regiment into three commands.

During my fight with the Indians I had the heartiest support from officers and men; but the conspicuous services of Brevet Colonel F. W. Benteen I desire to call attention to especially, for if ever a soldier deserved recognition by his Government for distinguished services he certainly does. I inclose herewith his report of the operations of his battalion from the time of leaving the regiment until we joined commands on the hill. I also inclose an accurate list of casualties as far as it can be made at the present time, separating them into two lists — A, those killed in General Custer's command; B, those killed and wounded in the command I had.

The number of Indians killed can only be approximated until we hear through the agencies. I saw the bodies of eighteen, and Captain Ball, Second Cavalry, who made a scout of thirteen miles over their trail, says that their graves were many along their line of march. It is simply impossible that numbers of them should not be hit in the several charges they made so close to my lines. They made their approach through the deep gulches that led from the hill-top to the river, and when the jealous care with which the Indian guards the bodies of killed and wounded is considered, it is not astonishing that their bodies were not found. It is probable that the stores left by them and destroyed the next two days was to make room for many of them on their trains.

The harrowing sight of the dead bodies crowning the height on which Custer fell, and which will remain vividly in my memory until death, is too recent for me not to ask the good people of this country whether a policy that sets opposing parties in the field, armed, clothed, equipped by one and the same Government, should not be abolished. All of which is respectfully submitted.[65]

M. A. Reno
Major 7th Cavalry
Com'd'g Regiment

For almost a hundred years now speculation has been rife as to what actually happened to Custer and the five companies under his immediate command. Dead men tell no tales. While most of the hostiles engaged survived the battle, little credence could be placed in what they had to relate about it. An Indian's sense of time was altogether different from a white man's. When engaged in battle he often ran together or juxtaposed the time sequence of its different events afterward. His vision of a battle was very limited. He saw only that part of it which related to him personally or to those nearest to him. The Indian warrior's ego was very well developed. His personal participation in a battle was the be-all and end-all of it to him. It was absolutely essential for him to boast about his own prowess in it afterward. In any case, after he had been thoroughly subjugated and was, in a sense, a prisoner, he told his white interrogators what he thought they wanted to hear. Too, his white interrogators usually didn't know his language or mode of thought, his questions being put through an interpreter, who was usually grossly incompetent. Consequently most Indian testimony is wildly at variance not only with most of the known facts, but contradictory. In all fairness it must be admitted much of the testimony of the 7th's survivors under Reno and Benteen together with that of their commanders is equally untrustworthy.

Benteen said he thought what had happened on Custer Field had been "a panic-rout". Naturally, Benteen, while inspecting its bloody debris, saw only what he wanted to see, his psychopathic hatred of his commanding officer somewhat distorted his vision. Most of the officers with Custer were brave and experienced soldiers. Even if Custer himself had been killed at the beginning of the battle, (as some writers have alleged), his brother, Captain Tom Custer or Lieutenant Cooke or Captain Keogh, to name only a few, would have taken command and prevented "a panic rout." It is therefore inconceivable anything of that nature occurred.

Many of the surviving hostile chiefs and warriors alleged it took only a half hour or hour at the most to wipe out Custer and his battalion. Naturally, again, Benteen and the other Custer haters in the regiment agreed. Tying in very neatly as it did with the "panic-rout" theory. Too, it absolved them from any charges of having dragged their boots in going to Custer's aid. Yet, Benteen confessed he counted "only two" dead Indian ponies on Custer Field. It is evident, then, the hostiles did not over-run Custer and his battalion in a charge en masse. If they had done so there would certainly have been more than two dead Indian ponies. It is also evident the Indians fought almost entirely on foot, which again precludes "a panic-rout." In any case, Indians never charged head-long en masse into even a small body of well-armed troops. It formed no part of their way of fighting. They had far too much sense. This in no way implies the average Indian warrior was any whit inferior to the average white trooper in courage. His tactics were simply different. He preferred fighting from cover or making circling attacks. Undoubtedly the former

65. The Report of the Secretary of War for 1876; Volume I.

was used for the most part against Custer and his battalion. Such tactics naturally suppose a more or less lengthy engagement, certainly one lasting more than half an hour or an hour. In any case, most of the testimony of Reno's and Benteen's men clearly indicated the action on Custer Field was of several hours duration.

Probably, it was Custer's original intention after sending Reno across the Little Big Horn to march along its bluffs until he found a practicable ford for attacking the hostile's encampment from the flank. It wasn't until he actually sighted the vast aggregation of tipis that he realized what he was up against. True, he knew from experience a large village was just as apt to disperse as a small one. But, for once in his life, at least, Custer had decided to play it safe. He had sent a message back to Benteen ordering him to bring up the regiment's reserve ammunition packs. "BENTEEN: COME ON. BIG VILLAGE. BE QUICK. BRING PACKS. W. W. COOKE. P.S. BRING PACKS." He would wait for them before attacking, fighting a holding action in the meantime. The 7th's senior Captain would be along shortly.*

Granted, all of this may be considered conjectural. But, it is based upon known facts. With this in mind, we may legitimately conjecture Custer and his battalion did fight a holding action until near the end of the battle, expecting Benteen to appear any minute with the regiment's reserve ammunition. It may well be this was a fatal mistake. But how could Custer have known Benteen would not be along — ever?

But what if Custer had not elected to play it safe? What if he had charged across the river into the hostile encampment? There were then few warriors to contest his crossing. This is one piece of Indian testimony we can safely rely on. Wouldn't there have been confusion compounded among the warriors still in it? The troopers would have been shooting, yelling, blowing bugles, setting fire to every tipi within reach, while women, children and old people would have been running helter-skelter, screaming at the top of their voices, getting in each others way and that of the few warriors present, dogs barking and howling, ponies rearing and neighing. The warriors streaming back from Reno would only have added to the confusion, dust and smoke obscuring everything. In short, it would have been one helluva donnybrook, a la GarryOwen! Even if Custer and his battalion had still died with their boots on, to a man.

Let us try to re-construct the actions at the Little Big Horn, from recent material gathered, basing facts originating from various authentic sources presented.

Custer turned his battalion away from the river to the prominence now known as Custer Hill, on which the monument stands. Here he dismounted his men, every fourth trooper being a horse-holder. There was little cover, but they wouldn't have to fight a holding action for very long. Benteen would soon be along with the regiment's reserve ammunition. A long range sniping contest then ensued. The hostiles, now gathering in full force, were also dismounted, their cover much better than that of the troopers. Armed mostly with bows and arrows they kept up a continual arcing shower of barbed shafts upon the pony soldiers, causing considerable casualties. Galling though it was, the troopers stood it manfully. Benteen would be along soon.

As the minutes slowly ticked by Custer was continually scanning with his field glasses, the direction in which he expected Benteen to appear. He hadn't sent him that far on the scout to the left of the 7th's line of march! He was only to find the valley of the Little Big Horn, "which was supposed to be nearby and to pitch into anything" he

---

* Trumpeter John Martini, who rode back to Benteen, carrying Custer's famous "last message," evidently failed to inform Benteen of Custer's last known position. Instead of moving cross country in his direction, Benteen kept on line of Reno's advance.

Courtesy U.S. Signal Corps (Brady Collection)

When the Army returned a year later, they found the field scattered with bleaching bones. Now and then a shoe or half a boot dotted the ground. Lonely wooden stakes, half tilted, towered above the bones, other markers were washed away. The grim task of identification and re-burial began.

might find. It was evident he hadn't found anything "to pitch into". Custer had!

Custer focused his field glasses on what afterward came to be known as Weir Point. Movement could be seen on it even through the dust and smoke of Custer Hill, flashes of blue, of sunlight striking metal. By God! There was one of the 7th's guidons! Benteen at last!

Swiftly Custer decided he must open a corridor for Benteen. Calling his officers around him, he ordered his brother Captain Tom Custer and Lieutenant A. E. Smith to take their companies down Custer Hill to the southeast. Then he ordered Captain Myles Keogh and his brother-in-law Lieutenant James Calhoun to take three companies along what is now known as Battle Ridge to the east of his command post, Calhoun diverging onto a ridge to the southeast.

Some men, we do not know how many, Custer kept with him at his command post. Taking up their assigned positions, Tom Custer, Smith, Keogh and Calhoun prepared to facilitate Benteen's arrival, expected momentarily. At his command post Custer anxiously scanned Weir Point for movement toward him. There was none! It looked like the troops on Weir Point were retreating instead of coming forward.

Tom Custer and Smith from their positions below Custer Hill could see nothing of this. They only knew there was no indication of Benteen's coming. They were under a galling fire, men were falling right and left, they couldn't hold their ground any longer. Trying to beat a hasty retreat back to the command post, most of the two companies were lost, a host of warriors under Lame White Man, seeing their chance, engulfing them in a red wave. Tom Custer and Smith and a handful of their men made it back to the comparative safety of the command post. They would live a little while longer.

Courtesy U.S. Signal Corps (Brady Collection)

Troopers usually marked their clothing. Socks, shirts, clothing—all were searched for markings hoping to establish some identification at that location. Many boot tops were cut-off by the Indians and used as moccasin soles, throwing the lower portion away. Note upper right corner.

Keogh and Calhoun found themselves in the same predicament. Both had dismounted their men upon taking their assigned positions, every fourth man a horse-holder. They, too, had come under a fierce fire with no sign of Benteen. It is evident from the positions of Calhoun and his men, as their bodies were found afterward, they had held a skirmish line to the end, the only such line to be found on Custer Field. Calhoun had once written his brother-in-law if ever the latter had need of him he would not be found wanting. Calhoun certainly kept this promise! Possibly, seeing Benteen wasn't coming he had determined to give Custer every chance, no matter how slim, to save what was left of the battalion. We do not know whether he advised Keogh of what we presume to have been his decision, or whether he would have been able to do so. In any case, it is evident from hostile testimony and the positions of the bodies of Keogh and his men, the fighting Irishman tried to lead a retreat

Courtesy U.S. Signal Corps (Brady Collection)

Shallow graves were dug. Only a few shovels were in the command. Hunting knives cut sections of sod to place over the victims. Boards from empty ammunition and hardtack boxes were used to identify officers who had fallen. Wooden stakes marked the troopers. Empty cartridges with rolled up paper inside for identification were driven into the stakes.

back to the command post, but they were wiped out en route. Calhoun and his command had probably fallen to the last man before this.

Custer now had only about 40 officers and men left at the command post, most of them perhaps wounded. Probably, he had seen the slaughter of Keogh's and Calhoun's commands through his field-glasses. For whatever reason, Benteen had not come. It was all too apparent "Custer's Luck" had run out! He now realized he and the remanent of his battalion were doomed. All that was left for them was to sell their lives as dearly as possible.

For their part, the hostiles could see this last portion of pony soldiers could also be wiped out to a man with small loss to themselves. All they had to do was to worm their way closer and closer from cover to cover, picking off these enemies by ones, twos and threes, until a mounted charge could over-run the very few left. This they proceeded to do. According to hostile testimony, only seven troopers managed to

Courtesy U.S. Signal Corps (Brady Collection)

Bones, from every part of the field were piled in heaps. Human remains were mixed in and hard to identify. Wolves dug up what they could find of soldiers and scattered their remains.

evade the final onslaught, making a futile break for the Little Big Horn. They were swiftly ridden down, being tomahawked, lanced or shot in their tracks. It was all over. "We have killed them all!"

Again all of this may be considered as conjecture. But it is logical, being based upon the few new facts we admittedly possess. We know the terrain of Custer Field, which hasn't changed much since 1876. We know a person using field glasses can easily descry Weir Point from Custer Hill and anything appearing upon it. We know the Indian method of fighting. Some Indian testimony, after the wheat has been separated from the chaff, rings true. The same may be said for much of the 7th's survivors testimony at the Reno Court Of Inquiry in 1879.

There are certain things that are evident of themselves. It is evident from Custer's last order to Benteen, the famous "Bring packs," he had decided to fight a holding action until the 7th's senior captain joined him with the ammunition packs. It is evident he knew Benteen could join him in a short time. It must have been evident to Custer most if not all of the hostiles had concentrated against him. Therefore, either Reno had been wiped out or his own appearance across the Little Big Horn from their encampment had diverted their attention from the Major to himself. Probably Custer thought the last assumption to be the correct one. Benteen, then, could pick up Reno's battalion and hurry with it and his own and the ammunition packs to join him.

As we have pointed out, Custer must have seen the appearance of the rest of the 7th through his field glasses on Weir Point. It is evident Benteen must have thought so, since he testified at the Reno Court he had had one of the 7th's guidons planted there so Custer would know where the rest of the regiment was. He could then fight his way through to it. Still, it must also have been evident to Benteen from the "Bring packs" order Custer expected him to do just the

Courtesy U.S. Signal Corps (Brady Collection)

Captain Nowlan and another man (unidentified) pay their respects to old comrades. A wreath of tall grass was made up and placed on Keogh's marker. Others in the background continue with their gruesome chores.

Courtesy Library of Congress

Captain C. K. Sanderson's camp at the Ford in 1879 while gathering bones and building the monument. (See Graham's "The Custer Myth", pages 369-371). Photo from a stereo.

Courtesy U.S. Signal Corps (Brady Collection)

After the battle of the Little Big Horn, the bodies of Custer's men were buried in shallow graves where they had fallen. Rifle butts, cups and knives were used to dig the graves. A year later, the Army returned and re-buried the bodies properly and with honors. Soldier putting finishing touches on wooden monument.

Courtesy Author's collection

The remains of three soldiers killed in the battle of the Little Big Horn were unearthed in an archeological research in June 1958. The National Park Service reported the finds on the eve of the 82nd Anniversary of Custer's famous last stand.

Courtesy Author's Collection

Just below the Reno-Benteen Monument are (left to right) Robert Bray, Archeologist; and Don Rickey, Jr., Historian (in trench coat). The other two men (behind Rickey and Bray, also far right) are not identified. Findings were a lime formation about the bones of one soldier. Several buttons, blue cloth, and a roll of bandages. The author was privileged to be there at that time.

opposite. Therefore, Benteen was to join Custer, not the other way 'round.

In the event, what would have been more logical for Custer than to have ordered the troop dispositions we have conjectured he did in order to facilitate Benteen's arrival. In this we agree with the late Dr. Kuhlman.* In any case, the positions where the bodies of Tom Custer's, Smith's, Keogh's and Calhoun's men were found bears this out. Unless we accept Benteen's wholly untenable theory it was all "a panic-rout."

Despite the faulty cartridge ejection of most of the 7th's weapons, the troopers were far better armed than the hostiles. Consequently the 7th's firepower was much greater. We may be sure the hostiles were well aware of this fact, acting accordingly, utilizing every bit of cover available to them, exposing themselves very little. As an inspection of the whole terrain of Custer Field shows, the Custer battalion was far more exposed. But, Custer didn't expect his holding action to last very long. Therefore he expected his casualties to be light.

It is only logical to assume if he had not seen the rest of the 7th on Weirpoint, deducing therefrom the swift arrival of Benteen, he would have sought a better defensive position he could hold for any length of time necessary, or as long as his ammunition held out. It does seem to us this may have been the crux of the matter. From Indian testimony it is evident the hostiles were successful in stampeding most of the 7th's mounts, their saddle-bags carrying most of the trooper's ammunition. This happened after Custer had made the troop dispositions we have recounted. Did Tom Custer's, Smith's, Keogh's and Calhoun's men run out of ammunition after their horses were stampeded? How long the Custer battalion's ammunition would have lasted if he had sought a better defensive

---

*Custer and the Gall Saga; Billings Mont., 1940. Legend into History; The Custer Mystery; Harrisburg, Pa., Stackpole Co., (1951).

Courtesy Custer Battlefield Museum

The remains of a trooper at Reno Battlefield, excavated June 1958. The three unknown soldiers were buried in the National Cemetery. Note the single row of brass buttons indicating a shell jacket worn.

position and had simply sat tight with his whole battalion it is impossible to say. The hostiles would still have tried to stampede the pony soldier's mounts. But it is doubtful if they would then have been as successful, for Custer would have done his utmost to safeguard the precious ammunition reserve he had with him.

Whether Custer could have held out as long as Reno and Benteen is a good question. However, until he had made the troop dispositions we have recounted, the battle, if it could be so termed, had been a long-drawn-out sniping contest, as was most of the Reno-Benteen engagement on Reno Hill. This did not use up much ammunition. It is possible Custer might have held out until the arrival of Terry and Gibbon. We know Reno and Benteen did.

We also know the hostiles made no all-out effort to overrun the Reno-Benteen positions. In fact, they didn't even try to wipe out Reno when he made his *sauve qui peut* to the bluffs from his position in the timber. This they could easily have done, incurring very few casualties themselves. They merely seemed content to have driven Reno away from proximity to their encampment. Of course, at the same time Custer was making his appearance opposite their encampment, which probably drew the hostiles' attention away from Reno and to him. This, together with the arrival of Benteen at about the same time, probably saved Reno.

While the defensive position Reno and Benteen selected on Reno Hill was better than any Custer would have been able to find where he was, it wasn't all that good. That is, if the hostiles had been as determined as white troops in a similar situation, they would have launched a head-long charge en masse on Reno Hill. And that would have been a Reno-Benteen Last Stand. But, this would have meant heavy casualties for them, so they were quite content to keep these pony soldiers effectively corraled away from their encampment. Isn't it possible they would have treated Custer's battalion in the same fashion if he had not made the final troop dispositions he did? Even though he was much closer to their encampment?

Actually, it is evident the hostiles acted almost throughout as defensively as the commanders of the 7th. Most hostile testimony states unequivocally their intention of not fighting at all. If forced to do so to

Courtesy Author's Collection

Custer Battlefield relics. 1. Remington new model Army cal. revolver. (Notice hammer screw replacement), probably Indian. 2. Sharp's hammer and lock plate. 3. .44 Henry pointed 4. Spencer .52 cal. 5. Spencer .52 cal. 6. Spencer .52 cal. 7. 50/70 8. 45/70 9. 50/70 10. Spencer .52 cal. 11. .50 caliber slug 12. .69 caliber ball 13. .44 caliber ball.

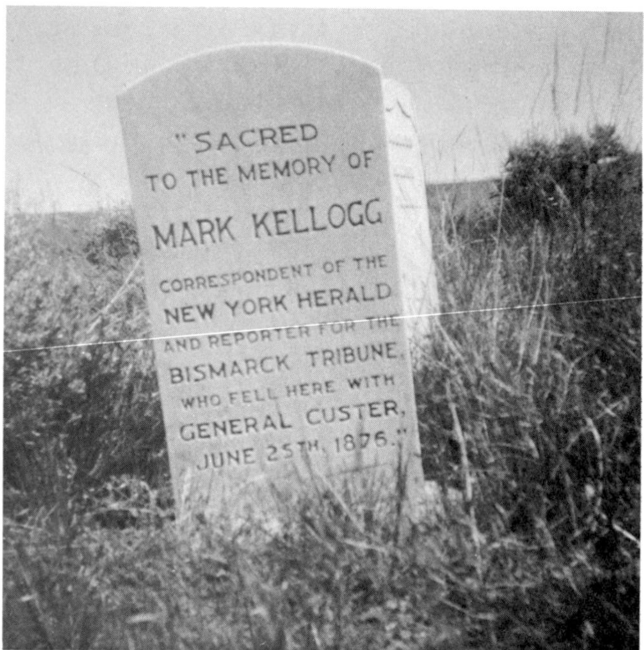

Courtesy Author's Collection

Mark Kellogg's last entry in his daily log, written June 24, 1876 reads, "I go with Custer and will be at the death."

fight defensively, buying time for their women, children and old people to escape the pony soldiers. While this may be taken with a grain of salt, the evidence strongly suggests it is true.

In short, the whole Battle of the Little Big Horn was partly a comedy of errors and could have resulted in a draw instead of only that portion of it fought by Reno and Benteen. There simply wouldn't have been a "Custer's Last Stand" and "Custer's Luck" would not have completely run out. Still, the key to the disaster it did become, was due to the actions, or rather, the lack thereof of Captain Frederick William Benteen; for whatever reason.

It may truthfully be said battles are seldom fought logically, regardless of how

Courtesy U.S. Signal Corps (Brady Collection)

General George Crook in a Civil War uniform. Crook, who had brought the Apaches on reservations, was transferred to the Department of the Platte in March, 1875. He was going to teach the Northern Indians to 'walk the white man's road.'

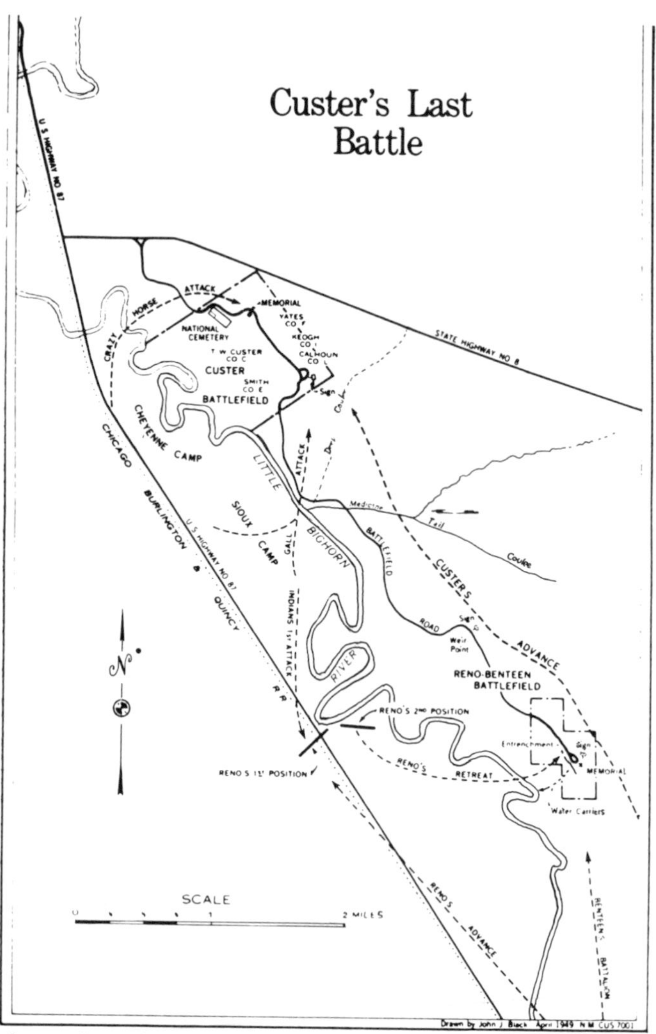

Courtesy National Park Service

Map — Custer's Last Battle

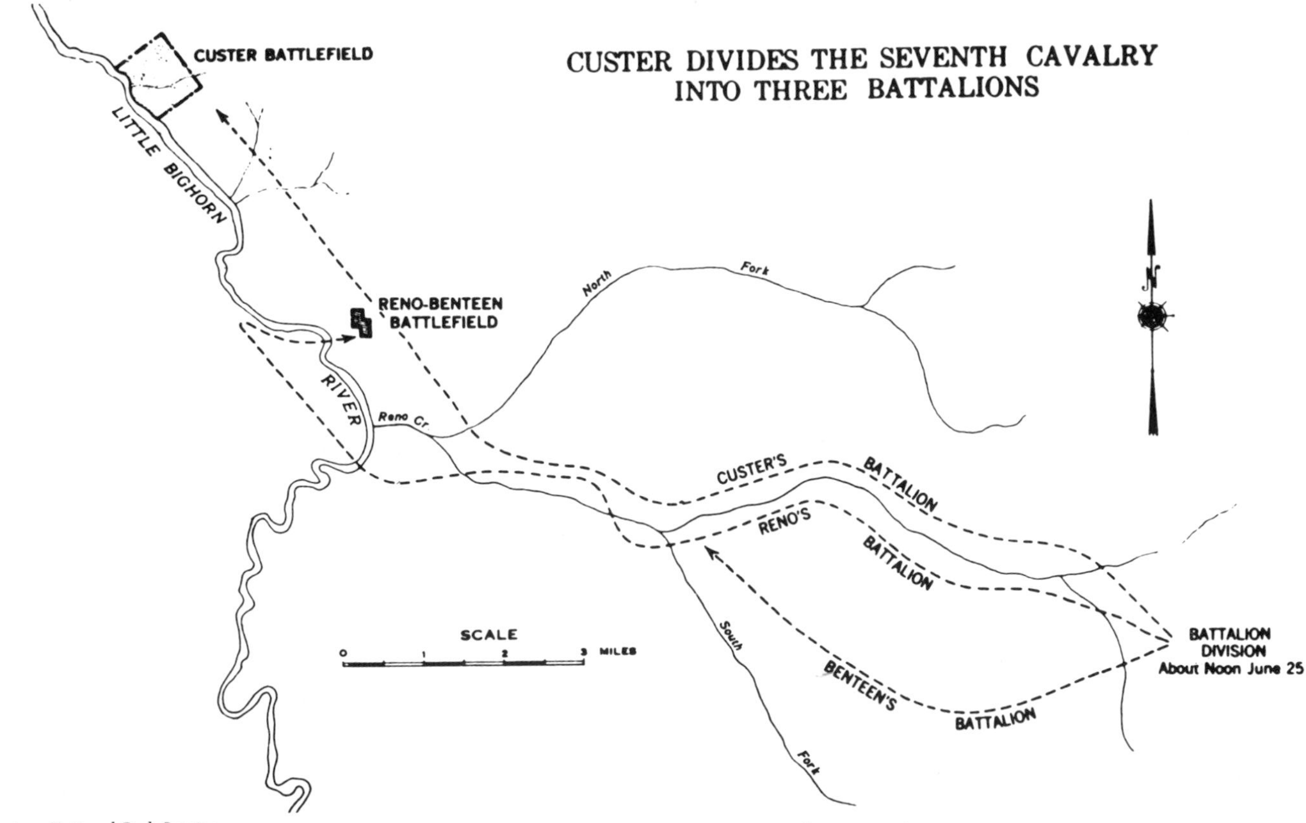

Courtesy National Park Service

Map — Custer divides the Seventh Cavalry into three Battalions.

THREE PRONGED MOVEMENTS
IN THE SIOUX EXPEDITION
OF 1876

FORT SHAW
Helena
Bozeman FORT ELLIS
GIBBON'S COLUMN
YELLOWSTONE RIVER
Billings
CUSTER BATTLEFIELD
Sheridan
CROOK'S COLUMN
FORT FETTERMAN
FORT LARAMIE
FORT D. A. RUSSELL
CHEYENNE
FORT LINCOLN
Bismarck
TERRY-CUSTER COLUMN
GREAT SIOUX RESERVATION
BLACK HILLS
MISSOURI RIVER
North Platte River
YELLOWSTONE NATIONAL PARK
SCALE
0 50 100 150 MI

Courtesy National Park Service

Map — "A three pronged march."

Officers killed at the Little Big Horn.

logically their commanders planned them. Far too much of the human element enters into them. However, once a battle has been fought and is brought into the light of the study lamp, a certain logic emerges, consisting of cause and effect, the sequence of events, the known facts, a knowledge of human nature. So it is with the Battle of the Little Big Horn, even though there were no survivors of a portion of one side engaged and much of the testimony of those who did survive on both sides is worthless. We believe we have elucidated this logic insofar as it can be. For those who may disagree, we can only say let them light their own study lamp and ponder far into the night.

EYEWITNESS OR LIAR?

By early afternoon on June 25, 1876, elements of the U.S. Army's Seventh Cavalry, under the command of General George Armstrong Custer, had been annihilated by a vastly superior force of Indian warriors, led by Sitting Bull. No survivors remained to tell details of the battle tactics. Even news of the event was weeks in reaching the civilized world; much of it was sketchy, imcomplete — and frustrating. What happened on the Little Big Horn?

It is fair to say that no other single event in American history has captured the imagination of the public more completely than "Custer's Last Stand." Although most Americans are aware that the Indians gained a victory at the Little Big Horn, few are familiar with the details of the events of that day. In considering the reasons for this, it is well to note the time during which this event took place. In 1876, accurate reporting of historical events was slow and uncertain. A newspaper reporter accompanied the Seventh Cavalry detachment under the command of General Custer. He was killed during the battle of the Little Big Horn. Had he survived and written about the campaign, it is entirely possible that a great deal of time would have passed before his reports reached public attention.

Ulysses S. Grant

A scant 10 years prior to Custer's defeat, this vast, untamed wilderness of south-central Montana had been known as a part of the Great American Desert. Many contemporary historians referred to Custer's last stand as a "massacre," although that term implies the slaughter of those who can make little or no resistance. In Custer's case, it was a bloody battle between armed antagonists, after the aggressor had attacked the Indians.

The lack of eyewitness reports from the battlefield has done much to confuse the situation. This frustrating condition has caused the event to remain shrouded in mystery. Yet there may be a clue to the events of that fateful day. Some months after the battle, a newspaper article appeared in the Minneapolis Tribune of September 8, 1876, and headlined, "Custer's Butcher." The Minneapolis Tribune and the St. Paul Pioneer Press had published an interview with a trapper by the name of D. H. Ridgeley, who had been in the Yellowstone country of Wyoming for many months. Ridgeley was aware of great Indian activity in the area in which he was trapping, and consequently took steps to avoid marauding Indian war parties. In late March 1876, he was captured by the Sioux and taken to the camp of Sitting Bull, where he was kept prisoner until the battle of the Little Big Horn. He was stripped of all his possessions and great mockery was made of him because of his thin build and facial whiskers. Forced to perform any tasks given him by the Indians, Ridgeley was subjected to daily degradation; other than that, his meals were regular and animal skins provided him warmth. The newspaper account continued, with Ridgeley supplying details of the Indians preparing for a great battle.

By the 25th day of June, 1876, the Indian nations under the leadership of Sitting Bull stood ready for an attack. This was the day of the battle against the long-knives of the U.S. Cavalry. A great number of Indians climbed the side of the hills overlooking the site of Custer's march down the valley along the Rosebud River. Examining the site where the Indian nation was encamped, we note that it was divided by a large bluff or ridge, the front of which ran well down toward the Rosebud and in the direction of the available fords along the river. It was as though Sitting Bull realized that this would be the site of a great battle for his people. He had divided his nation into two separate encampments. Some 25 teepees formed a village which could be visible to troops moving up the Rosebud River toward the bluff. However, another 75 teepees in a much larger village were located on the other side of the bluff, not visible to anyone moving up the river. The Indians had crossed the Rosebud to camp by this bluff along the available ford at the lower end of the bluff; Custer had followed their trail down to the water's edge. He noted the smaller village from across the river, and it was this village which he attacked first. He was immediately met by a strong force of 1,500 to 2,000 Indians in a regular order of battle, every movement by the Indians being made in a form of military precision. The trapper Ridgeley had been moved to the side of the hill, where he had a broad overview of the action taking place below him. He was still being kept prisoner, but he was not more than one and a half miles from the actual site of the fighting.

According to the Ridgeley report published in the Minneapolis newspaper, General Custer began his fight in a ravine near the ford where he crossed the river, fully one-half of the command immediately engaged and unhorsed by the first fire from the Indians. The cavalrymen immediately retreated toward a hill in the rear, and they were cut down on the way to that hill with astonishing rapidity. Ridgeley reported the commanding officer falling from his horse in the middle of this engagement, an astonishing admission and a notable discovery, if true. The battle continued to rage for

Courtesy Dr. L. A. Frost

Battle map to scale of the Little Big Horn, showing Custer's route (in white).

ARMY OF THE UNITED STATES.

To all whom it may concern:

Know Ye, That William E. Smith a Private of Captain [illegible] Company D of the Seventh Regiment of Cavalry who was enlisted the [illegible] day of September one thousand eight hundred and Seventy to serve Five Years is hereby discharged from the Army of the United States in consequence of Expiration of [illegible]

Said William E. Smith was born in Rouses Point in the State of New York is Twenty seven years of age Five feet 5½ inches high Dark complexion Grey eyes Dark hair and by occupation, when enlisted a Farmer

Given under my hand, at [illegible] this Twelfth day of September in the year of our Lord one thousand eight hundred and Eighty

[illegible]

Major Seventh Cavalry Commanding

CHARACTER.

Excellent in all respects.

[illegible]

A.G.O. No. 98.

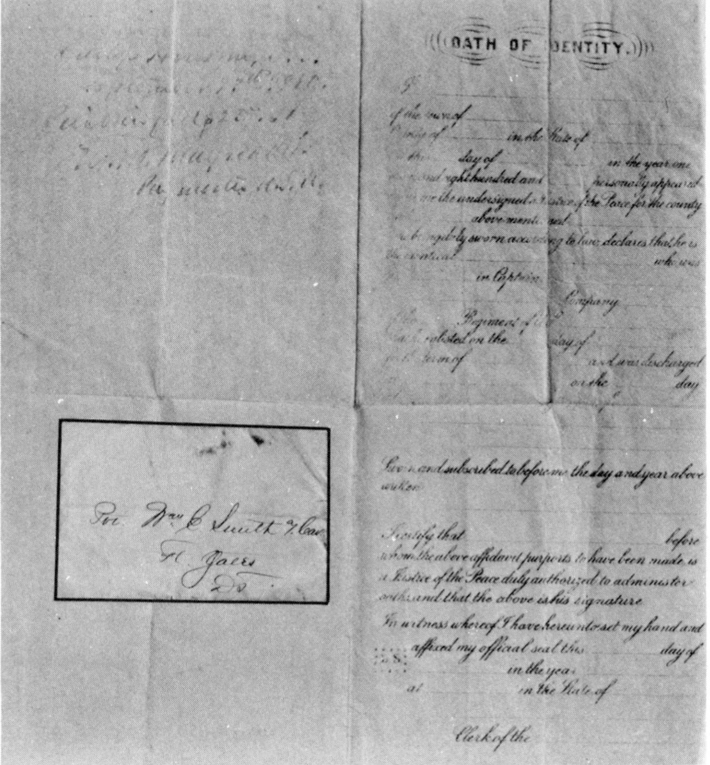
OATH OF IDENTITY.

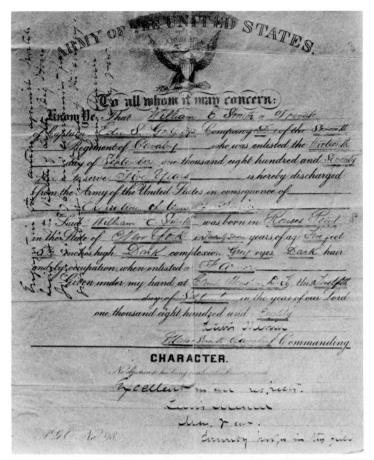

Courtesy Dr. Elizabeth Lawrence

Discharge of William E. Smith, Company D (Private). Company D was one of the four companies under the command of Major Reno. Thomas B. Weir was Captain.

another half to three-quarters of an hour until the last soldier had been killed. At the conclusion of the battle, the Indians returned to their camp with 6 soldiers as prisoners. They were delirious with joy over their successes. The soldiers having been taken prisoner were tied to stakes at a large wood pile in the village around the point of the hill, whereupon the wood was set afire and all soldiers burned to death, the bodies dropping to the earth a blackened, roasted and hideous mass. Apparently not content to allow them death in this fashion, Indian boys were allowed to fire red-hot arrows into the flesh of these soldiers. This incredible "amusement" was allowed to continue until each of the unfortunate victims had fallen a corpse. Ridgeley stated that the sight was so horrible that it could never be erased from his memory.

This grisly scene concluded, the Indian women, with their children, armed themselves with knives, whereupon they proceeded to the field of battle to rob the dead of clothing, valuables, trinkets and such else as they could find. They further mutilated the bodies of the soldiers in a manner too shocking and sickening for description.

During the time when the six soldiers were being burned to death in the village, another force attacked the Indian village, and the Indians turned their attention to meeting this attack. Undoubtedly, this attack was led by the forces of Major Reno. All during this second attack, the soldiers were kept burning and subjected to every imaginable torture. Ridgeley estimated that the time which elapsed was 45 minutes to an hour and a half; he was not permitted to speak to the soldiers before their horrible death. He could not, therefore, give any indication of their identities. Possibly important is his description of one of the soldiers as being of small stature, with grey hair and whiskers. These physical attributes may lead to the identification of one of the unfortunate prisoners.

It was evening by the time all of the Indians returned from the field of battle. Many returned to their camps to drink whiskey, captured during the battle, and admire new weapons and clothing taken from the fallen soldiers. During the revelry, squaws performed the duty of guarding Ridgeley and two companions. Names of the other two men with Ridgeley were not mentioned, nor did Ridgeley state whether or not they were cavalrymen. Much pandemonium reigned during the night after the battle, and the guards became drowsy. At the first opportunity, Ridgeley and his companions slipped away from the main group. Groping through the darkness, they came across several Indian ponies and mounted them to make tracks toward civilization, only to find the countryside literally crawling with Indian war parties. There seemed to be no alternative but seclusion, so they came to a halt and hid in a section of woods for 4 days, concealed from all searching eyes. Discovering, after 4 days, that it was apparently safe to travel again, they moved on slowly and steadily, encountering numerous straggling Indians along their journey, and studiously avoiding contact with them. On the fifth night away from Sitting Bull's camp, Ridgeley's pony stumbled, throwing him to the ground and causing him to break his arm in two places. The men traveled generally eastward, north of Fort Abraham Lincoln, as they were fearful that small war parties moving west to join Chief Sitting Bull might stumble across them. They strove for Fort Abercrombie, and, after reaching that destination safely, one of the two men traveling with Ridgeley was afflicted with erysipelas and died a few days later. The other man joined his own friends and family at home in northern Minnesota, nevermore to be heard from.

Unquestionably shaken by the events which had taken place, Ridgeley himself reached his hometown of Minneapolis shaken by the Indian massacre and his broken arm. When he came among his friends, one of whom was Mr. Hall McCleave of the firm of Warner and McCleave, undertakers and furniture dealers, Ridgeley recounted the story of his events. Mr. McCleave insisted that the trapper tell his story to a local newspaper editor and allow it to be printed, leaving out none of the reported atrocities he had witnessed.

Reviewing the newspaper article, we note that Ridgeley described Chief Sitting Bull as a large man, a half-breed, and very intelligent. He reported that, owing to some sort of injury, Sitting Bull's right foot turned outward and the deformity affected his walk noticeably. Sitting Bull claimed that every white man would be driven from the Black Hills, and he would stand and fight if soldiers came. Noting that Red River carts had been in the camp of Sitting Bull 5 weeks or so before the Custer fight, Ridgeley concluded that regular supplies of powder and lead from Canadian traders was flowing to the Indian nation. He further mentioned that there were apparently two chiefs in Sitting Bull's camp who were believed to be white men; they could speak English quite well. Of further interest is Ridgeley's report that the Indians were maneuvered like soldiers, displaying a surprising knowledge of military tactics.

Ridgeley's integrity and his truthfulness was not in question at the time that his report to the newspaper was made; therefore, little reason to doubt the substantial accuracy of his narrative was voiced. Although Ridgeley's story surpasses anything of the imagination, his credentials were sufficient to lend credence to his report. The story was published in Minneapolis on September 8, 1876. The effect of its publishing was really no surprise to anyone. Over night, Ridgeley became a celebrity. The New York papers picked up the story immediately, reprinting it almost word-for-word. The New York Grafic published the following: "There ought to be a purse raised as a testimonial to the bravery and mendacity of that alleged white man who escaped from Sitting Bull

The New-York Times.

VOL. XXV......NO. 7742. NEW-YORK, FRIDAY, JULY 7, 1876. PRICE FOUR CENTS.

THE LITTLE HORN MASSACRE.

LATEST ACCOUNTS OF THE CHARGE.

FORCE OF FOUR THOUSAND INDIANS IN POSITION ATTACKED BY LESS THAN FOUR HUNDRED TROOPS—OPINIONS OF LEADING ARMY OFFICERS OF THE DEED AND ITS CONSEQUENCES—FEELING IN THE COMMUNITY OVER THE DISASTER.

Special Dispatch to the New-York Times.

The dispatches giving an account of the slaughter of Gen. Custer's command, published in THE TIMES of yesterday, are confirmed and supplemented by official reports from Gen. A. H. Terry, commanding the expedition. On June 25 Gen. Custer's command came upon the main camp of Sitting Bull, and at once attacked it, charging the thickest part of it with five companies, Major Reno, with seven companies attacking on the other side. The soldiers were repulsed and a wholesale slaughter ensued. Gen. Custer, his brother, his nephew, and his brother-in-law were killed, and not one of his detachment escaped. The Indians surrounded Major Reno's command and held them in the hills during a whole day, but Gibbon's command came up and the Indians left. The number of killed is stated at 300 and the wounded at 31. Two hundred and seven men are said to have been buried in one place. The list of killed includes seventeen commissioned officers.

It is the opinion of Army officers in Chicago, Washington, and Philadelphia, including Gens. Sherman and Sheridan, that Gen. Custer was rashly imprudent to attack such a large number of Indians, Sitting Bull's force being 4,000 strong. Gen. Sherman thinks that the accounts of the disaster are exaggerated. The wounded soldiers are being conveyed to Fort Lincoln. Additional details are anxiously awaited throughout the country.

CONFIRMATION OF THE DISASTER.

DISPATCHES FROM GEN. TERRY RECEIVED AT SHERIDAN'S HEAD-QUARTERS—THEORIES OF THE BATTLE—PROBABLY TEN THOUSAND SIOUX IN POSITION—THE ATTACK CONDEMNED AS RASH BY OFFICERS OF EXPERIENCE—DISPOSITION OF THE WOUNDED.

CHICAGO, July 6.—At the head-quarters of Lieut. Gen. Sheridan this morning, all was bustle and confusion over the reported massacre of Custer's command. Telegrams were being constantly received, but most of them were of a confidential nature and withheld from publication. It is known that the unfortunate command broke camp on the North Rosebud on June 22 for the purpose of proceeding in a direction which would bring it to the point named about the 25th, at which place a bloody fight is reported to have taken time. The following dispatch, the last received at head-quarters in this city previous to the news of the massacre, confirms the accounts given to the extent of showing that Custer intended to go to that place.

CAMP ON THE NORTH ROSEBUD, June 21, 1876.

Lieut. Gen. P. H. Sheridan, Commanding Military Division of the Missouri, Chicago:

No Indians have been met with as yet, but traces of large and recent camp have been discovered twenty or thirty miles up the Rosebud. Gibbon's column will move this morning, on the north side of the Yellowstone, for the mouth of the Big Horn, where it will be ferried across by the supply steamer, and whence it will proceed to the mouth of the Little Horn, and so on. Custer will go up the Rosebud to-morrow with his whole regiment, and thence to the head-waters of the Little Horn, thence down the Little Horn.

A. H. TERRY,
Brigadier General Commanding.

A dispatch received at the quarters of Gen. Sheridan this morning at 11 o'clock confirms the first reports received. The dispatch states that the forces were falling back, and that the wounded had been sent to Fort Lincoln. No details were given, but the officers at head-quarters regard it as a full confirmation of the engagement reported. In reply to an inquiry as to whether the attack was made by Gen. Custer of his own accord, or under orders from the department, an answer was given that Custer made the charge of his own volition. A still later dispatch from Lieut. Kinzie, of the Seventh Cavalry, was received, asking that he be transferred from the department where he is now on duty to the scene of action. This is also regarded as another confirmation of the bloody massacre reported. Gen. Custer's family are at Fort Lincoln, to which point the wounded are being conveyed.

So far as an expression in regard to the wisdom of Gen. Custer's attack could be obtained at head-quarters, it was to the effect that Custer had been imprudent, to say the least. It is the opinion at head-quarters among those who are most familiar with the situation, that Custer struck Sitting Bull's main camp. Gen. Drum, of Sheridan's staff, is of opinion that Sitting Bull began concentrating his forces after the fight with Crook, and that no

thinks the first dispatch giving the details of the battle was mislaid, or else some enterprising newspaper correspondent bought up the messenger and sent the account East, thus keeping the War Department in ignorance of the occurrence. From what he knows of the occurrence he believes that Gen. Custer attempted a battle without reconnoitering the position, and that he was too bold. He does not think the slaughter so great as at first reported. The first dispatch received by Gen. Sheridan was as follows:

CAMP ON YELLOWSTONE, NEAR MOUTH OF BIG HORN, July 2.

On the evening of the 28th we commenced moving down with the wounded, but were able to get along but four miles, as the hard litters did not answer the purpose. The mule litters did excellently well, but they were insufficient in number; therefore, the 29th was spent in making a full supply of them. On the evening of the 29th we started again, and at 2 A. M. the wounded were placed on the steamer at the mouth of the Little Big Horn. The afternoon of the 30th they were brought down to the depot on the Yellowstone. I send them to-morrow by steam to Fort Lincoln, and with them one of my aids, Capt. E. W. Smith, who will be able to answer any questions which you may desire to ask. Col. Sheridan's dispatch informing me of the reported gathering of Indians on the Rosebud reached me after I came down here. I hear nothing of Gen. Crook's movements. At least a hundred horses are needed to remount the cavalrymen now here.

(Signed,) ALFRED H. TERRY,
Brigadier General.

The second dispatch was as follows:

CAMP BIG HORN, July 2.

I think I owe it to myself to put you more fully in possession of the facts of the late operations. While at the mouth of the Rosebud I submitted my plan to Gen. Gibbon and Gen. Custer. It was that Custer, with his whole regiment, should move up the Rosebud till he should meet a trail Reno had discovered a few days before, but that he should not follow it directly to the Little Big Horn; that he should send scouts over it and keep his main force further toward the south, so as to prevent the Indians from slipping in between himself and the mountains. He was also to examine the head waters of the Tullaska Creek, as he passed it, and send me word of what he found there. A scout was furnished him for the purpose of crossing the country to me. We calculated it would take Gibbons' column until the 26th to reach the mouth of the Little Big Horn, and that the wide sweep I had proposed Custer should make would require so much time that Gibbon would be able to co-operate with him in attacking any Indians that might be found on the stream. I asked Custer how long his marches would be. He said they would be at the rate of about thirty miles a day. Measurements were made and calculations based on that rate of progress. I talked with him about his strength and at one time suggested that, perhaps it would be well for me to take Gibbon's cavalry and go with him. To the latter suggestion he replied: "That, without reference to the command, he would prefer his own regiment alone. As a homogeneous body, as much could be done with it as with the two combined. He expressed the utmost confidence that he had all the force that he could need, and I shared his confidence. The plan adopted was the only one which promised to bring the infantry into action, and I desired to make sure of things by getting up every available man. I offered Custer the battery of Gatling guns, but he declined it, saying that it might embarrass him, and that he was strong enough without it.

The movements proposed by Gen. Gibbon's column were carried out to the letter, and had the attack been deferred until it was up, I cannot doubt that we should have been successful. The Indians had evidently prepared themselves for a stand, but as I learned from Capt. Benton that on the 22d the cavalry marched twelve miles; on the 23d, twenty-five miles; from 5 A. M. till 8 P. M., of the 24th, forty-five miles, and then after night ten miles further, resting, but without unsaddling, twenty-three miles, to the battle-field. The proposed route was not taken, but as soon as the trail was struck it was followed. I cannot learn that any examination of Tullaska Creek was made. I do not tell you this to cast any reflections upon Custer, for whatever errors he may have committed Custer's action is unexplainable in the case.

A. H. TERRY, Brigadier General.

These dispatches were all that either Gens. Sherman or Sheridan received up to midnight, and were sent to the Secretary of War.

boys approached the river, but the attempt was made, and though one man was killed and seven wounded the water was gained and the command relieved. When the fighting ceased for the night Reno further prepared for attacks.

There had been forty-eight hours' fighting, with no word from Custer. Twenty-four hours more of fighting and the suspense ended, when the Indians abandoned their village in great haste and confusion. Reno knew then that succor was near at hand. Gen. Terry, with Gibbon commanding his own infantry, had arrived, and as the comrades met men wept on each other's necks. Inquiries were then made for Custer, but none could tell where he was. Soon an officer came rushing into camp and related that he had found Custer, dead, stripped naked, but not mutilated, and near him his two brothers, Col. Tom and Boston Custer. His brother-in-law, Col. Calhoun, and his nephew Col. Yates, Col. Keogh, Capt. Smith, Lieut. Crittenden, Lieut. Sturgis, Col. Cooke, Lieut. Porter, Lieut. Harrington, Dr. Lord, Mack Kellogg, the Bismarck *Tribune* correspondent, and 190 men and scouts. Custer went into battle with Companies C, L, I, F, and E, of the Seventh Cavalry, and the staff and non-commissioned staff of his regiment and a number of scouts, and only one Crow scout remained to tell the tale. All are dead. Custer was surrounded on every side by Indians, and horses fell as they fought on skirmish line or in line of battle. Custer was among the last who fell, but when his cheering voice was no longer heard, the Indians made easy work of the remainder. The bodies of all save the newspaper correspondent were stripped, and most of them were horribly mutilated. Custer's was not mutilated. He was shot through the body and through the head. The troops cared for the wounded and buried the dead, and returned to their base for supplies and instructions from the General of the Army.

Col. Smith arrived at Bismarck last night with thirty-five of the wounded. The Indians lost heavily in the battle. The Crow Scout survived by hiding in a ravine. He believes the Indians lost more than the whites. The village numbered 1,800 lodges, and it is thought there were 4,000 warriors. Gen. Custer was directed by Gen. Terry to find and feel of the Indians, but not to fight unless Terry arrived with infantry and with Gibbon's column. The casualties foot up 261 killed and fifty-two wounded.

THE SCENE OF THE MASSACRE.

DESCRIPTION OF THE REGION BY MAJOR GRIMES, WHO REMOVED THE FORTS IN 1868, UNDER THE TREATY.

Special Dispatch to the New-York Times.

ST. LOUIS, July 6.—The news of the massacre of Gen. Custer with seventeen commissioned officers and 315 men, near the Little Big Horn River, has created an extraordinary sensation here. Subsequent advices received at military head-quarters in this city substantially confirm the terrible news. Your correspondent this evening had a conversation with Major J. W. Grimes, one of the military officers stationed here, and who is very familiar with Indian affairs in the West. He is well acquainted with the country where the fight took place. He was detailed by the Government in 1868 to remove all the forts on the Powder River route, in accordance with the provision of the Fort Laramie treaty of 1868. The battle occurred about twenty miles from the mouth of the Little Big Horn River, which empties into the Big Horn, and the latter into the Yellow Stone. The fight took place on the Crow reservation, about forty miles east of Fort C. L. Smith, the most northern of the Powder River Road forts, removed by Major Grimes in 1868. The country is diversified by mountain ranges and deep cañons, with intervening plateaus of sage brush prairies.

Ex-Gov. Fletcher, who was a member of the Peace Commission that went out last Summer, stated to-night that the present desperate condition of affairs is only a legitimate result of the present peace policy pursued by the Government toward the Indians.

THE CAUSES AND CONSEQUENCES.

and now gives a history of the fight through a Minneapolis paper. We will keep all money sent to us for that purpose." In the tumult over celebrating Ridgeley's reports, many would forget Custer and his brave men who lay dead on the hillsides of the Little Big Horn.

For 17 days, Ridgeley basked in the reflected glory of his reports. On the evening of September 25, 1876, a small column appeared in the Pioneer Press and Tribune in Minneapolis, puncturing a hole in Ridgeley's story, and bringing his period of exuberance to an end:

To the Editors of the Pioneer Press and Tribune:

I saw in your paper the other day, a statement of the trapper Ridgeley about the Custer fight on the Little Big Horn. Now, as I know this man Ridgeley well, and also knew his whereabouts since the first of July, 1875, I thought that a few words from me might be of interest to you and your many readers. Ridgeley claims he had been absent for two years on a trapping expedition. Now, Mr. Editor, he worked for me all through haying and harvesting in the summer of 1875; he left my place about the 25th of September of last year, but I saw him several times in October. He says he, with others, was captured by Indians in March last, and was still a prisoner in Sitting Bull's camp at the time of Custer's annihilation on the 25th of June. Now, I saw Ridgeley and conversed with him about the middle of April last, on the Platte River, in Morrison county, in this state; he was then at work for Hill Bros., in their logging camp on Platte River. More over I received the following letter from him early in July:

Sauk Rapids, Minn., July 3, A.D. 1876. 'Mr. Ward, Der Sir I wish that you Wold let me Know What the chance is Down there for Work in haying this yer, if there is a good chance and Wages I will come Down thare to Work this yer again plese let Me Know as soon as you git this good By From Your friend D. H. Ridgeley.'

Now, Mr. Editor, I am prepared to prove every statement made by me should our friend Ridgeley desire it. Why Ridgeley should invent such a story, of course is beyond my comprehension. He is of an imaginative mind, and is continually telling something to stir up a confusion.

Yours Respectfully, T. A. WARD, Anoka, Minn.

How could anyone now believe the account which Ridgeley had given? It appeared foolish to do so, as T. A. Ward seemed so certain of Ridgeley's whereabouts. Yet no published reports are made of any response Ridgeley might have made to the accusation by Ward. Did he have an answer on his whereabouts? Did he truly write the letter of July 3, 1876? How did he explain his report of the Custer massacre in such a short period of time?

History is ready to welcome another hero to its ranks. Had he not been pitching hay at the time of Custer's last stand, perhaps D. H. Ridgeley would have joined the ranks of national heroes. Yet who can say today whether or not things happened as Ridgeley reported? It is a nagging question which troubles historians and which, some day, may have an answer. Our "17-day hero" is lost to history.

INDEX